Congo missionary Del Carper
(far right) follows wounded survivor
of Stanleyville massacre
into giant rescue plane

OUT OF
THE JAWS
OF THE LION

OTHER BOOKS BY HOMER E. DOWDY

The Bamboo Cross

Christ's Witchdoctor

*For I know the plans I have for
you, says the Lord, plans for welfare
and not for evil, to give you a future
and a hope.*

—JEREMIAH 29:11 (RSV)

OUT OF THE JAWS OF THE LION

Homer E. Dowdy

Harper & Row, *Publishers*

NEW YORK

TO THE LOVED ONES OF

THE CONGO MARTYRS,

FROM WHOSE DEATHS

WILL SURELY SPRING FORTH

MUCH NEW LIFE

Library of Congress Catalog Card Number: 65-20450

A-Q

Contents

Picture Section follows page 94

Preface

Perhaps like most persons in this busy age, I was too preoccupied to be concerned about the plight of missionaries and other foreign residents in the rebel-controlled section of Congo until one day in November, 1964, a telephone call startled me out of my indifference.

"Sixty of our missionaries are held hostage behind rebel lines. We haven't heard from them in four months . . . but any day now something will happen by which all may be freed or killed."

The caller was the Rev. Ralph B. Odman, general secretary of Unevangelized Fields Mission. He was on his way to Congo to be there when, hopefully, his people might escape from their rebel captors.

"I want you to go along," he said. " . . . there's a story in Congo to be told, not just of what man is doing to man, but of what in the midst of terrible happenings God is doing *for* man."

In a short while we were in Leopoldville. The people who had come through the horrendous massacre of Stanleyville just the day before began telling of their experiences. Others escaped to "Leo" from Paulis and Poko and Bunia and Aketi and other towns with strange-sounding names. From the testimonies of the escapees has come this book.

I have attempted to reconstruct the events in northeast Congo as they happened in 1964; if there are passages of suspense or doubt or near despair, they trace the unfolding of the actual story when the participants, not knowing what would come next, went through suspense and doubt and near despair. In an effort to be accurate I

4

interrogated dozens of eyewitnesses on the most minute details, even to dialogue and pent-up emotions.

I trust that those who provided the material will forgive me for not interrupting the narrative to give proper attribution, but I have elected to acknowledge their indispensable contributions here. I greatly appreciate the willingness of so many to share with me their experiences; several granted me long interviews even in their deepest hours of grief.

It was a proud yet humbling experience to be the only writer to accompany Dr. Paul Carlson on his last, lonely journey to the Ubangi; for two days after the funeral party had left the area I was able to talk with Congolese who knew the doctor well. I of course found it impossible to interview everyone emerging from rebel territory whom I felt essential to the story; some left Congo before I could get to them. But to augment or to corroborate the testimony of others, I later tracked down many evacuees in Europe, the British Isles, and the United States.

I returned home with copious notes and with tape recordings that transcribed to about five hundred typewritten pages, many of them single-spaced. I am deeply grateful to the Rev. B. Lehman Keener, Unevangelized Fields deputation secretary, and his hardworking crews from Elizabethtown and Mount Joy, Pennsylvania, for transcribing the tapes. I also thank Mr. Odman not only for much practical assistance but for the sense of inspiration he continually brought to this project. I express appreciation also to Mrs. Gordon Fairley for her gracious hospitality at Leopoldville's Union Mission House; to Mission Évangelique d'Ubangi for the kindnesses their missionaries extended to me; to Dr. Frank J. Manley, director of the Mott Foundation, and to Dr. Henry R. Brandt, president of Christian Leadership Training, institutions in Flint, Michigan, with which I am associated, for saying "go ahead" when the opportunity arose to go to Congo; to the individual missionaries, their families, their several mission societies, all of whom co-operated unstintingly; to the members of my adult Sunday School class who regularly prayed for me throughout the writing of the book; and, by all means, to M. L. Arnold, Edward Ziegler, Eleanor Jordan, Beverly

Lancaster, and Lucia Withers, who, among others at Harper &
Row, possess insights and judgments which I value highly.

From the accounts here of those who lived through the Congo
rebellion of 1964 will come, I trust, greater understanding of those
trying days. I hope, for example, that the reader will understand
that it was not primarily racial hatred that brought about the atrocities, but cold calculation for political power. It is my hope, too,
that the testimonies in this book will move young hearts to fill the
decimated ranks of God's noble army of workers.

Finally, I am indebted to God for allowing me to witness the
emergence of spiritual triumph in the awful tragedies of Congo. If
the reader absorbs something of this victory, it will have been God's
doing that turned my faltering words into a meaningful ministry.

H.E.D.

1

How Will the Day End?

Daylight ordinarily awoke the prisoners in the Résidence Victoria at Stanleyville. This morning it was sound, not the sense of sight, that brought a stirring to the hotel deep in northeast Congo. On the second floor Alfred Larson was the first in his room to react to the roar of an engine outside.

"That was a plane!" he shouted. "Did you fellows hear that plane?"

He sprang over a less alert body, one of two that shared his bed, and bounded to the window. He leaned out to scan the pearl-gray sky. He began to count aloud. "Two—three—*four* planes!"

Overhead, a B-26 bomber skimmed the roof of the Victoria. He glanced up, saw that rockets clung to the wings. Higher up, another plane passed in and out of the cloud cover. A huge craft, it carried no explosives.

Larson drew back into the room.

"Del! Chuck!" he called. The man named Chuck stood at his elbow, peering out.

"Chuck!" he said, grasping his arm. "Chuck, there's a transport . . . they're not all fighter planes. A transport! You know what that can mean?"

Larson was a short, stocky man of thirty-six, an intense person who seldom hid his emotions. At this time his body trembled with excitement. He crossed to the bed, shook the one who still slept.

"Wake up, Del!" He bent over the bed and spoke directly into the other's ear. "There's a transport plane overhead!"

The sleeper roused. For a moment he lay still, unsure of what Larson had said. When arrested three weeks before, he had lost his hearing aid to a rebel soldier. Foreign equipment, especially unfamiliar electronic equipment, was highly suspicious, and so it was taken from him. He had found hearing extremely difficult since then.

Now he saw more than heard Larson's agitation. He jumped out of bed and ran to the window.

The other man, Chuck, was also on edge. He pointed excitedly.

"Look!" he said. "There's another transport . . . Do you suppose they could be carrying paratroopers?"

Al Larson turned and looked at Chuck. He half smiled, then gravely pursed his lips. "This is it," he said. "The next hour should tell the story."

For almost four months the three men had been among hundreds of foreign residents of northeast Congo whom the insurgent government held as prisoners, either under actual guard, as some three hundred were in the Victoria, or under house arrest all over the city. The rebels called themselves "Lions," or in the Swahili tongue, "Simbas." Larson believed they had lived up to their name.

Did these planes overhead mean that today, November 24, 1964, an attempt was to be made to wrest the helpless prey from the Lions? Larson thought so. For two days a rumor had circulated throughout the Victoria that Belgian paratroopers would arrive in American planes to rescue the foreign population of Stan, which was the abbreviated name the inhabitants gave their city. But how the effort would be accomplished—or whether it would succeed at all—he did not know.

He looked up. A hurtling plane was aiming straight at the hotel.

He watched as its silhouette grew larger, listened as the quivering struts of its wings screamed against the resisting air. It came closer and closer, its engine whining, its shattering percussion rattling the walls of the room and the very teeth in his head. It nosed up abruptly, clearing the hotel by an uncomfortable margin.

Other planes buzzed the streets as if they were trying to read the building signs. They zoomed, wheeled, and dived over Stan. They doubled back to the airport, which lay along the Congo River a mile and a quarter below the heart of town. Then the smaller planes joined the huge transports, which all the while flew in majestic circles over the landing field. The airport was strategic; if rescue came, Larson knew it would play a major role.

He looked at his watch. Six thirty. He looked down to the nearly deserted streets. The moist morning air lay heavy on the city and in a moment between sorties all seemed to be peace. Palm trees stood motionless along the broad streets and in the traffic roundabouts, their verdure highlighted by the soft shades of the buildings. Only a few Simbas walked the streets. Some wore the uniform of their rebel army, a haphazard garb that was complete only when a patch of fur had been sewn to it somewhere. Many had stripped themselves of all evidences of being Simbas—except for their automatic guns, their rifles, or their occasional spears that they carried with them straight from the bush. This morning, Larson could see, the Simbas wanted to look like ordinary townsfolk, except that ordinary people were not out today.

No Congolese laborer walked to his job as sweeper at Sedec Moteurs or as vat cleaner at the big brewery, and no country woman carried a basket of vegetables on her head to sell at the market. The Africans had heard and seen the planes; they knew that this was not to be a day for pursuing a livelihood in Stan.

Larson turned from the window, pulled on his shirt and trousers, socks and shoes.

"They seem to be staying close to the airport now," Larson said, and speaking loudly so Del could hear, he added, "We'd better get something into our stomachs. After a beginning like this, who knows how the day will end?"

"All we've got is a papaya," said Del. He split it into three parts as fairly as possible. The guards would hardly be around this morning with their usual pot of coffee from the hotel kitchen. Well, all right; they'd eat their fruit without coffee.

"Let's pray, fellows," said Larson. Reverently, he gave thanks for the food that had been provided.

"And, Father," he prayed, "whatever Thy will shall be today, let us accept it. Give us the wisdom to know what we ought to do and when we ought to do it."

Someone started to read aloud from the Bible, but a hubbub somewhere off in the building made it difficult to pay attention. The noise grew louder. Suddenly, it moved onto their floor. Then it exploded in the corridor right outside their room. Simba soldiers were running up and down the hall. They shouted and banged on doors.

"Appel! Appel! Roll call! Roll call!" they shrieked. One kicked open the door to the room. He lurched forward and in near hysteria thrust his Sten gun in their faces.

"Get out!" he cried. At this point-blank range Del heard without his hearing aid. "Colonel's orders! Out!"

The soldier trembled with fright. Larson could tell that any delay might set him off, so he nodded his compliance. The Simba waved his gun to point where the men were to go, then darted to the neighboring room to call out the prisoners there.

The floors above had been the first summoned to roll call. Hastily clad men and women, nearly all Belgians, some carrying or pulling along crying children, scrambled down the staircase under surveillance of rebel guns. From a second-floor room a Simba with fixed bayonet pushed out an old couple. According to what could be made of his tirade, they had tried to escape detection by crawling under their beds.

Al Larson and his roommates stuffed the last of the fruit into their mouths. From the desk Larson grabbed his passport and ID card, his Bible, and a plastic pack of vitamins and dysentery pills. He had been on an *appel* before; these were items he knew they might need. Del picked up his valise; he had never unpacked it.

Chuck collected whatever things of value he could slip into his pockets.

Larson looked at his watch again. Nearly seven. He took the watch from his wrist and dropped it in a pocket. Simbas liked watches; so far none had seen his. Quietly, they walked to the stairs and waited there for the way to clear. They fell in at the rear and began to walk down.

Were there paratroopers in those planes? Larson said to himself, "God be our help if rescue doesn't come!" A plane flying overhead always set the rebels off on a rampage. So many planes had maneuvered over the city this morning that the Simbas were driven to a frenzy.

But a greater danger lay in another direction. Less vague than the rumors of paratroopers were the reports of the mercenaries driving toward Stanleyville from the south. The Congo government of Moise Tshombe had retained this force of hired soldiers to lead his national troops in the war against the Simbas. They were driving on, now, under the direction of a South African named Mike Hoare. Ironically, this advance posed a deadly threat to the prisoners.

"Call off your mercenaries," the chief of the rebels had radioed to Tshombe. "Let them touch Stanleyville and we'll kill every foreigner in sight."

His threat did not end there. He went on to explain, in detail, how his Simbas would slaughter their hostages.

By all calculations Major Hoare and his crack column would strike at Stan at any time. For two weeks Hoare had been progressing almost at whatever pace he pleased. He figured on liberating Stan—all reports agreed—and breaking the back of the rebellion. He planned to do so before the end of November. That gave him a week.

Al Larson knew, and so did every foreign resident in Stan, whether in confinement or merely under house arrest, that as the mercenaries marched closer to Stan, nearer also drew the day of doom.

"This is it," Larson thought as he walked down the stairs.

"Today the crisis comes." How often the rebels had threatened to
kill the prisoners! Larson believed that at some time they actually
would kill them. In his mind he had tied the fateful day to the
arrival of the mercenaries. Now perhaps there was fresh hope.
Within the hour they should learn whether those planes carried the
means of liberation.

At the bottom of the stairs Larson spotted men he knew from an
upper floor.

"Some excitement today?" he asked as he greeted his friends.

"Yes," nodded a thin man in his mid-thirties who stood back to
wait for Larson. He probably had been handsomer before losing so
much weight. As they walked together Larson noticed that he
looked as if he might be ill and as if each step were an effort.

"What could you see from your window, Paul?" Larson asked.
He did not hear the answer, however; Simbas had taken up posts
in the hotel lobby to usher the prisoners through the front doors
and out into the street. There rebels prodded them to get along
faster.

"Move ahead! Move ahead!" a fellow wearing only a tattered
loincloth screamed angrily.

"Hurry along, there," another with wild-looking eyes shouted.
His nervous chatter blended grotesquely with the stutter of automatic gunfire somewhere in the distance. "You've got to catch up
with the others."

There were six of them moving along together—the three from
the second floor and three from a room above them. The six were
American missionaries. In recent days they had had to draw
deeply on their faith while they suffered because of their nationalities. Now it was evident that a new testing of spiritual stamina
lay somewhere along this side street of Stan down which the
column of some two hundred fifty prisoners moved.

"Are there paras?" Larson asked the thin, weary man from the
upper floor.

"Yes," he replied, puffing heavily. Brisk walking had become an
ordeal for him. "From our floor we saw them dropping."

"Dr. Carlson," called Chuck over his shoulder to the one who had spoken, "just what on earth is going to happen to us out here?"

"I don't know," Carlson replied. "You can hear the gunfire. Obviously the paratroopers are fighting their way into town. They are coming to us, or we are going to them. Perhaps when we meet we will provide the rebels with a human shield."

The missionaries closed ranks with the main body of prisoners, which had slowed almost to a stop. Larson stepped to one edge of the column to see what had caused the slackening. The head of the line turned a corner and stretched up another street. The people forward had stopped, and now the whole line was still.

"Sit down!" barked a commanding voice.

Larson's gaze halted just short of the turn. There on the grass a handful of Simbas were feverishly trying to load a machine gun. Its hideous barrel pointed directly at the halted hostages.

There had been so many rumors, so much confusion. Just yesterday the prisoners believed that Jomo Kenyatta, the former Mau Mau leader who was now prime minister of Kenya, would mediate the Congo crisis. He would come into Stan and arrange for the release of Belgian and American prisoners on the condition that Belgium and the United States stop giving aid to Tshombe's government. For this reason, the rumor had gone, the Simbas had cleaned out the Central Prison and the military camps and the other places where prisoners were held and had transferred them to the Victoria. The hotel was a more acceptable setting in which to exhibit the prisoners to an outsider.

But here in Avenue Sergeant Ketele, under the watchfulness of nervous Simba guards, Larson knew the time for negotiation had passed. He was afraid it might be too late for the paratroopers to help the prisoners. One look at the activity around the machine gun made clear the intent of the Simbas. The question was, why had the rebel army—indeed, why had so many of the people of northeast Congo—turned in fury on the foreigners with whom they once lived peaceably?

The Rev. Alfred Larson and his wife Jean had arrived in Congo

in 1953 to spend the rest of their lives in missionary work. Even at
twenty-four, which he was then, his balding crown and penetrating
eyes gave him the look of severity when pensive or troubled and
not smiling. Yet he was not a harsh person—except with himself.
He possessed unlimited energy, all of which he threw into his
calling.

His mother died when Al was an infant; he grew up in the
depression days in a Brooklyn orphanage. A nearby Baptist con-
gregation took an interest in the children at the home. The men
played ball with the boys; the Sunday School made the orphans
welcome. At thirteen this hard-luck boy might have graduated to a
street gang; instead, he gave his heart to Jesus Christ. At seventeen
he dedicated his life to missionary service.

Upon his arrival in Congo years later, he felt that the same
selfless interest that had won him would win the Congolese to
Christ. He fused this spirit of dedication with his natural drive. It
worked. His first field assignment was as an instructor in his mission's teacher-training school. He did more than instruct. He
begged musical instruments from friends in the United States and
started a band. With a knowledge of French learned during a year
in Belgium, he immersed himself in Lingala, and later Swahili, the
trade tongues of the people. He plunged into the bush to preach
and teach, to listen and observe, and to soak up African life.

Five years later his fellow workers in Unevangelized Fields Mission made him their assistant Congo leader, and in 1961 completed the shift of responsibilities onto his sturdy shoulders.

UFM, a nonsectarian society with headquarters near Philadelphia and in England and Australia, sponsors missionaries on
four continents and in New Guinea. Congo is one of its oldest and
largest fields. As Congo leader Larson became a co-laborer with
the principal Africans of the Evangelical Church of Upper Congo,
established in the 1930's by the UFM. He also grew to know and
respect the missionaries and national workers of other missions
throughout the country. He learned of the rough times of many
Congolese leaders. In a country being torn in bloody shreds, these

men of God depended on maturity and devotion to keep their churches free of destruction from both within and without.

But the year 1964, the half of it that remained after he and Jean returned from furlough in America, seemed one of considerable promise for the work of the Lord in northeast Congo. At nearly year's end, however, the promise somehow faded, and he found himself seated in a street in Stanleyville, looking on helplessly as Simbas hurried to feed a belt of bullets into a machine gun.

Delbert Carper—quiet, unassuming but resourceful, deep-thinking Del,—had been in Congo for ten years. He was a teacher and trainer of teachers and enjoyed good fellowship with the Africans, though that fellowship was now interrupted by the Simbas. The fellow Chuck—Charles Davis—was a brand-new missionary. His dreams were all future. He, too, was caught up in the nightmare.

Two others, Gene Bergman and Jon Snyder, had come to Congo in recent months as Mennonite objectors to war and military duty. But in their service in lieu of duty they had been caught up in war.

The sixth man in their group, Paul Carlson, had left his practice as a surgeon in California to work in Africa for Covenant World Missions. In his year in Congo he spent several months serving God and the Africans, the remainder of it suffering as few other captives had suffered.

Stanleyville was home to hundreds of foreigners, Belgians mostly, but also many Greeks, Italians, Pakistanis, Portuguese, and other nationalities. Always a part of Stan, the non-Africans differed among themselves in their mode of living. A planter might marry an African woman, a river boat captain claim no other home or allegiance. On the other hand, those who preferred isolation created a home-country island on which to live in a sea of African culture. For the most part the foreign residents strove to be neutral in Congo politics; a few tried to court the rebels, as they had fawned upon those before them, hoping by it to prosper in their shops or on their rubber or coffee plantations.

Regardless, however, of how they had lived, of their affinity to the African, here they all were—*commerçants,* doctors, technicians, missionaries—either seated in the street like unwary deer in the sights of crafty bowmen, or holed up in their houses, praying that violence would not come when reason said that it would.

Perhaps none puzzled more over the changes than veteran missionary Herbert Jenkinson and Alice his wife. This Britisher had walked into Congo by way of the White Nile forty-four years before. He battled malaria and blackwater fever and heat and superstition—and won. In soil that love and patience tilled he planted the seed of the Gospel. Then from England he sought helpers to tend the fragile shoots.

Among his recruits was a young woman whose vigor and freshness of life matched his. She became his bride. Over the years the color in her hair faded, but she made small allowance for other aspects of advancing years.

Jenkinson was fairly tall and very erect, with no stiffness or stuffiness about him. He also still possessed the physical force and the inquiring mind of the pioneering days.

For years he was his mission's field captain, until finally Al Larson succeeded him. He had baptized the oldest of the African believers. The people of the bush had found it hard to say "Jenkinson." The closest they came was "Kinso"—so Kinso and Ma Kinso it had been since any could remember.

Above everything else a humble man, Kinso habitually climbed into the back of the truck for a trip, letting others ride up front where by position he should have been. Proud to be an Englishman and as reserved as one, he nevertheless picked up many American ways through travel and association with the American missionaries who came to work alongside him. Though he might justifiably have looked back, he strove to be up to date, to search for fresh viewpoints, to consider new ideas. He welcomed change if by change they could further the Gospel in Congo.

In these days of rebel occupation Kinso had often gazed out, as he did this morning, from the window of his second-story flat over the bookshop he tended as the latest of many missionary duties.

Day after day he had to ask himself, "Are these the Africans I've lived among for nearly fifty years?"

And time after time Kinso thanked God that one could not generalize. The Christians, he knew, abhorred the violence, as did many others. But did not some of them feel that the political aims of the rebellion were right? Even among the military there were "good" Simbas and "bad" Simbas. The day's events, and the people's reaction to them, seemed to hinge on whether at the moment the good or the bad had the upper hand.

Five miles beyond the city at a compound called Kilometer 8 lived twenty-five missionaries, counting children, who were subject to these shifts in control. Among them were the Larson, Carper, and Davis families, left behind when the three American men were jailed. Not all the families belonged at Kilometer 8. The house was UFM's Congo headquarters, hence the residence of the Larsons. But the other missionaries, in transit for one reason or another, were trapped there as the rebels took over Stan nearly four months earlier. It mattered to them who was to have the upper hand today.

Out through the vast rain forest, in every direction, lived other aliens, hundreds of Roman Catholic priests and nuns among them, and scores of Protestant missionaries of many societies. What happened in Stan today could alter their lives. There were, for example, Joseph W. (Jay) and Angeline Tucker, of the Assemblies of God, in the city of Paulis northeast of Stan. If a lion's den ever existed, Paulis was one. Just the past August they had landed squarely in it—quite a reception for the beginning of their second quarter century of missionary service.

And upriver from Stan, past the treacherous Stanley Falls, resided the Cyril Taylors and the elderly pair, Muriel Harman and Mary Harrison. They carried on in their area the work of Worldwide Evangelization Crusade, a ministry begun by one of the great pioneers in missions, C. T. Studd.

There was Mary Baker at the all-Christian village of Bopepe— "dear Mary Baker," people usually said, "she's more African in her ways than most Africans."

After Congo's first prime minister was murdered in 1961, she was the only non-African around who was not taken in for questioning. People simply regarded Mary Baker as one of the local citizens.

She felt that someday the missionary might give up his life in order to witness of Christ; she never thought that strange. "After all," she wrote in letters to her home church in Richmond, Virginia, "Jesus died for me. Why shouldn't I expect to die for Him?"

And there were others: the brilliant medical couple from London, Dr. and Mrs. Ian Sharpe; young, energetic Bill McChesney, out from Arizona; the Chester Burks from Western Canada; the John Artons, so happy to have their teen-aged Heather down from England to spend her school holiday with them.

Serious trouble had enveloped these folk before. During Congo's turbulent independence days of 1960 the planters, the transport men, the missionaries, had suffered. Torn between a Congo government that asked them to stay and their national embassies that pressured them to get out, fearful and uncertain, most of them evacuated. Kinso stayed on; Al Larson remained until finally he felt he must leave.

The bloodletting stopped. The Congolese asked their foreign residents to return. Individual churches issued calls for individual missionaries to come back, much as a church in the homeland calls a pastor.

After a two-month absence Larson returned. At church one day two pastors flung their arms around him in glad reunion. Suddenly, he felt a squeeze on the calf of his leg. He looked down to see a toddler hugging with all his might. The boy had broken from his mother's grasp to have a part in welcoming back the missionary.

"Independence has brought its bewilderment," wrote Kinso and Larson jointly to their fellow missionaries. "Jesus came not to be ministered unto, but to minister. If you can't come to Africa in that spirit, don't come at all."

Those who would return would have to come with a clear understanding. In the new day of independence they would take orders from the Congolese, relinquish their personal rights, and accept with grace the overruling of their opinions and the corrections of their African brethren.

Almost all the missionaries returned, eager to begin work again. So did the merchants, the health officers, the vegetable dealers, the brewers, the planters.

And now in the current tension the plea to stay had once more been made. On this morning of November 24, 1964, the ones who remained found themselves under strict house arrest . . . or lying on damp concrete floors in the putrid prisons of the jungle hinterland . . . or numbly obeying the command to be seated in a Stanleyville street under the loaded guns of nervous rebel soldiers.

To learn "why" one perhaps had to go back before the terrifying days of 1964, even before the virulence of Independence, further back, and then trace the sorry facts of history until finally they built a stage for the present melodrama. Surely Africa had not forgotten the days when foreigners raided her villages for slaves to stock the empires of Europe. Nor had Congo erased the memory of Leopold II. For twenty-three years until 1908 this king of the Belgians considered the rich, tropical Congo his own private preserve, and the rest of the world stood by and let him. What village youth had not heard from his father or grandfather how Leopold's entrepeneurs set production quotas for rubber and diamonds and gold, and accepted bushels of native right hands to balance short accounts?

Then came Belgian colonialism and a new standard of living guaranteed by the firm paternal hand of an all-powerful triumvirate, the Belgian government, Belgian business, and the Belgian church.

European administrators pushed out into the bush to give to Congo law and order and justice, and jealously guarded the prerogatives their offices provided. Monopolies formed in Brussels transformed jungle trading posts like Stanleyville into modern, bustling cities boasting the convenience of the telephone, the cosmopolitan flair of international air travel, radio, seven-story buildings. The Catholic Church, the humanizing oil in this colonial machinery, raised chapels and hospitals and conducted schools, the latter its exclusive field until it was later shared with the expanding Protestant missions.

The standard of living was the highest of any colony in Africa. What more could Congo want? Only one thing: Independence.

On June 30, 1960, the Republic of Congo was born. Immediately, the new government of Patrice Lumumba faced civil war. Mutinies by the army, riots, African falling upon African in tribal conflict, an attempt at secession by the mine-rich province of Katanga, the frenzy of mob violence—all these events turned Congo into a flaming furnace. Non-Africans felt its heat, and for some the fire was fatal. Lumumba himself, clearly the people's choice, though to some a strange and dangerous mystic, was shunted aside and brutally murdered.

The United Nations had dispatched a peace-keeping force to hold Congo together. Eventually, conditions returned to near normal, though always in Congo's nine hundred thousand square miles some spot heaved in turmoil. The economy picked up. The first medical student among the fourteen million Congolese was graduated from a European university. For the churches the work of evangelism, teacher training, and village medicine thrived again. Much of the church's function rested in the hands of the national Christians—the Evangelical Church of Upper Congo had become self-governing in 1960 before independence.

"We are keeping in the background," missionary Hector McMillan wrote home to Canada. "For the most part the work continues to be indigenous."

But the president of the church association, or the local pastor, or the teacher never wanted the missionary to be far away.

Then shortly after 1964 began, disquieting news emerged from the heartland of Congo. From clandestine jungle hideouts wild bands of young men were striking out to terrorize villages, government posts, monasteries, and mission stations.

In Kwilu Province, Auguste Eicher, of Baptist Mid-Missions,

was pulled from his house one morning before sunup. His tormentors beat him, then made him kneel. Someone produced a
sledgehammer.

"Aren't you afraid?" a grinning youth teased.

"And you"—the fellow, now fondling the handle of the ham-
mer, addressed the missionary's wife—"aren't you afraid of what
will happen when your husband is dead and you are alone with
us?"

By this time the sun had risen on the isolated mission, but the
hour was dark for the Eichers. Yet somehow within themselves
there welled unusual courage. First he, then she, was able to say
truthfully, "No, I am not afraid."

Their courage had its effect. A dissenting member of the band
intervened; after four more hours of threatenings the brigands allowed the villagers to take the missionaries to the forest. There the
couple hid for a week, then were flown out to safety by a pilot of
Missionary Aviation Fellowship.

At the Catholic mission of Kilembe in the same province three
Belgian priests were not so fortunate. One midnight the fathers
heard a banging on the door of their house. The father superior
drew on his robe and went to investigate. Hands reached swiftly
through the darkness to grab him, and, once having him, beat him
until he died.

A second priest crossed to the door to see about the commotion.
He, too, was seized and murdered. The assailants waited for the
third. He failed to come out. He couldn't; a hip cast immobilized
him. The attackers entered, dragged him from the room, and
slashed him to death with butcher knives.

2

No Longer Academic

From various places came rueful accounts of house and even village burnings, of long nights of terror, and of days filled with forebodings. Then flashed the news of an attack on women.

Irene Ferrel and Ruth Hege conducted a quiet Baptist work in the Kwilu bush. With evidence that the menace around them was growing, they decided they must go. One night in a simple service in their living room they took leave of their faithful African workers: the pastor, the male nurse in charge of the dispensary, a teacher in the Bible School, a few of the students. Irene unfolded her portable organ to play for the singing. Then they read the Bible and prayed together and said their good-bys. The women retired, anticipating the arrival of a helicopter to take them out the next morning.

A little past midnight a youth gang stormed the lonely station, hurtling rocks through the windows and crying for blood. They rushed into the house, snatched the women from their beds, and pushed and pulled them to a grove of trees fifty feet away.

How odd that the moon should shine so prettily that night. It seemed almost that the grappling figures, brandishing their bows and arrows and knives, danced a ritual deep from the forest. In the light that shone through the trees, however, Ruth Hege witnessed a scene of horror. A boy in his teens had shot an arrow into Irene's neck.

She saw Irene pull out the arrow. Then she heard her say quietly, as if speaking of the day's routine, "I'm finished." Irene took a few steps, collapsed, and died.

Ruth, too, had been hit by an arrow, but less seriously. She fell beside Irene. Cold and frightened, and drenched from the dew that dropped from the trees, Ruth prayed for calmness. The answer lay in her ability to feign death, even when a man pulled out a handful of her hair.

Eventually, the assailants ran off into the night. Ruth had escaped further harm; yet, how many times in the awful days that followed was she to think of death as possibly the better course!

The violence in the central forests formed a pattern: Idle young men, disillusioned that independence made them neither wise nor wealthy, had banded into units of a loose-knit organization called the *Jeunesse*. Undisciplined and not knowing their own purpose, they robbed, pillaged, threatened, tortured, killed, and destroyed. Africans and foreigners alike were their victims. It became apparent, however, that these were more than disenchanted youth; they were the makings of a growing army. The communist-trained Pierre Mulele was their inspiration, though it was not clear whether he himself was alive or dead. The rebellion, if such at this point it could be called, had been supercharged by the taste of blood. It needed yet a plan and a cadre of officers to carry out the plan. By midyear of 1964 it was to have both.

The United Nations pulled its peace-keeping troops out of Congo on June 30, after having vainly begged its dissenting members for funds to keep them there. Defense was now up to the Congo government, which was so weak that for it to maintain order beyond Leopoldville was almost impossible. The way thus opened for opposition leaders to return from exile, to emerge from the special camps Red China had set up to indoctrinate in the communist technique of subversion.

They came back, arriving with their plans perfected and their cadres appointed. What better time than the present to put theory into practice?

The plunderings of the Kwilu became full-fledged revolts in Lomami and Maniema Provinces, then in the Kivu and in all of east Congo. The target, however, was Stanleyville. This keystone of the great northeast was to be the capital of the new People's Republic.

The missionaries of the northeast kept abreast of developments in central Congo. Contrasting them to their situation, Hector Mc-Millan wrote in July to friends, "It is hard to imagine trouble in Congo when in our area all we know is peace."

Yet even in the McMillans' tranquil village there appeared signs of possible trouble ahead. A man at the mission spoke bitterly of the local governmental official.

"Very soon," he said, "this enemy of the land will die. Other people will come, people who will give us jobs and money and the things we like to have in our houses."

Many persons, like this man, were looking for anyone who would bring them a better deal. The only dust on the horizon was in the south where the rebels were busy kicking it up.

But could the rebel army penetrate into the area around Stanleyville? Fresh troops had arrived from Leopoldville to strengthen the defenses. Yet, should the rebels overpower the government frontally or by stealth, what then?

The missionary, for one, had to decide on a course of action. July was a month of considerable discussion. Missionaries of the UFM met at Mary Baker's station at Bopepe to air the question of evacuation. Other groups gathered to weigh the issues.

Suppose that the northeast fell to the rebels? the reasoning ran. Nicholas Olenga, who as military chief called himself a general, held his insurgent soldiers under control. A Simba was not permitted to molest women. He could not touch so much as the hand of a foreigner nor take anything from him directly. He could not steal. Violation of a taboo might bring on death. If the faithful soldier observed the vows and certain practices of witchcraft, he became invincible in battle.

Even Olenga, a one-time clerk, appeared to believe in the power of his military sorcery. Stories spread even faster than the rebel advance that General Olenga obtained his strategy from a well-known meduim in Kindu, an important city en route to Stanleyville from the south.

Whether true or not, Olenga pushed his troops steadily toward Stan. Tension in the city mounted. Then the strain under which the foreigners lived was eased somewhat by a message from Olenga. Flushed with victory and confident of the future, the rebel general telegraphed:

> I HOPE THE FOREIGN POPULATION WILL REMAIN IN THEIR POSTS. OUR FIGHT IS NOT AGAINST THE FOR-EIGNER. YOU HAVE YOUR WORK TO DO. DO IT.

During the last week of July Al Larson met with some of the missionaries in the Kinso apartment in Stanleyville. They talked again about whether they should leave or stay. From Kilometer 8 Al spoke over the mission's new inter-station radio network, raising with missionaries outside Stan the question of evacuation.

In answer one of them said, "Why not learn from Independence?" From hindsight it appeared that perhaps none of them really had to leave then. Was not Stan engulfed in rebellion briefly in 1961? At that time the missionaries endured many threats, but met little actual interference with their work. Some of the rebel leaders in that revolt were leaders in the present action. Would not the parallel favor staying?

"Here at Bongondza everything is peaceful," said Ian Sharpe, taking time from a busy surgery schedule at the UFM hospital north of Stan.

"We've just been on trek through the bush and the people were never more friendly nor more appreciative of our visit," someone else reported.

"Ought we not stay by our African Christians?" another asked.

"Are we or are we not a part of the African Church?"

"We are!" cut in still another. "By their invitation we are. And if by staying we can help the Congolese stiffen their backs against the wrong, shouldn't we stay, even if possibly it means we lay down our lives alongside them?"

Larson summed up for those on the network what they had said:

"God called us to Congo. I think we're willing to pay the price of serving as long as He allows us to serve."

He then added:

"I can't order you to stay, but I'll ask you all to stay. If any one of you feels he ought to leave, feel free to do so."

He suggested they seek by prayer to know the will of God, and then report back at three o'clock that afternoon. This was done. The calls were all the same:

"We will stay."

It was of course not certain that Stan would fall to the rebels, so perhaps their decision had been academic. The reinforced army guarded many strategic points on the route up from the south—the iron bridge at Wanie-Rukula, for example. An invader had to cross that bridge. Block the road at either end and the lay of the land would thwart an advance. Disperse the rebel army there and likely the march on Stan would collapse.

Present at the Kinso flat during the discussion were Volker and Elsi Gscheidle, a German missionary couple. Their station forty miles from Stan would be the first to know if the talk had been only idle conversation. Their house stood not far from the north end of the bridge.

"Volker," said Larson, much concerned for their safety, "keep in touch by radio every two hours. Let us know when the rebels approach. If they cross the bridge—"

"The bridge is mined," broke in Gscheidle.

"If they succeed in crossing," Larson continued, "you and Elsi beat it into town. How the rebels behave may affect all our plans."

On Sunday, August 2, Larson tried vainly to contact the Wanie station. Because of the silence he looked all day for the Gscheidles to drive into Stan. But they did not. On Monday, it was rumored that a high-ranking rebel had slipped into town to convince the national soldiers they should throw down their arms. That afternoon a curfew sounded, spreading further alarm among the already skittish inhabitants. Tuesday morning the American consul in Stan summoned Larson to his office.

"I need not dwell on the uncertainties here," the consul said. "I wanted to tell you that two planes will arrive here this afternoon to take out the dependents of our consular staff, United Nations personnel, and others to the point of capacity. There are nineteen seats available to you."

Suddenly, the question of going or staying was somehow not academic in the least. But Larson deliberated for only a moment.

"Thank you, sir," he replied. "You are not leaving?"

"No," the consul said. "My men and I will stay."

"The shopkeepers and the beer makers and the auto mechanics are not leaving," Larson said. "When trouble comes, should the missionary be the first to run?"

He thanked the consul for his offer. "We cannot accept," he said firmly. "We are going to stay."

The planes came, as the consul had said they would come. Anxious men placed their wives and children aboard and watched the planes take off into the lowering sun, off to the sanctuary of Leopoldville. At five o'clock the streets of Stan were disturbed by the sporadic firing of guns.

Surely, this couldn't be Olenga's army! The latest report had placed them about one hundred fifty miles beyond Wanie-Rukula. In the apartment Kinso hummed a tune as he removed a book from the bookcase and thumbed through it. By his nonchalance he hoped to calm the minds of his wife and Mary Rutt, a missionary from Pennsylvania who assisted in the work of the bookshop and who shared quarters with the British couple.

"Merely practice shooting," he said with a shrug. "There's not enough for fighting."

Meanwhile, Al Larson had run from place to place all afternoon, first to seek permission to drive the road to the Wanie station to check on the German couple, and then, that request denied as suicidal, to promote a reconnaissance flight. On this, too, he gathered only refusals.

Earlier in the day he had summarily dismissed the notion of evacuating. Now with the day closing out, he worried about the Gscheidles. His fear for their safety mounted with each *ping* of a ricocheting bullet. He headed home to Kilometer 8 and weighed his decision in the fog of doubt. Had their reasoning been faulty? What if, contrary to Olenga's assurances, the rebels turned their war against the foreigner, against the missionary, even against the children?

But in resolving to stay, had they—and more particularly, had he—tied the choice to what a rebel might or might not do? Or were they seeking the will of One to whom a Simba was only a part of an all-encompassing plan?

Larson knew that in the days ahead they were certain to find the answers to these haunting questions. The army of the People's Republic had breached the defenses of Stan and the noise of the battle now reached even to the house at Kilometer 8.

3

Proving Themselves Lions

Practice, was it, that firing in the streets of Stan? Before the evening ended Kinso had to admit that things outside were a trifle upsetting. The late news on the BBC reported that the Stanleyville airport had fallen to the rebels.

"Now *that* I don't believe," said Kinso to his wife and Mary Rutt. "They'd have to go past our place to get to the airfield, and we haven't heard that much fighting."

The apartment, over the bookstore of Librairie Évangelique au Congo, a joint-mission undertaking known as "LECO," faced directly on the Central Prison. It stood a block from the *État-Major,* the local headquarters for the national army. The next morning the main body of rebels arrived. The shooting centered about LECO, sending the missionaries for cover.

But by noon the fighting subsided. The government troops had shown no strong will to resist. From his window Kinso looked down at the triumphant rebels milling before the Central Prison and realized why surrender had come about so easily.

The maelstrom in the street centered on four witchdoctors who in full regalia had danced into Stan at the head of the invading column. Even to one who attached no spiritual meaning to their

29

persons were the sorcerers downright frightening; being wrapped in
jungle superstition made them seem to possess a power that held
one in awe. It was from panic that Stan's defenders pitched aside
their bazooka guns and scattered.

The four had whitened their faces by a paste of the manioc root;
the chalk accented the black pupils of their glassy eyes. They covered their bodies with grass skirts and feathers, and their heads
with hats of leopard skin. Goat horns protruded from one hat and
gave its wearer the look of a forest devil. Around each neck hung a
fetish bag, the precious pouch that contained the mysterious source
of a witchdoctor's power.

The sorcerers were as much a part of the rebel army as any
officer and could share the credit for its successes. Kinso knew that
the soldiers down in the street acknowledged it freely.

The soldiers themselves were scantily clad in rag tatters of short
pants or in still briefer loincloths. Some covered their chests with
palm fronds and their faces with dots of the chalky white. The
forehead over the nose bore fresh knife cuts. Like the sorcerers,
each man wore a bit of animal skin.

For those unable to obtain leopard, monkey or rhino was acceptable. Men possessing caps attached the skin to them; the others wore it on a wrist. This was the symbol of being Congo's lions.
In Swahili they chanted wherever they went:

"Simba! Simba! Simba!"

The intonation of a hundred trotting warriors had a way of chill-
ing the marrow of one's bones.

The cutting of the forehead was a part of the preparation for
battle, as was a daily baptism. The ritual, which was performed
by a sorcerer if one were around or, second best, by the soldier's
commanding officer, guaranteed that should a bullet strike a Simba
so prepared, it would turn to water on impact. To be thus impreg-
nable, however, a rebel must be faithful to the conditions of his
baptism. He was obliged to honor the taboos concerning thievery,
women, and the touching of another person, even accidentally, as
well as any personal vows he had made—perhaps not to eat manioc
greens in palm oil.

If a soldier less than perfect died, he did not really die. He only slept, the Simbas were assured, and in three days would wake up to fight again.

The Simbas in the street had undergone a final step in preparing for combat. They smoked a hypnotic hemp called *bangi,* or else rubbed a narcotic substance into the forehead cuts. Excitable by nature, they went wild on receiving the *dawa,* or spiritual medicine. The drugs pushed a man to do what even a savage would shrink from doing—for one thing, to run headlong into the enemy's fire.

The rebel army, fearless and fully ready for its most important undertaking, proved its invincibility at Stan. By Thursday, August 6, two days after the first elements invaded, the Simbas of the People's Republic gained control of the city.

Word penetrated behind the closed doors of shops and homes of how the citizens of Stan should welcome the rebels: No one would dare appear on the street without a flower or a leafy branch to wave in gratitude for having been liberated. Flowers and gunfire, a strange mixture; to it would be added other strange combinations, sadism and bureaucratic protocol, social justice and sorcery, rigid laws and anarchy.

The fall of Stanleyville gave substance to the shadow government of the People's Republic. At its head was Christophe Gbenye, a bearded, mercurial man who claimed the title of president. He was once minister of interior in the central government and in 1961 had been a leader in the short-lived rival regime in Stan after Lumumba's death. Gbenye looked on himself as the spiritual heir of the martyred Lumumba.

Baba—"Daddy" in Swahili—announced that he was savior of the nation.

He rode in a Rolls-Royce, but dressed in blue jeans. He orated with little persuading. One day over the radio he said with proud confidence:

"From Stan we'll push on to Leopoldville, then to Brussels, and on to New York. Someday the world will be ours."

Slightly less bold was his announcement that all thievery in Stan would stop. His government would also see that jobs were found for the idle. He ordered closed shopkeepers to reopen. Except for the merchants the people cheered when he cut all prices exactly in half.

Second in power was Gaston-Emile Soumialot, minister of defense, an ordinary appearing man who had read the communist manuals and followed them line upon line. Gbenye, Soumialot, and General Olenga put a wild-eyed, seemingly crazed local politician named Kingese in charge of Stan's affairs.

The affairs at this time were really only one, vengeance on "the people's" enemies.

Kingese aimed his cleanup at any who had served in Moise Tshombe's national government or who could be accused of non-African ways. Before the last of the invasion shots were fired, Kingese took to Radio Stan to summon the people as jurors in huge public trials. Convicted by acclamation, administrators, newsmen, magistrates, and Congolese businessmen met death by firing squad or by the practiced hand of spearmen.

Most of the executions occurred at a monument erected to honor Patrice Lumumba. Situated on a central square near the post office, the tile-and-marble memorial resembled a sentry box. Its main feature was a larger-than-life painting of the ardent nationalist. Behind protective glass, Lumumba stood in full color, his left arm resting on the world, his right arm raised as if to bless all who conquered in his name.

Many persons had long mounted the five marble steps to bring fresh floral offerings daily or to worship the slain hero. Once Kinso walked past and observed a man who removed his shoes, knelt, and genuflected. Larson had seen another who prostrated himself in praying to Lumumba. Now in a new phase of this religion, the Simbas ushered before the altar those hated ones whom they believed their patron would delight to accept in sacrifice.

On the steps and on the wide sidewalk in front, the crowds grew larger every day. From their apartment two blocks away the missionaries could not quite view the monument, but they saw and heard the mobs. Neither could they help knowing every time the Simbas thrust a luckless captive from the Central Prison and pushed or pulled him off to Lumumba Square.

On countless occasions that first week of occupation they heard the people's courts proclaim the guilt of someone haled before them. Then would sound the volleys of the firing squad, except that sometimes there were no shots. From accounts that reached them, they knew these silent executions to be the worst of all.

An eyewitness told of the day ten prisoners were led to the monument. Each was bruised from many beatings. Stan's deposed mayor, Leopold Matabo, was forced to look on as the men he had known so well lined up.

"Kneel!" the executioners commanded. Nine of the ten knelt. The founder of a local political party now in disgrace stood defiantly.

"I will die standing," he said.

He began to speak to the crowd, hoping to remind them that they knew him to be an honorable man. He toppled with the others, however; the submachine guns of the rebels showed no partiality to courage.

Matabo was not to find death so sweetly abrupt. The Simbas marched him to the public market. There a laughing officer disemboweled the mayor, and in view of the dying man feasted on his vitals.

By the first Saturday night the blood of the judged had stained the monument sidewalk a sickly red. Few of Stan's native citizens had been able to avoid jury duty at the monument.

On Sunday, Kingese was to unwrap his biggest spectacle.

Early that morning the Kinsos slipped out of the flat to worship with the handful of Africans who would dare to gather in a church. It was not advisable for an unmarried woman to appear yet on the street, so Mary Rutt stayed home. A missionary in Congo since 1946, Mary had never expected to escape the rough and raw of life; but what was happening in Stan now frightened her.

She stood at a window of the apartment, watching an unending stream of humanity flow through the channel that was their street. Since before the Kinsos went out the Congolese had been walking, running, riding past on bicycles. A few—provided they were soldiers of privilege—rode in cars or trucks. All pushed toward one objective, the city's soccer stadium.

For the most part what Mary saw was a pleasure-bent crowd, noisy, carefree, living for the moment.

"Mai mai, Mulele!" sang out a marcher. He solicited the blessing of the Kwilu rebel who was said to have died a second time and to have come back to life once more. The water—meaning the spirit—of Mulele would keep them from harm.

"Mai mai, Olenga!" cried another.

"Mai mai, Lumumba!" That touched the heights—to invoke the name of the martyred. For several moments the chant rocked between the LECO building and the Central Prison. Then as the marchers gradually fell back to lighter vein Mary's attention rested on a hulking, gaudily dressed woman obviously in from some country village. Shuffling by, the woman raised her head; her eyes met Mary's.

"You foreign woman up there in the window," she bellowed, shaking a fist. "You come down here and join us. We're going along to the stadium to see what they're going to do next."

Mary quickly drew back from the window. The woman's words plumbed the depths of her fear. What would they do next? More of what they had already done. Mary slowly shook her head. This crowd today would love it!

She had never realized so many people lived in Stan as were hustling by beneath her window. The stadium's few seats would of course have been occupied hours before, and these still on their way would stand with the thousands already there. Where once they had cheered a soccer team they would now echo an orator in his loud call for blood. An assortment of suspects would be tried, charged with treason against the People's Republic. Though evidence might be slight, perhaps a neighbors' quarrel or a tribal feud as the only offense, the verdict from twenty thousand throats would be loud, the execution certain.

That afternoon Mary stood again at the window as the people returned from their outing. No more the hilarity, however; no raucous shouts, no laughter. No holiday mood as they walked with heads down or rode their bicycles with unusual orderliness. Maybe they had spent their voices in shouting out the death penalty: shooting for one, a spear for another, death by blows of the machete for a third, and so on down the long line. Maybe now the people preferred to keep silent.

But theirs was a brooding silence. Plainly, many were worried and frightened.

But why? This was just another day in a series of days of execution. Perhaps it was the accumulation, or the planned aspect of the spectacle, or the sight of responsible men, as today's lot had certainly been, cut down in a ruthless quest of man for power.

Whatever, there had been quite enough to sober any people.

Out on the edge of Stan, Kilometer 8 escaped the shock of the invaders' gunfire. It was set at the edge of a dense rain forest, out from the city on a road that at one time had been important but was now bypassed by a better highway. The compound was a peaceful place, pretty with mango trees that lined the long drive-way and with rose bushes that were just beginning to bloom.

Three buildings far back from the road consisted of a large main house of solid construction in which Al and Jean Larson and their two-year-old Carol lived, a still larger structure which because of its uncompleted interior they called "the hangar," and a small house in the rear in which African servants had lived when Belgians owned the property.

The compound bustled at this time with UFM families. Some had stopped en route home from vacations in East Africa; others were there to pick up their children who had arrived from the American school near the Uganda border. All were caught up in the sudden rebel take-over of Stan.

One of these families was the Hector McMillans. Called by his first name by everyone, Hector considered himself a servant of the servants of God. He could not say "no" to people because he never

wanted to spare himself. He was, among other things, a builder, a
fix-it man. If a motor quit at some mission station or a carburetor
misbehaved, people invariably said, "Wait until Hector gets here.
He'll fix it."

This nearly six-foot two-hundred-pound man with very sparse
hair loved life, every bit of it. He always had a string of jokes to
tell. His own high-pitched cackle, so out of character, stirred as
much laughter in others as his stories did.

He seldom walked when he could run. "Come on, I'll race you,"
he would frequently say. A devout person, he rose at five thirty
each morning to search the Scriptures. Every day he would ask
God for a promise from the Bible for each of his six sons who
were away at school. At week's end he would compile the passages
in his letter to the boys and encourage them to look back over the
week to see in what ways God's hand had moved upon their
lives.

Hector had dropped off Ione his wife and four of his boys in
Stanleyville and with second son Paul drove overland to get Kenneth, the oldest son, who had come back to Congo from high
school in Uganda. To meet Ken they had to travel to Boyulu
mission, which pioneers of the UFM had planted on the trail once
used regularly by the slave traders. The first missionary passing
that way had seen the Boyulu jail crammed with murderers.
Twenty years after establishing the mission there he noted that the
jail was empty and the mission chapel full.

A church, a school, a dispensary, and other facilities had sprung
up at Boyulu. But growth in the Christian community demanded
more construction. Faithful to duty as always, Hector McMillan
loaded his truck with lumber before leaving Stan. Upon his arrival
at Boyulu he changed his mind about returning immediately.
Wanting to push the building of the new school along, he decided
instead to stay over another day to haul bricks for the project.

His eagerness to serve others placed him and the two older sons
at Boyulu on the day the rebels streamed into the Stanleyville area.
He and the boys started for Kilometer 8; about halfway there
they met a car coming from Stan.

"Turn back" the driver said in great excitement. "The rebels are closing in on Stan. They will kill you if you try to go there."

They went back to Boyulu. Had they not taken the time to haul the bricks they would have arrived in Stan before the rebels. But now the McMillan family was split. In a few days Hector despaired of seeing Ione and the four younger boys again. He contracted pneumonia; at one point he seemed to be on the verge of death.

There was no communication at this time with Kilometer 8, so no one there knew he was sick. But because the rebels forbade travel the folk at Kilometer 8 could not have done anything to help had they known of his sickness. Perhaps this lack of knowledge was a kindness to them. As it was, they now had more than enough to contend with at the headquarters compound.

The Simbas had discovered Kilometer 8.

The first visit occurred on the day Kingese staged his sadistic circus in the Stanleyville stadium. Dressed in palm branches, which signified they were ready to fight, and with paint splashed on their faces, they presented a frightening sight as they walked up the long driveway from the road. Their appearance, however, was worse than their conduct. The four who came merely ambled through the house.

"What are you looking for?" Al Larson asked as he accompanied them from room to room, thinking it wise to stick at their heels.

"Tshombe's soldiers," they replied.

Robert McAllister, a robust Irishman, moved in to join the inspecting party. He had served in the United States Army during World War II and now twenty years later could have licked the four had not prudence and the mellowing of his missionary calling prevented him. Instead, in the distinctive brogue of his native Belfast he barked:

"You won't find any soldiers here."

"If we do," one of the Simbas replied, halting his search to address them so they would thoroughly understand, " . . . if we do, we will shoot not only soldiers, but missionaries, too."

"We are not involved in politics," said Larson. "We are here to preach the Gospel. That's all."

The rebels acknowledged their search was fruitless, and they left. Two Congolese teachers came at that time to give the missionaries whatever protection they could offer. They were in the main house when a second carload of Simbas pulled into the driveway. Larson thought it best for them to slip out of the house before the rebels found them there. They retreated to the homes of the Kilometer 8 houseboys which were nearer to the forest's edge. In the main house the Simbas discovered the radio transmitter that Larson used to contact the other mission stations. He heard them exchange excited whispers about the *phonee,* their term for a radio used as a telephone. More than any other piece of equipment that foreigners possessed, a *phonee* upset the rebels. Even the most backward Simba from deep in the bush had heard it said that the owners of such magical boxes sat at them all day long and called in airplanes to rain destruction on the rebel forces.

The Simbas did not take the transmitter, nor even talk about it to the missionaries. They left the house peaceably, still accompanied by the men of the station. But once outside and on their way to the car near the road, they loosed a terrifying barrage from their guns.

"Why did you do that?" asked Larson.

"Oh," said one who had emptied the clip of his rifle and now replaced it with another, "we do that just to scare people."

The Simbas may well have frightened the women and children, for they ran out the back door. But in others the fusillade prompted a display of fidelity and courage.

From the Congolese houses at the edge of the forest walked a determined group of men, women, and children.

"Uhuru!" They shouted the cry of Congo independence and waved palm branches as they approached the main house. At first it appeared that the teachers and houseboys had joined the revolution. Then it became clear that they were coming to gain a hearing from the rebels.

The Simbas, however, had left, and the sentiment of the demonstration was limited to the missionaries to appreciate. The teachers had alerted the houseboys to the Simba visit. Fearing that perhaps their friends would be harmed, the group started toward the house; and hearing the shooting, they were sure the missionaries needed their help. So they marched in defiance of rebel behavior, even if all they were capable of doing was to take a stand with their friends against anyone who might mistreat them.

The day following the visit of the Simbas the order went out for all foreigners to turn in their transmitter sets. Bob McAllister and Del Carper carried the Kilometer 8 set into Stan, but after searching the city over for half a day could find no one authorized or willing to accept it. They went in again on Tuesday and this time got rid of the *phonee*. But on that trip they received so much heckling about having a car that they parked it behind the house at Kilometer 8 and determined not to drive again as long as the Simbas would cast covetous eyes upon other people's vehicles.

At Kilometer 8 now were the Larsons; the McAllisters with their three children; Del and Lois Carper and eleven-year-old Marilyn; Ione McMillan and four of her boys who had moved out from Stan; and three single women missionaries, Viola Walker, Olive Bjerkseth, and Mina Erskine. Wherever missionaries congregate there is bound to be a lot of talk. This was true here. And sooner or later the conversation always worked around to the rebel situation.

"They certainly got the support of the people in a hurry," someone observed.

And why not? In many villages the teachers had not been paid by the national government for nearly a year. The men who worked on the roads had gone payless for months.

"The money came through from Leo," Larson said. "Graft and corruption put it in the wrong pockets."

"How long can the national government hold on?" someone else asked. "The rebels are beating the army back on every front."

"Tshombe is bringing in outside help," Larson said. The prime minister had asked for troops from other African nations, but they favored the rebels. Larson added, "The BBC said this morning that Tshombe has hired mercenaries from Belgium and Jo'burg."

One ventured that if the killing of local leaders kept up the rebels would soon alienate the people.

"With their leaders dead, how can they resist?" countered Bob McAllister.

Frequently they expressed grave concern for the president of the Evangelical Church of Upper Congo. He was a man who by his education and refinement the rebels would certainly class among the hated elite. His name was Asani Benedict. He was one of the outstanding Christian leaders of Africa.

Asani and his twin brother Bo Martin became Christians in their youth. Now thirty-nine, they had for many years worked as a team. Bo was the first born, but Asani, said to have been longer in the womb, was counted as the elder brother. Asani grew to be a natural leader, a man worthy of note in the white suits he usually wore, outgoing, aggressive, a powerful preacher with a tremendous burden for his people.

Bo Martin's chief characteristic was his utter faithfulness—to a task, to a friend, to the Lord. Asani's fiery preaching drew hundreds from their pagan altars to Christ. Bo's pastoral ways confirmed them in their faith. The twins personally established twenty-three churches and chapels. They pioneered the Christian village of Bopepe, and it was here that Bo Martin served as pastor.

Asani was elected head of the Upper Congo church. He studied a year in France. Recently he filled the office of president of the Congo Protestant Council and currently of general secretary of the Evangelical Fellowship. If ever there was a man for the rebels to liquidate for being a leader, Asani was that man. And Bo Martin was not far behind him.

But Asani was not in the Stanleyville area. After meeting with missionaries and church leaders at Bopepe in mid-July, Asani took his ailing wife to a mission hospital near the Uganda border. Yokana Jean, the director of UFM schools, met them there after attending a conference of Congolese educators in that vicinity. Whether it was better that these two key men had left the danger zone of Stan was a question no one at Kilometer 8 could answer.

From the reports that filtered in, no place in northeast Congo could any longer be considered safe.

The missionaries were equally concerned for Volker and Elsi Gscheidle, the German couple at Wanie-Rukula. For two weeks they had not been heard from. Al Larson and Kinso racked their brains for a way to get to Wanie. But the road was barred in several places by military checkpoints, and neither possessed the pass that would get them through.

Nevertheless, two such enterprising men could not have lived in Stan as long as they had without making friends in strategic places. One of their friends was a young English businessman named Peter Rombaut, a tall, handsome fellow with a kindly countenance and dark, wavy hair. He was every inch of his height a gentleman. He had served his London firm in Kenya as well as in Congo, and now doubled as honorary British consul in Stan.

Kinso spoke to Rombaut about the Gscheidles. Rombaut, proving himself to be brave as well as urbane, stretched his diplomatic privilege; he recruited a Simba guard to do the talking at the roadblocks and headed for Wanie on a rescue mission. He found the couple and returned them to Stan. All along the route the Simbas leveled threats against his life as well as against theirs.

At one place they saw a group of rebels tie up and beat an African man.

"We'll do that to you one of these days," a Simba said to them as they waited to pass through his checkpoint.

Another rebel laughed, but not out of humor. *"Mateka iko,* we'll make butter out of you," he said.

And this they might well have done. A week before on that same road a Greek plantation owner and a Belgian army officer were slain and their bodies partly eaten for no apparent reason.

The Gscheidles supplied an eye-witness account of the rebel advance across the Wanie bridge and an explanation of their radio silence.

"We watched them storm the bridge," said Gscheidle. "Four witchdoctors led the procession."

"In step chanting *'Mai mai mai,* Mulele'?" asked Larson.

"And *'Mai mai mai,* Lumumba,'" he answered. "But they needed no protection against bullets—not at the bridge, they didn't. The soldiers who could have held them off got a glimpse of the witchdoctors and ran away into the forest."

"But the bridge—" interrupted McAllister. "Wasn't it mined?"

"If it was," Gscheidle said, "no one remained to blow it."

Gscheidle would have passed the word to Larson over his transmitter, but the rebels swarmed on them so rapidly that he had no chance to do so. There was another reason also, about which he now spoke.

"Our house is closest to the bridge, so they overran us immediately," he continued. "They turned the house into a hospital, because the soldiers on our side of the river stood their ground for a little while and both sides suffered casualties."

Someone interjected that Elsi, being a nurse, must have been pressed into service to care for the wounded.

"I was," she replied. "But they permitted me to take care of only the Simbas."

"And," her husband added, "they said that if any of their fellows died they would hold her accountable."

"But about the radio," Larson said.

"Oh, yes, the radio," Gscheidle replied. "When the rebels came they asked one of our African Christians if the missionaries owned a *phonee.* He said they did not. We did, of course. He lied. He wanted to protect us from their anger."

To protect the Christian in turn, because his cover-up was certain to be exposed, Gscheidle quickly and quietly dismantled their set and scattered the parts among boxes in the attic.

The safe arrival of the German couple gave particular relief to

Al Larson, though as field leader he deeply felt a responsibility for some thirty or more UFM missionaries still spread over a wide region beyond Stan. There was nothing he could do for them, nothing that anyone could do. The Simbas were truly lions, and northeast Congo was their den. More and more the foreigner was was feeling himself to be a helpless prey. He would be all right as long as the lions were satisfied. But what lion did not develop sooner or later a voracious appetite?

During the latter part of August the raving Kingese declared over Radio Stan that Congo would be wiped clean of religion. Religious teaching was to cease in two weeks. And that other menace—America—was to be dealt with, too. Every American within rebel reach was to be arrested immediately.

4

Nothing to Do but Pray

Radio Stan belched invective against the Americans. "Tshombe has sold Congo to the Americans," quoted the official line. "We have become their slaves. Fight to free our land of the imperialists."

What they heard on the radio confused the houseboys and their families at Kilometer 8.

"Bwana Larson is from America," said Malenza, who had cooked for missionaries for many years and watched over the compound like a mother hen. "He is not like the men Radio Stan talks about."

"I do not want to fight the ones who taught us about Jesus," said the younger Fabian.

The two, in fact, were saddened to see the Americans at Kilometer 8 pack suitcases for the trip to prison. But no one called on the day of Kingese's order to arrest Americans, nor on the day following, nor on the day after that. Soon, living out of suitcases became inconvenient, so the missionaries gradually unpacked, though in line with a suggestion by Larson each maintained a case with essentials and important papers.

They asked each other uncertainly, "Was the order only a

threat?" Had they been aware of events at another station they could have answered the question themselves.

The rebels came often to Banjwadi, forty miles north of Stan. Here were located a seminary for pastoral students, a primary school for five hundred children, a dispensary, a bookstore, and of course a church. Both brick and mud-wall buildings nestled among flamboyant trees and neat gardens; the entire settlement enjoyed a magnificent view of the Lindi River, a tributary of the Congo.

Because of the great amount of activity here, most of the UFM missionaries had at some time lived at Banjwadi. Presently, a couple named David and Sonia Grant were assigned to the station. A new missionary family, the Charles Davises, had arrived five days before the rebels captured Stan. Margaret Hayes, a nurse and excellent midwife who teamed with Mary Baker up the road at Bopepe, was visiting.

The missionaries, the pastors, the Congolese nurses, the seminary students, all dreaded the rebel visits. Often truckloads of Simbas drove into the station. At least one defaming speech marked each visit. The missionaries stood in the road to listen to them, but Davis always seethed.

"I wish they'd speak in French," he muttered once under his breath. "I can't follow them in Swahili."

"Be thankful you can't," Muriel, his wife, whispered.

Davis had studied Swahili for three months in a town near the Uganda border. He and his wife and two small children had ridden down to Stan when the Hector McMillans brought their boys from school. Eager to start work, they went on the same day to Banjwadi.

He was on loan from another mission to teach in the seminary. A sensitive, sincere, and open person, he had in preparing for the mission field run the gamut from pastoring a country church in the mountains of Virginia to studying anthropology at Harvard. Muriel was determined to be a good missionary wife and mother.

The young couple frankly admitted that the frightful dress and graceless behavior of the Simbas sent chills up their spines. They had had no time to get accustomed to even the normal ways of a strange land, and already they faced daily bouts with doped or drunken men.

The Grants, missionaries for nine years, found the Simba visits hardly less exacting. One night the rebels confiscated their transmitter and Volkswagen bus. They also commandeered the bus owner. David Grant was forced to drive them in a search for food that lasted until midnight.

The next day the Grants heard Radio Stan broadcast the order to seize American citizens. They were Canadians—from Saint John, New Brunswick—and Margaret Hayes was English. So on their station only the Davis family came under the edict. They decided not to add to the disquietude of the young couple, so said nothing of Kingese's outburst.

That afternoon, upon hearing the roar of a speeding car, Grant rushed from his house to intercept it before it got down the station road to the Davis home. The car stopped, however, about halfway between the residences. A Simba officer in camouflage uniform jumped from behind the wheel. Two ragged soldiers got out on the other side.

"What is your nationality?" the officer inquired of Grant, who was just reaching the car. He spoke politely, and asked, rather than demanded, to see his ID card.

"We're Canadian," Grant said, and in his answer included Sonia, who with Margaret Hayes was approaching. Margaret returned to the house to get her card. Grant volunteered that she was British.

Just then Chuck Davis walked out of his house and to the gathering at the car. Grant had been hoping he would not show up. Now that he had, he hoped that Davis would be scarce with his answers to the rebel's questions.

"We are looking for Americans," the officer said, sounding disappointed that so far his trip from Stan had not been worthwhile.

"Oh, I'm American," Davis said. "My whole family is American."

Grant then wished he had warned Davis about the broadcast.

Yet, the officer seemed friendly; perhaps there was not much to fear. Grant felt he should make one point clear.

"We are missionaries," he said. "We are engaged in no political activity."

At this the officer drew from his shirt a letter which he said contained his orders. He refused to let anyone read the letter, but Grant noticed in handwriting on the bottom margin the names of Al Larson and Del Carper.

"My orders are to transport all Americans to Stan so they may be issued travel papers," the Simba said.

So that was it. Perhaps the American consul had negotiated a release for his people. And if the Americans, maybe other nationalities would be treated similarly. There was more assurance still when the Simba said they would be driving to the airport. Grant sighed with relief.

Margaret Hayes went with Chuck Davis to help him and Muriel pack. The Grants invited the officer into their house for coffee. He drank the coffee, but politely declined the cookies that Sonia offered. A taboo prevented him from eating food prepared by a woman.

"*Bwana* Larson and *Bwana* Carper, they do not live here?" the officer asked.

"You will find them at Kilometer 8, on the old highway, not this road," Grant said, happy that something good seemed in store for his friends. "And while you're getting the Americans together, there is another person you should include . . . Mary Baker. She lives up the road at Bopepe."

The officer shook his head. "Not today," he said. "Later."

His coffee finished, the officer excused himself, saying they must leave. The Davises arrived, carrying several suitcases. The Simba held up a hand.

"No baggage," he said. He still spoke politely, but firmly.

"What do you mean, no baggage?" asked Davis. He had pieced together the officer's gestures with his own rudimentary knowledge of Swahili.

The officer turned to Grant. "They will need nothing. Papers will be issued today. We then will return them here."

The couple did, however, transfer a few essential items for the children to a handbag. While they did this the officer took note of the children, four-year-old Stephen and twenty-month-old Beth. He smiled. Given more time, he might have won their confidence.

The young soldiers placed the handbag in the trunk of the car, a two-door blue Opel with a window in the roof. Chuck Davis and his wife and children climbed into the back seat, the officer and his men into the front.

A number of seminary students and other Congolese who lived on the station had gathered around the car. They waved good-by to the missionary family. They heard the rebels' parting cry.

"*Mateka iko?*" the officer asked. He grinned broadly and gunned the motor to race away as fast as he had come.

"*Mateka iko!*" the two soldiers were heard to answer.

The Grants and Margaret Hayes did not know the phrase. But the students did. It caused them to freeze suddenly with fear. One suggested that they pray right then and there.

"But what did they say?" Grant asked. He had to coax the explanation from them. One finally revealed the Simba's intention to turn his passengers into butter.

David Grant threw up his hands to his face. What danger had this young couple so blithely walked into? And Larson and Carper and dear Mary Baker—he had revealed their whereabouts to the officer. What now would become of them?

Yes, they'd better pray. There was nothing else they could do.

Neither Davis nor his wife appreciated the long, vicious spear and the bulky club with which the soldiers in the front seat had armed themselves. But they soon despised more the officer's revolver. At the frequent stops they made en route to the city he flashed it before cowed villagers. By showing off his importance he lost the illusion he earlier had gained of being the perfect gentleman.

They arrived in Stan in late afternoon, sweaty and burned from

the sun's rays through the open roof. For some while they drove
through city streets, passing one landmark or another several times
but never seeming to approach the airport. In one totally unfamiliar area the car stopped in the middle of a mob of shouting,
pushing, fighting men.

"Why doesn't he go and get out of here?" Muriel asked her
husband.

"He can't budge this thing," Chuck answered. The swirling
crowd, throwing fists and kicking at one another, completely enveloped the car.

"Oh, Chuck!" gasped Muriel, terrified. "What can we do?"

"Pray, honey," he said.

"I'm scared—"

The blast of a gun interrupted. For a brief moment it quieted the
crowd. Then in the wake the clamorous tide rolled in; through his
window Davis saw a crumpled body in the street.

"Kill him! Kill him!" cried many voices together. They lashed
out not at the one already dead by the gun blast, but at another,
perhaps at the one who had done the shooting.

Most of those in the mob were Simba soldiers, identifiable by
palm leaves covering their chests and the animal skins on their
hats or arms. They carried an assortment of guns, spears, and
clubs. With such profusion of weapons they couldn't struggle long
until someone else would die. Those in the car, both Simbas and
missionaries, wondered whether the victims might not turn out to
be they.

The mob jostled the car.

"Daddy!" shrieked little Stephen. "They're going to tip us
over!"

It certainly seemed they would. The rebel officer was trying all
his worth to drive the car forward through the mob, but it offered
no match for the force that had stopped it. Darting a glance at
their driver, Chuck Davis knew he was as frightened as they. Then
his eyes swept past the driver; a man sprawled on the hood of the
car. In a moment he was hurtled to the ground. In the next split
second his body was riddled with bullets.

"Daddy! They've killed him!" sobbed Stephen. "Oh! They've killed that man!"

Davis buried his son's head in his lap, but still the boy screamed and cried uncontrollably. His sobs angered the reckless throng. Simbas habitually killed any who mourned one of their victims. Through the front windows eight or ten men thrust the smoking barrels of their guns into the rear of the car.

"Dear God," Davis choked, "take us all together. Don't leave the children alone with them. Oh, don't leave them! Kill us all together!"

He turned from the steel that shook nervously in his face. He looked at Muriel. Beth cowered in her mother's lap, afraid, but too young to know why she was afraid. Guns pointed at his wife. He saw that she, too, was praying. More than hearing her, he read her lips, "God, let us die together."

But as suddenly as the guns thrust into the car, they withdrew. The mob's frenzy seemed to have abated. Two deaths—they appeared to appease the lust for blood for the present. The men dispersed. The officer pushed down hard on the accelerator; the car spurted ahead.

"We'll get to the airport now," he called back to his passengers.

If they had expected an airplane to be waiting to sweep them off to the safety of Leopoldville, their arrival at the terminal could have carried no greater disappointment. Here they faced another angry crowd. Their driver had had enough. He ordered them out of the car and hurriedly drove away.

They had no idea of the cause of the bedlam, but they sensed that their arrival further incensed the mob. A fist shot out and struck Muriel.

"Leave her alone! Can't you see she's pregnant!" Chuck Davis was almost blinded by his hot, stinging tears.

An undetermined number pushed guns into their backs.

"Over here!" a Simba soldier ordered. Roughly, he guided them into a run-down building, down a narrow hallway to a door that led to a women's toilet. A guard shoved a knife blade into the spring lock that secured the door. As the door opened he pushed and kicked the Davis family into the room. The door slammed shut behind them.

The room was small, the light from a high window dim, the stench sickening. These conditions one might expect to find in a public restroom. The shock was to discover the room jammed with people—nearly a dozen Africans, Davis noted as his eyes adjusted to the semi-darkness, and a few foreigners.

A man pushed forward toward them.

"For heaven's sake! You're Americans!" he exclaimed. "What are you doing here?"

"You sound like an American," Davis answered. "What are *you* doing here?"

"I'm Mike Hoyt—"

"You . . . you're the consul?"

Michael Hoyt explained that he was. The four members of his staff were in the room. They had been prisoners of the rebels almost since the day that Stan capitulated.

"How long have you been here?" Davis asked.

"We slept here last night," Hoyt said. "If you could call it sleeping. Nineteen people in this cubicle. We make use of the stalls, too." He pointed to two compartments that contained toilets. Both fixtures had overflowed; slimy water covered the floor.

In about forty minutes the door to the hall opened again. The Africans were taken out. The rebels were interested in gaining tribute money from the Congolese, most of whom appeared to be businessmen. But the Americans they pulled out for a lesson in humiliation.

"The woman and the children will go," a Simba said, separating Muriel and the youngsters from Chuck.

"You can't take her from me!" Chuck said with pleading in his voice.

"Go home!" the soldier ordered Mrs. Davis.

"My home is far from here," she said. "I don't want to go there without my husband."

"Go home!" the soldier said again. Others stepped forward to lead her away. Davis tried to give Muriel the handbag with Beth's things. Someone, thinking he was trying to go with her, pushed him to the floor.

"You stay here," he growled.

Davis' mind seemed to numb as his wife and children slipped out of sight, heading, he was sure, to a car that still smoked from the blast of guns. But as he and the consulate staff were thrust back into the room, he snapped back to the present. There they were made to strip to their undershorts. The guards pushed them again to the corridor outside.

A half-dozen Simbas, taking advantage of a temporary absence by their officers, had hauled the men out to have some morbid fun at their expense. Suddenly, Davis felt cold filth trickling down his back. The one who threw it doubled over in laughter. Another found his aim good, right in the head. Several joined in the bombardment; they roared each time they scored a hit on one of the men.

The Simbas pointed to the bare feet of the prisoners. They slapped their sides. How funny to see a foreigner without shoes trying to stand up in the watery mess that flowed under the door to where this game was being played. One fellow struck Davis with the flat of his bayonet.

"They won't kill you," said Mike Hoyt. "They'll just make you feel as low as a human can feel."

Chuck Davis, however, was too frightened to learn much from the lesson in humiliation.

After twenty minutes an officer came by. He chased the merrymakers away, sent the prisoners back to their fetid cell. Someone else returned their clothes—minus the contents of the pockets.

"You can sleep in the hall," one who appeared to be in charge informed them.

Sleep? Though half sick from weariness Chuck Davis would not be able to sleep. The horrible things that had happened today were still too much with him—the man shot and killed beside the car, the smoking gun barrels in their faces, and filth running down his back, his wife and children gone, snatched away by evil men.

Why had it happened? Because he was a missionary? Not really.

The cause was political. Yet he suffered in the line of duty—and his duty was being a missionary. He had every right to be secure in the providence of God, and this he believed he was.

But in terms of the moment he felt terribly afraid. If fear was unbelief, his only prayer was, "Lord, help my unbelief."

Not having a choice, Muriel Davis carried Beth to a waiting car, and Stephen stuck close to his mother. Two young Simbas sat in the front seat. An angry fellow with a heavy stick pushed Muriel and the children into the rear seat, then crowded in beside them.

"Daddy!" cried Stephen. "I want Daddy to come!"

"Be quiet!" the angry Simba shouted in Swahili, raising his stick to menace the boy. He then spoke curtly to Muriel:

"Where do you live?"

She said something in French, which only brought a curse from the soldier.

"This woman doesn't even speak good French," he complained to his partners.

That she understood, and knew he was right. So summoning her best effort she said, "Take me to Kilometer 8, if you please."

"No," replied the rebel. "That is too far." He said they were low on fuel.

"You said you would take me clear home to Banjwadi,—but I don't want to go there."

Now he did not understand what she said; he accused her of speaking nothing but "pure English." He ordered the driver to start the engine and proceed to Camp Prince Leopold, a rebel army installation.

Camp Prince Leopold! She had no trouble understanding that. "Oh, no!" she gasped. An army camp was the last place she wanted to go to. But where in this strange city could she spend the night safely? She knew nothing about it, no one in it. In fact, to her it was wholly a place that boiled with violence.

Desperately she prayed, feverishly she searched her mind for some place of security, hoping against hope that she could get free of her captors before the fullness of night fell. But they were

speeding toward the army camp. She didn't know where it was—
just some location where the Devil lived.

Where else? Where else? And then without being able to explain
the process, from somewhere within she pulled a name that once
had come up in casual conversation at Banjwadi, but which until
this time had meant little to her.

"LECO!" she cried. "Take me and my children to LECO!"

"LECO?" the surly Simba asked, leaning over to stare at her.
"LECO? What is that?"

"I don't know—except they sell books there," she replied.

At slower pace now they cruised what might have been half the
streets of Stan. Finally the driver stopped the car. He called to a
European man who walked along a sidewalk.

"LECO . . ." the Simba said. "Tell me, where is LECO?"

The man knew its location. He said it was about a block from
Lumumba's monument.

In a few minutes the driver stopped again. "Here," said the
fellow in the rear seat, opening the door and pushing her and the
children out into the street. "You get out here."

She stumbled from the car. She took a firm grip on the children,
carrying Beth and pulling Stephen by the hand. She hurried around
the corner of a large building to get out of sight of the car. In the
quickly closing darkness she looked around. Across the street
stood a building that plainly was a prison, and this sight frightened
her. Stephen began to whimper, so she pressed his face into her
skirt. She dared not let the children cry here.

How awfully alone she felt. She was alone, alone in this strange
city that had given her only terror and grief, alone with two babies
and with the sickening sense that her husband felt as alone as
she.

Out of the prison guardroom drifted the vulgar laugh of a soldier. She stiffened. Then it seemed as though her knees would
buckle, that her whole body would fall on the sidewalk in a
heap.

Muriel Davis . . . missionary. Was it for this that God had sent
her to Africa?

5

Death
by Default

She had to pull herself together. Wasn't this the place of safety? Wasn't everything going to be all right now? She heard the car that had brought her drive away, so she looked cautiously around the corner of the building. In the gathering night she barely made out the lettering above the barred windows, "Librairie Évangelique."

If indeed this was LECO it was plain to see that the shop was shut. At that moment a Congolese man walked by. She spoke to him.

"Tell me, please," she said, mustering the courage to make herself heard, "how do you get to the apartments above?"

He answered politely that the door was on another side of the building, and led the way to it. While following, she noticed that a light shone in a window overhead.

"Hello, hello!" she called. There was no answer. She followed her guide to a doorway and gave him a faint smile for his trouble. She tried the door. It was locked. But someone had to be in this building, perhaps up the flight of stairs which she could see through the glass. Someone had to be enjoying the security of that room up there with the light. Suddenly another name popped into her mind . . . Kinso. The name of a man, she thought, connected somehow with LECO. Was that his given name, or his last name? It made no difference. She began to pound on the door and call him.

"Kinso!" she shouted in desperation. "Kinso! Kinso!"

"I'm coming," called a voice in English inside. "I'm coming right down."

Oh, what music there was in that voice! How reassuring! She hugged Beth tightly and dropped her face in the girl's hair. She squeezed Stephen's hand.

"Are we going in here, Mommy?" the boy asked. "What are we going to do, Mommy? Huh? What are we going to do?"

"Oh, Stevie," she said, half crying, half laughing. "A nice man is coming who will take care of us, a man that God has sent us."

The bolt slid back. The door opened. A tall man with a kind face stepped aside to permit her and the children to enter.

"My word," he said with surprise, "I thought it was Mary Baker—"

Almost as if she had not seen him, she brushed past and ran up the stairs, dragging Stephen and bobbling Beth on a hip. She stopped only when she met Ma Kinso in the hall and, sobbing, wilted in the older woman's outstretched arms.

In a moment or two they all moved into the apartment. Muriel Davis blotted her tears to look at the folk who had taken her in.

"You are the missionaries here?" she asked.

"We are," Kinso replied. "The name is Jenkinson, but most people call us the Kinsos." Mary Rutt came in from her room, and he introduced her.

"I'm—I'm Muriel Davis," she stammered, "the wife of Charles Davis. They've got Chuck in that horrible place at the airport."

Ma Kinso made sure that she was comfortable. She sat on the davenport; the baby lay in her lap and Stephen clung to her knees.

"We're the new missionaries on loan by the Africa Inland Mission to the seminary at Banjwadi," Muriel went on.

"Of course," broke in Kinso. "You arrived a few days before

the 'others' took over Stan. But you must be hungry."

"Not really," she said with a sigh.

"And tired?"

"The children are."

"I'll make some hot chocolate," said Ma Kinso.

"I don't want to burden you," Muriel said, pushing back the dark disheveled strands of hair that looked darker still against a face that the Congo sun had not yet browned. For herself, food held small interest tonight, and sleep was out of the question. She had to talk, to speak about the brush with death her family had experienced this day, the fright of her children and herself, the brutal treatment her husband might be receiving at this very moment . . . if, indeed, he wasn't dead.

"The first thing tomorrow morning we'll see what we can learn," Kinso said. "We have a friend . . . he gets about." The enterprising Peter Rombaut did get about. As honorary British consul he never allowed himself to be swallowed up in the fine points of protocol. Rather, being an extremely practical man, he gave himself fully to extricating any person, regardless of nationality, from a tight spot —and there were plenty of these in Stan. If anyone could do something for Chuck Davis, Rombaut could.

Ma Kinso and Mary Rutt settled Mrs. Davis and the children. Kinso sat alone with his thoughts.

Poor girl, poor, poor frightened girl. And those children. How hard it was without their father. What did it mean, now that the Simbas were locking up Americans—American missionaries? Whatever was going to be the end?

The mad Kingese, Olenga the general, brainy Soumialot, President Christophe Gbenye—these builders of the People's Republic were finding that their annihilation of the Congo elite, the leadership class, was starting to produce hostility. The executions in the stadium had sprouted mumbled protest. The continuing courts in Lumumba Square were making the people talk openly. They were saying that Kingese would have to go. There were too many religious people around Stan to swallow his edict of no religion.

But with the arrest of Charles Davis, might the rebels be moving obliquely against Christian teaching? What would stop them from jailing a missionary, if not overtly for his religion, at least on the excuse of his nationality?

The Americans, along with the Belgians, were becoming scapegoats of an insurgent government that had lost popularity for its crass brutality. Kinso saw it. So did Al Larson. Unite the people against the Americans as the hated imperialistic aggressors, and the blame for all unhappiness could be laid on them.

Somehow, the American missionaries at Kilometer 8 escaped the dragnet. Larson realized the situation was serious, however, and was getting worse. In the last broadcast on the mission network before losing the transmitter he said:

"You have no idea of how bad things are. If you have a chance to get out, you'd better go."

Toward the end of August the American government insisted that its citizens leave the troubled areas of Congo. The warning was too late, however, except for persons living in border areas not yet controlled by the rebels. A number of families of the Africa Inland Mission heard Larson's final broadcast and one by a veteran of their own mission; on the strength of their urgings they evacuated their stations, which were nearer to the Uganda and Sudan borders than most Protestant missions in Congo. Some escaped the closing rebel net by a very thin thread, perhaps none by a thinner thread than the William Stoughs.

In traveling to a point on the Uganda border the family encountered a washed-out bridge. And who besides the Stoughs should it delay? The advance party of the Simba army. The patrol wished to contact the main rebel force, but could not. So on Bill Stough's suggestion they helped him repair the bridge. They rejoined their outfit, which then began its push. The Stoughs arrived at the border and escaped across safely before the rebel army could stop them.

A large band of African Christians also forged toward the border. The company included Asani Benedict and his wife; Yokana

Jean; and two or three of their pastors. They walked from the AIM Hospital at Oicha.

The hospital staff, the ambulatory patients, and visitors such as Asani journeyed a week to attain the border. Constantly harassed, they often had to dodge a hail of rebel bullets. Some got sores on their feet, the legs of others swelled, some became ill; but they managed to escape without one dying. Asani and Yokana, key men in the church, were safe, but they felt in their exile that they had been shunted aside at a time when people in Congo needed them badly.

A UFM family, the Richard Siggs, escaped with the AIM missionaries. In Uganda Sigg met Asani when Asani and his people were hungry and almost without funds.

"We've trusted that God would provide," said Asani. His white suit was wrinkled and soiled, a mark of the recent struggle to escape the Congo rebels. But his eyes were still bright and his smile broad. He believed that God would look out for them.

God did, in the person of Dick Sigg. Sigg carried mission funds on him to distribute to needy evacuees.

This tall, athletic young missionary from Florida was to be useful in other ways at this time. He and Mimi his amiable wife served as houseparents in Rethy Academy, the school for missionary children. Sigg's work also consisted of doing whatever at the moment needed doing. Right now there was a need for someone to embark on a daring mission.

In the Uganda capital of Kampala, Sigg received a telephone call from a representative of the United Nations.

"We want a man who knows the Congo mission stations—where they are, who's on them," the officer said. "We leave tomorrow morning to carry out a plan of evacuation. Will you go?"

"Yes, I will," Sigg agreed.

The following evening a charter flight set Sigg down in Bunia, a tin-mining town at the edge of the mountains in east Congo, four hundred miles from Stanleyville. Tshombe's national troops still held Bunia, though the rebels pressed hard for a break-through.

Sigg debarked warily. Having heard that the field was closed to normal traffic, he wondered if the town was about to fall into rebel hands.

"Hey, Dick!" a voice called from the edge of the strip. Sigg looked up, recognized a missionary friend.

"Well, Mert Wolcott," he exclaimed, and went over to shake hands. In the next ten minutes the two caught up each other on their news. Wolcott, a member of the Immanuel Mission, served at the village of Nyankunde not far from Bunia. One of Congo's largest religious presses operated there.

"We haven't evacuated yet—not all of us," Wolcott said. "The families are gone, but Bill Deans is still there; so is our nurse . . . and me." William Deans was the American director of the station.

The two compared notes, found that the same rescue project had brought them both to Bunia.

The next morning they kept a rendezvous with officials of the United Nations and the United States. In one of the business houses of Bunia a big-shouldered Swede with a long brown beard and heavy mustache stepped forward to greet Sigg and Wolcott.

"I'm Captain Glantz," he said, extending an oversized hand. "Here I am the pilot of the rescue plane."

To lay out sorties for Captain Glantz the group worked for several hours over maps and lists of mission stations and personnel; they attempted to pinpoint where every missionary lived. The plan was to go into areas having landing strips and to drop instructions on other stations on how to get out of the country.

Bush flying was a nasty business these days. No one was more aware of this than the intrepid pilots who compiled a commendable record of snatching folk from dangerous situations throughout central Congo. In just recent days a Methodist mission flyer had died in the line of this perilous duty.

While flying above a station newly captured by the rebels, Burleigh Law peered down to see his co-laborers in trouble. They gestured that it was unsafe to land, and waved him off. But he was unwilling to leave them in their predicament and refused to take their advice. He set the plane down on the tiny airstrip to see what he could do to help.

Rebels who were armed to the teeth approached as he taxied to a stop. He jumped out to face them. Immediately they demanded his keys.

These he did not wish to give up. He reached in the cabin for the keys at the same instant a rebel stuck out his hand for them. Their hands touched. The rebel whipped out his gun and shot Law three times in the stomach.

The taboo that said a Simba should not touch another person had been broken. By it the rebel sensed he lost his soldiery power. The one means of restoration was to kill the one who caused the violation.

Friendly villagers carried the wounded pilot to a mission hospital. But the pilot died, breathing forgiveness on the one who had shot him.

Mindful of the danger, Glantz took off from Bunia on his mission. No one was to be rescued in this operation, however. The big Swede returned to Bunia, unable to land at any station because of rebel ground fire. The officials called off the rescue attempt as a hopeless job. The situation was more serious than anyone had thought. The rebels, it seemed, had dispersed over the whole of northeast Congo.

In the afternoon an American transport plane flew into Bunia from Leopoldville. Sigg and Wolcott were at the airport when it arrived. An officer of the American embassy, certain that Bunia was about to be overrun by the Simbas, ordered Sigg and Wolcott aboard for an immediate trip back to Leopoldville.

"I can't go," Wolcott protested. "There are two missionaries still at my station."

"Captain Glantz can fly over and drop them a note," the official said. "I'll instruct them to walk out through the mountains to Uganda."

The matter ended by Sigg flying to Leopoldville and Wolcott staying behind with the Swedish pilot. After the transport had left, these two felt it would be a mistake to send Bill Deans and the nurse on a precarious overland hike. So instead of dropping them instructions they drove in Wolcott's car to the station, picked up the pair, and then all flew out to Uganda.

The very day after they evacuated, Simba warriors fanned through the area the missionaries would have taken had they walked out. They bore down swiftly and sternly on the station.

"Where are the Americans?" they demanded. "We've come to kill them right now."

They also had a commission to liquidate an influential African editor who worked in the mission press. This man who was named Yosia Butso did not try to flee. On hearing the rebels come, he walked calmly to his office and began to work on a manuscript. In a few minutes a Simba poked his head through the window, which was open. Exhibiting a freshly sharpened machete, he said:

"I'm looking for Yosia Butso."

"Yosia Butso?" repeated the one who sat at the desk.

"Yes," the Simba said. "I intend to kill him."

Yosia Butso clucked his tongue a bit, then spoke in understatement:

"Well," he said, with a slight shrug, "I just work here."

"Hmmm," replied the rebel. "If you see him, tell him we'll be back tomorrow to kill him."

Three Simbas had raided the station that day. But they did not quite make it back the following day to carry out the threat against Yosia Butso. On the road outside the station they ran into an ambush set up by government troops. All three died.

There seemed to be no spot now that the rebels did not control. Not only was escape impossible, but free movement within rebel territory quite unlikely. The transmitters gone, a smuggled letter remained the last means of communication, and this was rare. No wonder then that the note handed to Al Larson by a truck driver down from the north created a stir at Kilometer 8. It was the first word in quite a while from Mary Baker.

Very often the missionaries at Stan talked about Mary and the do with contrary orders they told me that I was causing them a great deal of trouble."

She felt that she had not been singled out for harrying, so David Grant's inadvertence in calling the Simba officer's attention to her that day at Banjwadi bore no evident consequence. She believed others were having harder times. She accepted the confiscation of her small radio with philosophic calm. "Of course," she wrote, "I'm completely cut off from the outside world now, though in its present state I guess I'm just as well off."

She was not surprised that Bo Martin rushed to her aid the moment he heard the Simbas were in her house, nor that to reach her he recklessly pushed aside the armed guards who stood in his way, saying, "I will stand by Mademoiselle as long as she needs me."

She wrote about another instance in which rebel guns had been stuck in her face. ". . . this, of course, does not make me flinch."

She explained that she was not trying to be heroic, just that years ago she had settled the matter of "by life or by death—and there it rests." Who could disturb one so committed? Certainly not those whose worst power was to kill the body but not the soul.

"Yet, I am concerned for Bo Martin," she wrote. "Pray for him."

Long before these crisis days he and the teachers at Bopepe had taught the villagers about communism and how the communists sometimes used wicked means to achieve their ends.

"He is fearless," she went on. "I'm afraid he is choosing Scripture and delivering messages that are very pointed. While he is strictly keeping to the Word of God and is not making direct statements, the implications are there just the same. I have spoken to him about it, and he insists that he is only teaching what the Bible says about murder and rape and pillage, and that he will so teach as long as he is able to speak."

Bopepe lay a hundred miles north of Stanleyville. Nearly two hundred miles beyond Bopepe the hatred the rebels stimulated against the Americans hit hard against another mission station.

The mission at Ekoko was one of the largest among the UFM

believers in Bopepe. Congolese had pleaded with Mary to live their village. She consented, and nearly everyone spoke of h perfect the match was. Mary was short and stout, talkative, viv cious, filled with humor and sure of herself. She and the equal resourceful Pastor Bo Martin made an unbeatable team for th Lord.

Since Independence Mary had been joined by Margaret Hayes. But just now Margaret was with the Grants at Banjwadi. At Bopepe it was just Mary Baker and the people.

Left quite to themselves, the villagers of Bopepe had always worked out their problems according to Biblical teaching. But the letter just received from Mary revealed that they were no longer alone. The People's Republic had penetrated through the thick bush to find even little, secluded Bopepe.

"Twice I have been visited seriously," wrote Mary Baker, "on last Sunday even to the point of being menaced. The Simbas surrounded my house and held off the villagers by guns. I was asleep when they came, so went to the door in a half-stupor, which did nothing to make my visitors think more highly of me."

The Simbas turned the house upside down and inside out, and hurled every possible accusation at her. Some of the men approached her with evil intentions and two of them attempted to take hold of her, but, she wrote, "the Lord intervened."

She said the men had been drinking "and nothing I said or did would satisfy them; if I answered their accusations they told me that I was a woman of many words and much trouble; if I kept silent I had cheek in refusing to answer. They made me play my accordion to show them that it was for music, and when I didn't play one of their songs they berated me for that.

"They demanded to see my film-strip machine work and ranted that I didn't get it done in a hurry. (I had to get the transformer out and hitched up, plus the light plant going.) I was trying to open the drawers of my desk down on the floor on my knees and they yelled for me to open immediately the drawers of the files.

"One would ask me a question and when I would try to answer another would tell me to shut up, and when I asked what I should work. William and Dorothy Scholten and their five young children resided there, as did Pearl Hiles, a nurse from Pennsylvania, and Betty O'Neill, also a nurse and midwife from Northern Ireland. Though a new missionary, Scholten had made many friends among the Congolese. He taught in a school that trained African teachers, a job which as a university graduate he was well equipped to do. He communed easily with his students, always keeping hot a sociable pot of coffee. He conducted a unit of the *Flambeau,* a Boy Scout type of organization. He liked nothing better than to spend vacation periods trekking with his students through the dense jungle.

At the time of the rebel invasion, tall, thin Bill Scholten was thinner yet, for he was a sick man.

He suffered pain from malaria, parasites, and dysentery. In this condition he found the Simba inspections hard to take. One time a rebel soldier fired off five pistol shots close beside his throbbing head. Sometimes they made him and the women sit long hours in the blazing sun. The Simbas not only took away his carryall, but because they were generally poor drivers, they often forced him out of a sick bed to get behind the wheel and drive, and this usually at night when he was the sickest. Frequently a trip took him at constant gunpoint to some distant place; likely the day had dawned before he was allowed to crawl back into bed, seemingly more dead than alive.

Always he was greatly concerned over the welfare of Dorothy and the children, of whom the oldest was a boy of seven, and of the two unmarried women on the station. The treatment the rebels gave him and his worry about the others wore him down to the extent that it was a question of whether he would survive.

On Sunday, September 13, malarial chills convulsed him unmercifully. It was that day that the rebels chose to arrest him.

The order arrived from rebel headquarters in Stan to arrest *les mercenaires.* The local Simbas knew there were several *missionnaires* in the area. Not distinguishing between the two words they began to gather up *les missionnaires* who wore white robes and beards and those who, like Scholten, did not. They thought themselves extremely fortunate to find one that Stan wanted who not only fit the prescription but was an American as well.

Parting from his family was difficult for Bill Scholten.

"I'll see you in Heaven," he said. He was then led away to a truck that would carry Catholic priests as well as himself to the town prison at Aketi, sixty miles from the Ekoko station.

Late that Sunday the rebels stopped the truck at a checkpoint in Aketi. The barrier blocked the road in front of the home of Charles Mann, a missionary colleague of Scholten's. Mann, on seeing that a foreigner occupied the cab of the truck, approached it. To his great surprise that foreigner was his friend.

"Why?" he asked on learning their destination was prison. "Why you, Bill?"

The malaria attack had diminished for the time. Scholten was better able to view his situation with some detachment.

"They want mercenaries," he replied. "I suppose they think I'm one. And, too, I'm an American. And then there is the matter of the radio transmitter. There's one on the station . . . out of commish, but a transmitter nevertheless."

He said to Mann not to worry. "When they find I'm in no political affair they'll turn me loose."

But he was not released. Sunday night he lay on the dank floor of the poorly ventilated prison, more sick than he had ever been. Monday morning the prisoners were herded into a truck for the trip to Stan. But Scholten was too sick to go. The others drove away and he stayed in his cell.

Monday and Tuesday nights he was allowed to sleep under the stars in the prison courtyard. But all the time he suffered from chills or fever. On Wednesday morning, the 16th, a violent spasm shook his body. It was the last to torment him. Only his jailer saw him die.

In a note intended for his wife he had written:

"Dearest Dorothy, The Lord will not allow you to go through more than you can bear."

The rebels had told him that they planned to kill him by degrees in the presence of his family. They named many kinds of torture methods. But they had cheated themselves of their brutish fun. By contemptuous treatment of his sickness they killed him; in dying he found escape from having to face more than he could bear.

By secret messenger the word of his death reached Stanleyville. The news brought great heaviness upon the folk at Kilometer 8. Al Larson, his penetrating eyes devoid of their usual sparkle, looked his severest because he had a troubled heart.

"Bill is the first of our group to go, the first of us to pay with his life for answering Christ's call to Congo," he said quietly and almost without emotion. "He may not be the last."

From Stan the news moved east to Bunia. An older missionary couple who were able to carry on their work there in spite of rebel occupation slipped a message across the border into Uganda.

But outside Congo the world paid small heed to Bill Scholten's death. To be reasonable, hadn't the age inured itself to suffering and death so long as the ugly business stayed out of easy sight? Who far away in America or in Europe could really see the dangerous plight of the alien residents of northeast Congo?

Very few, it seemed, either saw or cared.

The people who were trapped in rebel territory and who felt that their situation deteriorated almost daily began to ask, "What must happen here to make the outside world see and care?"

6

Busy Days for Doctor Paul

In a sprawling, sturdy-built hospital of block walls and corrugated roof, four hundred miles northwest of Stanleyville, the examining physician glanced up quickly to see who entered the ward, then turned back to his patient. He smiled broadly.

"You can go home today," he said to the bandaged fellow who with wide eyes followed the doctor's probings and punchings. "Your rupture has healed to the point that you can work in your garden. But keep off your bicycle for a while. I don't want any nasty spills."

"Monganga Paulo—Doctor Paul," whispered the person who had come in and now stood at the doctor's elbow, "you must leave at once."

"In a few minutes, pastor," the doctor replied, moving to another patient. "There are eight more to check in this ward. And then I'd like to see the lepers once more."

"There won't be time. The rebels will be here soon," the anxious informer said.

"Go find Boniface and Kanga Joseph," the doctor directed quietly, asking for his male nurses. "Send them to me and I'll finish
68

quicker. Also, I want to leave special instructions for nursing some of the patients."

The pastor went out. The doctor continued his rounds. He stopped at the bedside of a patient in traction. A rigging of tree limbs supported the apparatus of ropes, a pulley, and a bucket of sand. He adjusted the suspension, smiled at the patient, spoke a few words of encouragement, then moved on to the next. He worked with deliberation and quite without hurry, yet wasted no motion or time. Hardly could a patient read the tenseness of the hour in the boyish face bent over him, nor in the dark, friendly eyes matched by the shock of dark, wavy hair and set off by the tropical whites he wore. This was Paul Carlson, the efficient healer and kindly counselor who found it impossible to turn away from anyone's problem.

To be even-tempered in a crisis was not unusual for Carlson. Since coming to Congo fourteen months before he had found life to be a chain of crises. But one met the demands of the hour by doing what he was supposed to be doing and not worrying that he failed to do something else.

Carlson loved life in Africa. He had not been in Congo long enough to consider the people and their ways as ordinary, and probably he never would. In letters to friends he always spoke of new and intriguing discoveries.

Until becoming a medical missionary Paul Carlson lived almost indistinguishably from thousands of other young American doctors. Yet in his fabric ran a peculiarly stout thread that tied him to God and the Bible.

His parents had dedicated Paul as a child to the Lord's service. In growing up in Southern California, he always found the church of prime importance. He made a special point of studying the Bible. He taught Sunday School. During a two-year hitch in the navy he remained faithful to his Christian ideals and looked past discharge to fitting himself to serve the Lord and mankind.

While an orderly in Swedish Covenant Hospital in Chicago,

where he had gone to study at North Park College, Paul Carlson fell in love with a striking blonde student nurse, Lois Lindblom. He often said that if she married him, which he hoped she would do, she might be marrying a missionary. He placed his name on the missionary volunteer list of the Evangelical Covenant Church, but no call for his services came.

He struggled to get through college and medical school and the years of interning and residency; and having won the pretty girl to be his wife, they could settle down, eventually to have two fine children, a comfortable home, and an office full of people asking to go under his knife.

As he moved into a promising career as a surgeon, Paul seemed to move away from the possibility of being a missionary. Yet he never completely gave up the thought that someday God might send him overseas.

One day in 1960 at their home in Torrance, California, Lois picked the mail out of the box and noted a letter from the Christian Medical Society. She was aware that this organization had been seeking short-term volunteers to fill emergency gaps on mission fields. She felt that through that letter God perhaps was raising His voice to the level of a call. She thought about hiding the letter from Paul.

"Probably they want him to go off to Africa or some such place," she said to herself. But out of loyalty to the one she loved dearly, she passed the letter to him with the rest of the mail.

It was indeed a call to Africa. The Congo Protestant Relief Agency needed help desperately. Paul Carlson answered the call in 1961, a few short months after the land's bloody introduction to independence.

He was assigned to the hospital at Wasolo in the Ubangi region of Congo. In five months there he treated countless cases of hookworm, yaws, tuberculosis, elephantiasis, goiter, malnutrition, and diet-induced hernias. During his stay he saw a vast population not only without adequate medical care but with insufficient Gospel witness.

In the wards and on the covered passageways of the eighty-bed Wasolo hospital and on the street of the mission settlement and in the nearby villages Paul Carlson exchanged a bond of deep admiration with the Congolese people. On completion of his term the Church of Christ in the Ubangi asked him to return.

"Bring your family next time," the church leaders begged.

He returned to California and prayed—and Lois joined him in his prayer—that God would send them as missionaries to Africa.

In early summer of 1962 their church dedicated Paul and Lois to missionary service. By fall of that year he was studying tropical medicine in England. Lois and the children joined him later for study of French in Paris.

They arrived in Congo in July, 1963, studied Lingala first at the Ubangi village of Karawa, then moved to Wasolo in October. He was one of only four physicians, all of them mission doctors, in the province.

"The good doctor—*Monganga Paulo*—is back." The word spread quickly through the dense rain forest. By road and path and by dugout canoes on the nearby rivers whole families came, bearing their sick. Mornings he spent in surgery and in making the rounds of the wards, afternoons in treating the walk-ins at the outpatient clinic until darkness would suddenly overtake the jungle clearing. And always to be sandwiched in somehow were the lepers with their specialized care, the baby clinics, the trips to neighboring villages.

There were buildings to build, the car to fix, surplus food to distribute, sermons to prepare and deliver, family life to maintain.

The family prayed together in the mornings. Paul Carlson prayed like a farmer talking to his horse—familiarly, intimately, effectively. Much of the family fun had to come in the daily routine —except with Paul there hardly was routine.

He thought nothing of interrupting his dinner to look at a new arrival, or of postponing it to watch at the bedside of one who was critically ill. Whenever he snatched a few minutes to relax in his house that sat on a small hill, he usually had his tape recorder working, playing good music. Sometimes late at night he and Lois would linger over a cup of coffee. Paul often remarked about the goodness of the Lord in leading them to Wasolo.

The first year went by quickly. One happy event not far into the second was the wedding at Wasolo of the hospital pastor's daughter on August 22. But within the week the rebel Simbas pressed dangerously near to Wasolo.

Paul decided he must take Lois, his son Wayne, his young daughter Lynette, and the missionary nurse Jody LeVahn across the Ubangi River to the safety of the Central African Republic. He drove them in the hospital truck during the first week of September. He was urged to stay out of Congo by other mission members who evacuated from other stations about the same time, as well as by United States consular personnel.

But Carlson said no. He was needed at the hospital. He thought that by going back he could prevent the collapse of the staff under the pressures the rebels no doubt would bring to bear on them. As for danger to himself, he thought the chances quite remote.

"Why should the rebels be interested in me?" he asked. "I'm only a doctor." He went back to the hospital that evening. Two days later he visited his family in exile, but stayed with them only a couple of hours.

A few days after the second return to Wasolo, the rebels penetrated as far as Yakoma, where the Bomu and Uele Rivers join to form the Ubangi, about twelve miles from Wasolo. Eight times the Simbas charged the defending soldiers' positions; seven times the troops of the national army held them off. That night Yakoma and the surrounding area went to bed uneasily, not knowing exactly what to expect from the rebel victors.

For the next several days the national and rebel armies engaged in skirmishes on all sides of Wasolo. One day the rebel commander of Yakoma sent a message to Carlson.

"Come, if you please," he said. "Bring your bag of medicine."

He drove into Yakoma. There he found numerous wounded

rebels in serious need of his care. He did what he could to patch them up, and the rebel force seemed to appreciate his efforts.

The commander invited Carlson in to tea. Before allowing him to leave, the officer pinned on the doctor's arm a white cloth band bearing a red cross.

"There now," he said, admiring his work, "go back to your hospital. Your patients need you."

Now that the rebels recognized him for what he was—a doctor —Carlson felt he had done the right thing in sticking at the hospital. One day he ticked off ten cases in which he had saved a life since returning. Yet at times he wondered if he ought to try to leave. It was no simple matter now; the Simbas controlled the roads, and snakes the swamps and crocodiles the rivers in the area. Once he was offered a lift out of the area by plane, but he refused to allow it to come in, believing that so dramatic a departure would endanger the staff and patients left behind.

On the night of September 17 Matthieu Bangi, the pastor, approached him about going.

"Escape to your family," cautioned the pastor, a man who was older than the doctor and who bore the marks of tribal cuttings on his forehead.

"What about my patients?" Carlson asked.

"The Simbas will no doubt permit Boniface and the others to care for the sick," the pastor replied.

"The commander said for me to keep on working," Carlson protested.

"But they have discovered that you possess a *phonee*," said Matthieu Bangi, "and that has made them angry with you."

The chief in a village near Wasolo, who had not wanted a mission hospital established in his area in the first place, had made a trip to Yakoma to report the doctor's *phonee*.

"He told them you talk on your radio every day," the pastor reported. And this Carlson did, to say a cheerful good morning to the outside world and in the past to consult with other stations on medical problems.

"He says you speak of Simba movements and call in planes to

bomb them," Pastor Matthieu continued.

"They can't be serious," Carlson said. "But if necessary, I can leave quickly."

That day the rebels killed seventeen villagers a few miles from Wasolo. The next morning a person who was in the know came hurrying to the pastor with the vital message that the Simbas would strike very soon.

"They will kill *Monganga Paulo,*" the informant whispered stealthily; his whole body shook so violently that he could hardly talk. "And they will kill Boniface and others who stay at their posts."

The pastor went immediately to the doctor in the big ward, broke in on him as he examined the hernia case and other patients.

"Monganga Paulo," he whispered excitedly, "you must leave at once."

But if the threat produced fear in Carlson, he did not show it. He made up his mind to leave, however, and would get started after completing his rounds. In fifteen minutes he would be gone. He would trust his friends somehow to get him through to safety.

The nurses he had sent for and another named Kokembe had hardly joined him in the ward when rifle shots announced that the rebels were there. Carlson and the nurses hastened to the door.

Outside, they saw two rebel soldiers approaching. Both were armed with guns. One lifted his weapon and shot. Boniface fell dead.

At that point Simba reinforcements arrived by truck, twenty-five or thirty more rebels. Their weapons were assorted—guns, knives, spears. One angry fellow who once had worked for the hospital stepped up to the doctor and struck him in the face with a stick. He hit Carlson's nose, which began to bleed.

"Why do you hit me?" Carlson asked his assailant.

"Because you use your *phonee* to call the planes to bomb us," the fellow, who trembled with rage, snapped in reply.

"Bring us your *phonee,*" ordered another Simba. Kanga Joseph and Kokembe were being tied with ropes. Kanga Joseph gained rebel attention by shouting:

"Untie me, and I will lead you to his *phonee*."

This they did. They forced the doctor to climb in the truck and at the nurse's direction drove him to his house on the little hill. Carlson thought that scarcely had he ever made a more difficult trip.

The blow with the stick by the disgruntled former worker—this he could take. But Kanga Joseph, this helper whom the doctor had trusted, this simple man who for all his simplicity had always proved himself a faithful fellow—it was difficult to accept his sudden move, even if fear was the man's prompter. He approached the house and his head hurt, certainly from the hard blow with the stick, but also from sadness.

Carlson watched as the Simbas looted his house of things of value. What they did not want, they broke into small pieces. Then, their pillage ended for the time, they drove him back to the hospital. Here they untied Kokembe. The group walked to the hospital entrance and there a Simba halted them. He ordered Kokembe to return to the truck.

"Watch him go, *monsieur le médecin*," an officer commanded Carlson. "Watch carefully now."

The officer quickly removed the pistol from his holster and shot the retreating nurse in the back of the head.

It is true, thought Carlson, the rebels have only murder in mind. He earnestly believed that he, too, would be killed right then and there.

The Simbas, however, ordered him once again to climb into the truck. One piece of equipment of his they had kept and not destroyed was the tape recorder which had supplied so many delightful hours of music.

"It is yours. You keep it," a Simba insisted. They could kill a man's co-laborers and tumble his work to the ground without a flinch and turn right around and insist that strict accounting be made for an item of only material worth.

En route to the jail in Yakoma the Simbas beat Dr. Carlson. He was imprisoned with thirteen other men in a room of about twelve square feet. For three days he wondered whether death might not come by suffocation.

West of Yakoma the national army had regrouped and was succeeding in pushing the rebels back the way they had come. In the bitter conflicts many Simbas were killed—and to the dismay of those who saw their comrades fall, none rose to fight again after their three-day "sleep." And many who were not killed were wounded.

The commander remembered he had a doctor locked up in the jail. He ordered him brought before him.

"My men suffer," he said as Carlson stood before him. "Will you take care of their wounds?"

Paul Carlson himself was painfully sore from the beating he had received, and stiff from the dampness of the cell. He did not wait long, however, to give his answer.

"Where are the wounded?" he asked.

The Simba pointed in the direction of the road through the forest.

"Get some medicines and let's go," the doctor said. "That's why I'm in Congo."

7

A Prison without Despair

In Stanleyville, Christophe Gbenye, the rebel president, summoned the foreign consuls to his residence for a meeting. The American consul and his assistant were brought from their arrest quarters in the Sabena Guest House at the airport. But just as they arrived, General Olenga drove up. He went nearly berserk with rage.

"The Americans are not supposed to be here!" he shouted. At his command, Simba soldiers began beating the two men with their gunstocks and fists. Olenga ordered them back into the car in which they had come.

"Take them to the Central Prison!" he demanded.

On the way there the guards stopped at Sabena to pick up the three other consular staff members and Charles Davis, the new missionary who was in detention with them.

The presence of Davis in the prison soon became known outside. Al Larson and Del Carper scoured the town to get him help.

"It's funny," Larson said to Carper one day during a break for coffee in Kinso's living room. "How do you explain that Davis is locked up across the street and we who are also Americans are sitting here, free to work on getting him released?"

Typical of rebel bureaucracy, the arrest order for Larson and

Carper, which David Grant had seen at Banjwadi at the time the
Davis family was picked up, no longer seemed to have importance.
But their attempts to help Davis had been futile, as had the efforts
of Peter Rombaut.

The British consul did, however, succeed in arranging for
Muriel Davis to visit her husband one day. And perhaps Rombaut's persistence was to bear more fruit than what appeared at the
time.

Davis and the other Americans found the prison was no guest
house. Cells opened onto a courtyard screened from the street by a
high wall. The beds were wood planks. There were no blankets, no
mosquito nets, not even a breath of air. Following their installation
here, the men received several beatings. Then on the fourth day
General Olenga himself arrived to recruit volunteers from among
the African prisoners to fight against the nationalist army.

His first action, however, was to stop at the cell containing the
six Americans. He sized them up, then singled out Davis.

"Are you the missionary?" he asked.

"Yes, sir," Davis replied uneasily.

"Stand there," Olenga said, indicating a place in the cell apart
from the others. For two hours Davis waited under a cloud of
anxious doubt while the general made the rounds of the other cells,
seeking to augment his army.

Eventually he worked back to the cell of the Americans. He
extemporized a particularly harsh censure in the French language,
castigating his prisoners for what he termed the despicable policies
of the United States against the rebel cause. In the indictment the
nervous, sweating Chuck Davis hopefully wondered if the reason
for his separation from the others had been forgotten. But suddenly Olenga centered his attention on Davis.

"Take him to the guardhouse!" the general ordered the soldiers
with a sweep of his hand. Davis walked out of the cell not quite
knowing how he was able to place one foot ahead of the other, he
trembled so. Why, he wondered, was he alone to suffer for what
the general saw as the diplomatic sins of America?

In the guardhouse, which stood in the row of cells, Olenga began to explain his action concerning Davis, and what Davis heard was far different from the death sentence he had been expecting. Olenga sounded rather apologetic as he spoke.

"You are not supposed to be here," he said.

Not supposed to be here! Davis, stunned with sudden hope for his life, felt his head swim. The throbbing of the blood in his temples interfered with his understanding. The way Olenga had said it, the decent look on his face as he spoke—the clear intent was to show some favor to his prisoner.

But why the sudden turnabout? After these days and nights of living a horrid dream Davis had actually heard the general say, "You are not supposed to be here."

In a moment Olenga chose to relieve Davis of his perplexity. He said that missionaries were good people.

"They help the Congolese," he asserted. Then before he went out he ordered that Davis be released.

But just to let him walk away from the prison was too simple a procedure for Simba officialism. An hour was required to process his discharge. Yet in that hour the soldiers showed Davis much deference. One pulled up a chair for him to sit in. Everyone spoke with politeness. The general had said that here was a good fellow, and they believed him.

Finally, an officer informed Davis he could go home.

"I don't want to go home," Davis replied. He said he wanted to go where his family had gone, to Kilometer 8. But they had no car in which to transport him.

"Give me two Simbas to walk me across the street to LECO," he then said.

And once in the street this new missionary who had spent almost as much time in detention as at his station did just what his wife had done on her release before him.

He called for Kinso.

Freedom was restored to one missionary—as much freedom as

anyone in this rigid situation knew. But one missionary was dead, as much a victim by the contempt for his illness as if a spear had run him through.

Al Larson thought he should try to pin down the responsibility for Bill Scholten's death.

"If we don't take a strong stand against what the Simbas allowed to happen to Bill," he said one morning to the assembled group at Kilometer 8, "we may jeopardize all our lives."

If the rebels could mistreat alien residents without a protest raised, what would stop them from picking off the foreigners one by one? The American consuls were still locked up; whatever the protest, the missionaries would have to make it.

The group decided that Larson and Bob McAllister should accost the lions in their den at army headquarters in Stan. Should something happen to Larson, an American, there was good chance that the Irishman would escape to carry on.

Late in September Larson and McAllister paid a call on Colonel Joseph Opepe, the second in command of the rebel military force. While they awaited admittance to the colonel's office in the *Etat-Major*, they tried to appear casual in the midst of threatening talk by the Simbas who loitered at headquarters.

"I killed an American at Bukavu," said one soldier proudly.

"I slashed *three* with my machete as if they had been pigs," said another. Still others boasted they could easily top such records of mediocrity if given half a chance.

Larson had no desire to prove whether the talk was factual or mere bravado, so felt distinctly relieved when an aide showed him and McAllister in to the colonel.

Opepe stood behind his desk. He was taller than most Congolese, broad shouldered, and had a very large stomach. A roundish face gave him an age of about fifty. He was neatly dressed in blue-gray shirt and trousers. Except for his oversized midsection, Opepe appeared quite soldierly.

Larson had heard of the colonel; at one time he had been a captain in the national army. It was said of him that he joined the rebels because he believed in their political cause. But it was apparent that his joining did not extend to the Simba witchcraft. Opepe wore no animal skin, *dawa* paint, leaves, or fetish. He seemed to rely on a military bearing and a correctly slung rifle to characterize him as a soldier.

Larson spoke a greeting in Swahili. Through an interpreter Opepe halted him; he knew little of the official Simba tongue. He instructed his aide to speak to the foreigners in French, and he himself would use Lingala. Larson seized on this break to speak to the colonel directly in Lingala.

"You speak my tongue?" the colonel asked, obviously pleased. Larson had gained a point with Opepe, and did not lose it even when the colonel asked his nationality and he replied, "American."

For several minutes Larson recounted the circumstances of Bill Scholten's death. Although McAllister, unable to speak Lingala, was left out of the conversation, he said to Larson later that Opepe looked like a father giving attention to a son. In the end, the colonel agreed to issue Larson a road pass to Aketi to enable him to visit Scholten's widow and children and possibly bring them to Stanleyville.

The other missionaries at Kilometer 8, and Kinso, refused to sanction the trip. They agreed with a Belgian trader who warned that with the hatred building up against the Americans, he would never make it alive to the ferry slip at Banalia, a town on the Aruwimi River between Banjwadi and Bopepe.

Larson did not go. But he felt they had made their point of protest with the Simba authorities. And in the process they had gained a friend in the growing atmosphere of enmity—not an ally or a defender, but at least a friend.

If the first visit by the Simbas to Kilometer 8 left the missionaries believing that life under rebel rule was to be peaceful with only stray shots in the air to shatter the tranquillity, subsequent calls set them straight.

The rebels came often, day and night. Weekends were especially bad. The Simba officers released their men from normal duties, so bands of undisciplined soldiers wandered through the area, often intoxicated or under the narcotic influence of hemp.

A precipitate visit at midnight would rouse the entire compound, for the rooms of each house were usually searched. The Simbas looked for *phonees* or for nationalist soldiers. And finding neither, they would turn to other bounty.

There was, of course, the taboo against stealing. But a Simba did not consider it a theft to point his gun at a person and say, "I am thanking you, *bwana,* because you are going to give me petrol for my car."

Most times they were meticulous in writing out receipts for things taken. They would often promise a new item for an old . . . "when we take over Brussels."

Sometimes the rebels dropped in just to harass. Once very late at night one banged on the door with a specific intent in mind. Al Larson answered his knock. The caller, a Simba officer, let it be seen that he had his gun out of its holster. He demanded to talk to a certain missionary woman.

Larson admitted him. "Say what you want to say, then leave," he said to him. The rebel went to the woman's room. Larson thought he ought to listen at the door. In a matter of seconds he burst into the room.

"Taking of women is forbidden to a Simba," he said sternly to the intruder. He stepped between the soldier and the woman.

"You are one to tell me what a Simba can do?" asked the rebel officer contemptuously. He raised the gun that he held and pushed it against Larson's stomach. "I want her. I will have her."

Within Larson welled the fighting spirit that had been a part of his early life on the streets of Brooklyn. He had faced bullies before—not one with a loaded gun, but bullies who could make life miserable if a person knuckled under to them. He was not about to let the Simba carry out his evil intention.

"Now look here," Larson said evenly but forcefully. "I know you've got a gun sticking in my stomach, and at any time you want to you can pull the trigger and I'll be dead. But that's the only way you're going to touch this woman—after I'm dead."

For several moments the Simba's hand quavered, and Larson could feel every pulsation transmitted through the barrel of the gun. He knew that any second could be his last; yet, strangely, he was not reviewing his life in one blinding flash, not thinking of all the unfinished tasks he had wanted to accomplish in life. Instead, he was telling this lustful soldier in a matter-of-fact way that he simply would not get what he had come for.

"You are not going to have her," Larson said. And, somehow, that was that. Without a word the man slowly lowered his gun, stepped back a pace, bowing to this voice of authority.

"Come on," said Larson, seizing the moment for action, "I'll take you on an inspection of all the rooms." He knew the officer would have to explain his presence in the house, perhaps to fellow Simbas who waited at the road; a search for *phonees* would provide as good an excuse as any.

The Simba visitations grew less frequent when the high command deposed Kingese, the mad ruler of Stanleyville who had vowed to end religious teaching and wipe the name of God from Congo. Yet a change of official policy—if indeed it was a true change, for rumor had it that Kingese would be kept on salary—a change in the thinking of those on top did not necessarily trickle down to the ordinary soldier. Or if it did, and he felt it better to disregard the change, the "little" Simba carried on the way he pleased, to the point that he got away with it.

So the inspections never ceased at Kilometer 8, even after Colonel Opepe had stated the people there were involved in no political affair. The first person to hear a motor on the road—and few but rebels drove vehicles these days—would shout "Car!" Everyone outdoors would walk, not run, to the cover of the nearest house.

The men always tried to meet the Simbas in the driveway. Because the houses sat far back from the road, they usually had time to intercept the inspecting party before it could charge into a house unannounced. And most often they succeeded in deflecting the Simbas from the back yard, where the mission vehicles were stored.

Generally, the first question was, "What is the nationality of the people in this house?"

Larson often would reply, placing emphasis on the key word, "We are men who speak *English*." If a particular set of visitors was not too inquisitive, that ended the hazardous discussion of nationality.

The ability to speak to the Simbas in Swahili proved helpful in softening their harsh demands. So did the knowledge of when and how to stand them off. None was more adept at this than Bob McAllister.

He only laughed when one day a Simba demanded to know why in the large group of people living at Kilometer 8 there were so few men, and another Simba cut in with the explanation, "Oh, these folk are missionaries. And missionaries, you know, have big families."

On another day McAllister was the spokesman for the missionaries when a Simba came demanding food.

"I need some meat for my rice," the soldier began. "We have a pot going down the road."

McAllister had a way of talking to the rebels that often caused them to forget what they came for. On this day he used mock anger.

"Oh, you want meat, do you?" he said. "Well, do you realize that we have twenty-three people to feed here every meal?"

"Twenty-three?" asked the Simba in surprise.

"Twenty-three," McAllister replied. "And eleven of them are children."

Pointing over his shoulder to the room where some of the children played, he continued, "Just look at those children with their open mouths."

He paused so the Simba could peer around him and see for himself. Then he resumed the attack again.

"You have rice," McAllister said. "You should be coming here and saying, '*Bwana*, can I give you rice?' Then you would be helping me feed these twenty-three people three times a day."

The soldier had heard enough. He backed away from the door.

"It's all right, *bwana*," he said. "I really didn't intend to take anything from you. I was just wondering how you were getting on. You are all right, aren't you?"

He then excused himself; he had to head down the road.

Two hours later he was back. He had brought two tiny avocados —"for the children."

He presented them to McAllister in cupped hands, the way of politeness in Congo. And in doing so he neglected the taboo of touching nothing that another touched.

Because Kilometer 8 was her home, Jean Larson bore the brunt of meal planning and preparation. With so many mouths to feed it was, in fact, difficult to maintain an adequate food supply. At times the missionaries could not buy food in Stan. But they never ran out. Sometimes the cupboards got nearly bare, but somehow a fresh supply would arrive and they would then be filled again.

Seldom did they have eggs, and fresh vegetables were in short supply. Stan merchants donated cases of mackerel or canned chicken or powdered milk from their private stores. Rice came from the big brewery.

"I don't feel bad at all about eating the brewery's rice," Bob McAllister said one day. "What we eat, they can't turn into beer."

One item that became a staple was sardines. If anything lacked, it was never sardines. Jean Larson liked having so many women at Kilometer 8; each produced a different recipe for serving sardines.

To transport the donations or purchases of food from Stan to the house was almost a cops-and-robbers game. Off-duty Sunday when the streets were less crowded proved to be the best time to move the supplies. Al Larson, with Del Carper or Bob McAllister, would cycle into the city, pedal to the establishment of a Greek or a Portuguese friend, then wait at the rear door for a man to happen along who had been authorized by the Simbas to keep and operate his truck. Into the truck would go the foodstuffs, the bikes, and the men. The thrill of the ride to the house was in the uncertainty of whether they would be highjacked along the way.

Their transportation helper was a Britisher named Bob Latham. This thin, stooped man in his middle thirties had migrated to

Congo "to see if its independence works." He hired on the United Nations peace-keeping force as a mechanic and transport officer.

Larson had known him since his arrival in Stan and always found him standoffish. Never antagonistic to the mission effort, but not one to believe that a man could enjoy a personal fellowship with God, he shrugged off every witness to the reality of Christ.

"Just what can God do for you?" he used to ask in skepticism. Yet in these somber days when living in Congo was more of a nightmare than an adventure, he drew close to the missionary circle.

The Simbas pressed him into service when they took over Stan, and because he kept in repair the vehicles they confiscated to use as their own, they allowed him to drive his truck. This is why he could come and go at will. His home lay about two miles beyond Kilometer 8, so nearly every day going to and coming from town he stopped at the mission home to offer rides for any having business in Stan or for transporting supplies.

More and more, it seemed, Bob Latham was timing his visits to coincide with the daily prayer meetings at ten in the morning or after supper in the evening. He took no part in them. He just seemed to want to be around.

Not all the foodstuffs Latham had helped accumulate at Kilometer 8 were for the folk living there. They had received word from the Artons and the Burks, missionaries at Boyulu, that the station on the old slave trail often suffered from hunger. Al Larson mentioned the problem at one of the prayer meetings. A few days later Latham said he had the answer.

He had asked for and received permission of the Simbas to drive toward Boyulu in his truck. He would carry soldiers to hunt for food the Simbas liked, and at the same time he would deliver a shipment of American and British supplies to the impoverished missionaries at Boyulu. And on the return trip he would give a lift to the missionaries who wanted to come to Stan.

This was how Hector McMillan and Kenneth and Paul, the two older sons, were able to join Ione and the four younger boys at

Kilometer 8. Also riding with Latham were Thelma Southard and her small son Larry. Marshall Southard, the husband, had been away at a conference when the rebels closed off Stan, so was caught in Leopoldville away from his wife during the siege.

Latham planned a second foray into the Boyulu area, but the rebels took his truck from him to use in another area. Hope thus was dashed for assembling all of the UFM people at Stan—for mutual encouragement and to take advantage of any Red Cross or other emancipating flight, though none was really expected.

"Where is the safest place?" someone asked.

"The place where the Lord puts you," another answered. At the moment, there were many different locations for many different persons.

Bob Latham often dropped off a bag of cement at Kilometer 8. That permitted Hector and Del to work on the interior of the building called "the hangar." As walls went up, the big missionary family—now numbering twenty-eight—spread out. But all the families ate their meals together in the main house.

Two tables occupied the dining room. A third was set on a screened back veranda that opened off the dining room through a large double doorway. A broad arch led from the dining room to a fairly large living room. Bedrooms and a bath opened off the dining room and another screened porch off the living room.

This house was the prison of sorts for the missionaries. The adults were determined that it should not be a place of despair. Parents and the "aunts" stretched their imaginations to keep the children occupied.

They allowed the children to play outdoors. At first the youngsters used the front yard; when their presence there caused passing Simbas to stop and investigate why so many foreigners lived at one house, they were banished to the rear. There the McMillan boys made swings of old tires. Some of the children tended gardens. Del Carper and Chuck Davis rigged up an old bathtub as a pond for fish taken from the stream in the forest behind the property. Davis built a jumping post for the boys; others erected monkey bars.

The small ones played "customs office," or were pushed in a homemade wheelbarrow; the older boys and girls walked through the forest to add to their collections of feathers and wild-life specimens. Hector McMillan led small groups, held down in size in order not to attract attention of passers-by, to the gently sloping roof over the garage where he taught them to pick out the constellations of the southern sky. Bob Latham helped the boys make model railroad cars; occasionally he took them to his home where he had an elaborate scale train, including an exact model of the station in his hometown in Wales.

Al Larson asked Chuck Davis to teach the adults three evenings a week from the Book of Acts. The lessons were good for the group, and the preparation for Davis. It lifted his mind from the sore troubles that had beset him and helped him to see that he wasn't the first to suffer imprisonment and beatings and humiliations as a child of God.

Each morning at six thirty Larson led a daily worship on the front veranda, and to these meetings the African Christians came faithfully. Sunday mornings the men of Kilometer 8 cycled up or down the road to worship with the Congolese in their neighborhoods. On Thursdays Jean Larson, Lois Carper, and Mina Erskine conducted sewing classes for the neighboring women. These classes were held in the home of Malenza, the houseboy.

Several spoke of the deep fellowship they were enjoying with their Congolese brethren during these difficult days. The bond between the believers, regardless of race and nationality, was aptly illustrated one day by the visit of Kaitenge Jeremy, a pastor from the seminary station at Banjwadi.

The missionaries had just sat down to a meal when he arrived on his bicycle, perspiring and winded. They made him welcome, and asked him to eat with them.

For a full minute or more, however, he stood absolutely still. He said nothing, just gazed upon them as if in his mind he were checking off the names of each one on a list. Then satisfied that all were accounted for, he shouted:

"Praise the Lord!"

He had pedaled the forty miles only to see whether the missionaries were still alive. After dinner he jumped on his bicycle again to go home. He said he was in a bit of haste. He had found out what he wanted to know, and others at Banjwadi would be anxiously awaiting his report.

Larson thought this time of enforced leisure would be good opportunity for the missionary to improve on his language ability. So he taught Swahili to those who were not very proficient. Others organized a school for the children—there were students in grades four through nine and in eleven. Viola Walker and Lois Carper undertook most of the teaching. Schoolbooks were limited—mostly a set of the *World Book* and a few Congolese texts and some French books from LECO. The older boys made a scale model of the mission compound and by this they studied art and mathematics. The lamps and electric motors they constructed introduced them to physics and to woodworking. Larson searched the house and came up with five musical instruments, so he started a band. Alma McAllister, Bob's wife, formed a choir. Her own clear soprano voice carried them quite acceptably through the "Hallelujah Chorus" and less demanding pieces. She gave the children lessons on the accordion and on the small, folding organ on which she accompanied the frequent "singsongs."

Al Larson introduced a course whose credits might not be transferable. It was, simply, survival. He sought to instill not fear, but discipline, in both adults and children.

"Kids," he would say, "don't cry when the Simbas are around." And to everyone he cautioned:

"You know how the Simbas are reckless with their guns. If at any time a Simba opens fire, drop to the floor and play dead. It may save your life."

On Saturday nights Larson led them in games. Sometimes they produced homespun dramas. A skit by Hector McMillan brought down the house one night.

"This is my haberdashery production," he explained from "off stage" to his audience. He then entered the room where they sat, and they laughed to see his arms hiked up in the sleeves, making the coat appear too large. He paraded before them, went out, and returned in a coat several sizes too small for his large frame.

For his next walk-on he carried a suitcase.

"I'm taking my suit to court," he said. Then he unfolded a stepladder and climbed it, suitcase in hand.

"I'm taking my case to higher court," he explained. The final act was to walk through the room in shirtsleeves.

"I lost my suit," he said.

Hector and Bob McAllister were usually at the center of the merriment. It was a tossup as to the better comic. Hector brought laughs by his string of jokes; Bob by his rare ability to see the funny side in everyday life. McAllister had a nickname for everyone. He was forever spinning off malaprops. Whenever the men returned home from a trip to the city, they always urged Bob to relate what had happened; he could find a light side to the most dire threat.

In the evenings Kilometer 8 might have been a gloomy place; they used only oil lamps because the electric lights shone like beacons and they wished to attract no attention from passing Simbas. But Hector's hen cackle and Alma McAllister's deep, powerful chuckle pierced the gloom and helped keep despair at bay.

Since Hector McMillan returned from Boyulu, where he nearly died from pneumonia, he had lost part of his love for funmaking. Occasionally someone would remark that he seemed to detach himself from life around him. He was not moody, but introspective, as if he possessed a foreboding of the future. Yet he himself said nothing about an apprehension; more likely he was to speak about Heaven.

One day in the heat of afternoon he came in from working on "the hangar." He drank a quart of cold water. "Someday," he said to Ione, his wife, "I'll sit down by the River of Life and I'll just drink and drink and drink."

More than anyone, Ione noticed the change in Hector. "He probably seems different," she said to one who mentioned it, "because he lost forty pounds during his sickness at Boyulu."

She was thankful to have her family together. She recalled that but for a change in plans Hector could not have come back with Bob Latham. The driver of the truck had intended to go to Boyulu three days earlier, but the Simbas were slow in granting a pass. Several of the missionaries expressed disappointment at the delay.

"I suppose they won't let Mr. Latham go at all," someone said. But he did make the trip, and had he gone when he first planned he would have found Hector McMillan sick with a high temperature and completely unable to travel.

Because they were under virtual house arrest and so mostly stayed home, the missionaries found opportunity for reading. In their unhurried quiet times the Bible took on new significance; familiar passages burned with fresh meaning. The Psalms especially voiced their inner feelings.

"Maybe the Psalms mean so much to us," Bob McAllister ventured one day during devotions after breakfast, "because David, who wrote so many of them, was a hunted, persecuted man."

"Yes," agreed Al Larson. "He was a man of great affliction, but in the midst of trouble he experienced great triumph."

An unpleasant Simba visit sometimes left them uneasy and discouraged. Olive Bjerkseth always urged them to pray. Viola Walker claimed a particular promise from Scripture that seemed to fit the occasion. And always, Ione McMillan's steady, smooth voice with just a hint of cheer to it reminded them of the words of the Apostle Peter, "Think it not strange concerning the fiery trial which is to try you, as though some strange thing happened unto you: but rejoice, inasmuch as ye are partakers of Christ's sufferings."

Ione was of medium height, was slender, and her hair was graying. She brought animation to a conversation, yet enjoyed the quiet times of reading. Among the books at Kilometer 8 she discovered a biography of Adoniram Judson, the great missionary to Burma. In settling down to read it, she thought back to the days of her girlhood when she had pledged her life for missionary service in Asia. She had been deeply moved by the martyrdom of John and

Betty Stam in China, and promised God that she would volunteer to help fill the gap created by their murder by Chinese bandits.

But China closed to missions before she could get there, so she turned to Congo instead. Now Congo was undergoing the convulsions that had shaken China, and it seemed conceivable that God would have his martyrs in this land also.

The fall months of 1964 wore on; the rebel government of northeast Congo found itself deep in trouble. The economy was near a standstill. Moise Tshombe's national army, led by mercenary soldiers, had begun to push the rebels back from their far-flung outposts. Clearly, desperate days lay ahead for the rebellion. Such conditions brought a tightening of the reins.

In October the visits by Simba soldiers picked up in frequency and bitter action at Kilometer 8. It hardly seemed probable that the missionaries could hold on to their vehicles for much longer. The rebels had begun to cast their covetous eyes on Bob McAllister's Land Rover, so Al Larson went to Colonel Opepe to ask him to exempt it from confiscation.

He was successful in his mission. Opepe agreed that mission vehicles should be reserved for the work of God. But the matter rested not with the top officials, but with the "little" Simbas who carried on this war in their own way.

Larson pedaled with all his might to get home to Kilometer 8. Swinging into the driveway, he waved the paper bearing the colonel's signature. But he was too late. Bob's Land Rover was already gone. Two very young boys who proudly claimed to be full-fledged rebels talked an officer into driving the car away.

That day Malenza paused in his preparation of the evening meal to speak confidentially to Ione McMillan.

"They are taking everything," he said.

"Our lives remain," she replied.

"And what if they take your lives, too?"

"Maybe they will," she said. "But if they do, perhaps some will remain. Perhaps some sons of mine will be left who will come back here to live among you and talk to you about Jesus."

Toward the end of October the missionaries began to think that Malenza's concern was no exaggeration. The hatemongers of Gbenye's People's Republic had stepped up their anti-American, anti-Belgian campaign. But on the 28th, a Thursday, they were determined not to look on the dark side. This day was the thirty-sixth birthday of their field leader. They wanted Al Larson to remember it as a happy occasion.

All at Kilometer 8 hunted around for gifts or busied themselves in making something for him. Someone produced a ballpoint pen from a dresser drawer. Mary Rutt sent out a can of peanut brittle from LECO in Stan. Jean opened one of her precious cans of frankfurters—which were reserved for birthdays and wedding anniversaries. She also baked her husband an eggless cake.

Larson was all set to blow out the candles when the radio, tuned to Radio Stan but kept low in volume, broke off its American jazz for a speech by Gbenye.

Every American and Belgian in rebel territory was to be arrested and thrown in prison, he said. The foreigners were now to be hostages, providing the rebel forces with a powerful weapon of defense. If Simbas were to be killed in the war, the hostages, too, Gbenye threatened, would die.

"The missionaries are like other Belgians and Americans," he said. "They are imperialists like their governments. Arrest them all."

No one now had much appetite for cake.

If the Americans were to go, that meant the Larsons, the Carpers, and the Davises. These couples packed their bags, as they had done at the previous arrest order. Then they waited for the Simbas to show up.

The next day Bob McAllister went into Stan to see what he could learn. Twice the rebels arrested him, but upon learning he was Irish, released him each time.

"If they take me to headquarters once more," he said on his return to Kilometer 8, "I'll insist that they place me on the payroll."

On Sunday afternoon four rebels swooped on the compound.

They had come to do the arresting.

"Everybody goes," the leader said. To him, all foreigners were Americans today.

"Colonel Opepe has cleared this house," protested Larson. He produced a paper with the colonel's signature to prove it.

"No matter," the rebel leader said. "Today is different."

"Do the women and children have to go?" asked Chuck Davis, hopeful that only the men would be taken. In a corner of the room Bob and Alma McAllister were praying quietly. Then McAllister broke off and confronted the Simba officer.

"You shouldn't take the women and children," he said. He pleaded earnestly that they content themselves by arresting only men.

"Everybody—"

"You can't—"

The Simba chief started to give his order again. But as he did he looked to the corner of a room. Muriel Davis, several months pregnant now, lifted her daughter Beth from a crib. The child buried her head in her mother's shoulder and cried.

"Everybody," the rebel said, determined not to soften.

Back to detention for Chuck Davis. He could feel the cold slime trickling down his back. Yet today was different from that terrifying afternoon in August. The bitterness was gone. The fear was lessened. In these weeks at Kilometer 8 he had observed great faith at work in the lives of his older, more mature missionary colleagues. He felt now that he was ready to face whatever lay ahead.

". . . not the women and children." It was Bob McAllister again.

"All right," the Simba said. "Not the women and children."

The rebels had come to make the arrest without any means of transporting their prisoners to Stan. Kinso's little Bedford bus, which he used in literature work, was stored at Kilometer 8. This the rebels commandeered to carry away the men—Canadian Hector McMillan and Irish Bob McAllister, as well as the three Americans.

An African boy stood by, watching the proceedings; he turned

Unevangelized Fields missionaries Alfred Larson and Hector McMillan (second and third from top) join Congolese pastors in baptism of new believers in peaceful days before McMillan was killed by half-crazed rebels (Chapter 12).

Stanleyville (above), a busy river port of 200,000 population, possesses a tropical charm. Square building at left is the Hôtel des Chutes, where for three weeks the rebels held as prisoners three American missionaries (Chapter 9). The Librairie Évangelique au Congo (LECO) and Résidence Victoria are at top center. Hidden among the trees is Lumumba Monument (closeup views below), a memorial to the late Congo nationalist Patrice Lumumba. The rebels executed hundreds of their enemies before the monument, and threatened to kill eight Americans on the marble steps (Chapter 10).

LECO (left, above), a literature project, served northeast Congo. Missionary children play in the yard of Kilometer 8 (above), where at one time twenty-eight UFM missionaries lived under house arrest. Hard-bitten mercenary soldiers wept when they came across evidence at the Banalia ferry slip (photo at left) that eleven UFM missionaries had been slain by the Simbas (Chapter 18). Stanleyville's Hôtel des Chutes (lower photo) became a mission station for three American prisoners, Al Larson, Del Carper, and Chuck Davis.

AL LARSON

Angeline Tucker records her experiences for this book on the upper veranda of historic Union Mission House in Leopoldville. Her husband, Joseph W. Tucker, was brutally murdered by the rebels at Paulis (Chapter 15). "Why did Jay have to die?" In desperation Mrs. Tucker asked this question—and in faith found a satisfying answer.

Charles and Muriel Davis and their children Stephen and Beth narrowly escaped death when they were caught up in a fighting, murderous mob of Simbas (Chapter 4). Chuck Davis was held a prisoner for seventeen days. He was trying to pull Dr. Paul Carlson over a wall to safety when the surgeon died in the Stanleyville massacre (Chapter 13).

Kinso and Ma Kinso have been a tower of strength for both missionaries and Congolese Christians in their more than twoscore years of service to Africa. Head of the literature work in Stanleyville, they became key figures in relieving the suffering of prisoners. Several times Dr. Paul Carlson visited their apartment for meals (Chapter 8).

Fellow missionaries termed Alfred Larson, field director for Unevangelized Fields Mission, "the bravest man in Congo" after he stood up against incessant rebel demands. Larson once protected his people from molestation despite the fact that an enraged Simba pressed a loaded gun in his stomach (Chapter 7). After surviving the Stanleyville massacre he organized and led a party through rebel gunfire to rescue twenty-five missionary hostages (Chapter 14). Finally evacuated and with no rest, he prepares a sermon for delivery in Leopoldville.

Upon their return to America from Congo, Ione McMillan and her six sons are able to smile in spite of the death of Hector McMillan, the husband and father. Kenneth and Paul, the two older sons to the right of their mother, were wounded by rebel point-blank gunfire (Chapter 12). Mrs. McMillan set aside her grief and helped others she felt to be in greater need (Chapter 17).

Republic of Congo President Joseph Kasavubu visits Kenneth McMillan as the missionary son recuperates in a Leopoldville hospital.

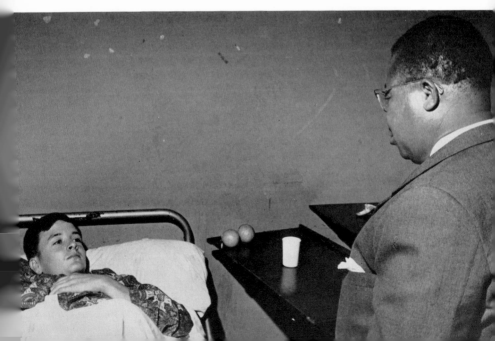

Missionaries Al Larson and Richard Sigg listen to Italian nuns as they describe the rebel killing of seven Catholic and six Protestant missionaries at Bafwasende (Chapter 18). Eleven nuns and three UFM women missionaries survived to share both terrifying and humorous experiences.

Bearded Père Charles Schuster chats with his old village mentor Père Kinsch (photo at left) in a street in Luxembourg after Père Schuster survived a horrifying massacre in Stanleyville's Rive Gauche section (Chapter 16). In photo below, UFM missionaries walk to an evacuation plane at the Stanleyville airport following their dramatic rescue from Kilometer 8. From left are Muriel Davis, Mina Erskine, Mrs. Marshall Southard and son Larry, and Alma and Bob McAllister.

Rebel officers (above) review troops during Stanleyville occupation. President Christope Gbenye (left) and General Nicholas Olenga (right) give Simba salute. Defense Minister Gaston Soumialot stands between them. Simba soldiers (left) pose with their weapons. A Simba youth (below) is identified by the leopard skin on his hat.

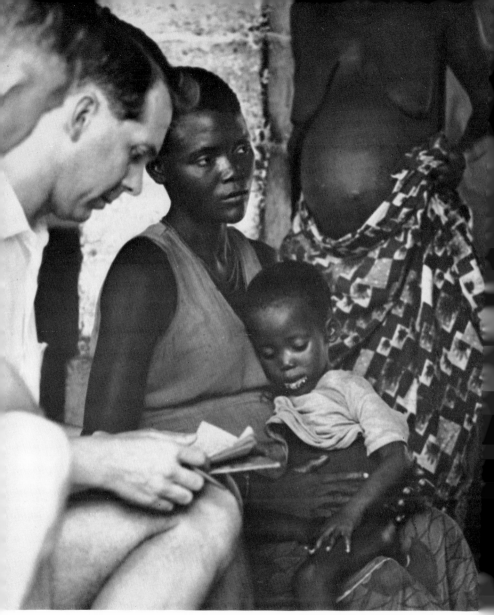

Dr. Paul Carlson, medical missionary of the Evangelical Covenant and Evangelical Free Churches of America, prepares to examine a child in the Wasolo hospital deep in Ubangi territory. Dr. Carlson was captured by the Simbas in September, 1964 (Chapter 6), later was sentenced to die on trumped-up charges (Chapter 10). The rebels, however, delayed his execution and held him instead as a hostage. He died just inches from escape in the Stanleyville massacre (Chapter 13).

In the Summer of 1964 Dr. Carlson received the help of Philip Little-ford, a Johns Hopkins University student who was sent to Africa by a pharmaceutical firm for training in jungle medicine. Always heavy, the work included surgical cases, lepers, and victims of a wide range of tropical diseases.

A marine honor guard drapes the body of Paul Carlson after it was flown from Stanleyville to Leopoldville following the massacre of November 24.

Honored by the Congo government, local villagers, fellow missionaries, and his family, Paul Carlson is laid to rest in the Ubangi village of Karawa (Chapter 17). Son Wayne comforts his mother, who bows over the plain wooden coffin.

After their own rescue from the Simbas, missionaries met often on the veranda of Union Mission House in Leopoldville to pray for their fellow workers still behind rebel lines. Clockwise are Mrs. George Kerrigan, Mrs. Al Larson, Kerrigan, Mrs. Hector McMillan and two of her sons, and Ralph Odman (back to camera), general secretary of Unevangelized Fields Mission, who flew to Congo to meet the missionaries as they emerged from captivity.

H.E.D.

Congo Martyrs

"There is no safe way to do missionary work and missionary deaths will yet be necessary to complete world-wide evangelization. This principle gives no license to spiritual dare-devilism or to recklessness. We must be prudent while depending on guidance from God, in forming our strategy and movements. It may well be that many more will seal their service with a martyr's death to join those who 'overcame him by the blood of the Lamb . . . and they loved not their lives unto the death.' "—Ralph B. Odman

The beloved missionary Mary Baker responds to the welcome given her by the Christians of Bopepe village. She holds aloft the hands of twin brothers Asani Benedict (in white suit) and Bo Martin, her partners in the work of the Gospel. Mary was killed by the rebels at Banalia, and Bo Martin may have died there in defense of the missionaries. Asani and his family escaped certain death by eluding the Simbas under gunfire and crossing the border into Uganda.

JOE WRIGHT

Joseph W. Tucker,
Assemblies of God

William P. McChesney,
Worldwide Evangelization Crusade

Phyllis Rine,
African Christian Mission

Dennis and Nora Parry
and children, two of whom
were killed by Simbas,
Unevangelized Fields Mission

James Rodger, WEC

Cyril Taylor, killed at Rive Gauche,
and his wife Joy and children, WEC

Laurel McCallum, UFM

Dr. and Mrs. Ian Sharpe, UFM

Muriel Harman, WEC

Hector McMillan, UFM

Chester Burk, UFM

William Scholten, the first of the UFM
Congo missionaries to die,
and his wife Dorothy and children

Irene Ferrel,
Baptist Mid-Missions

Jean Sweet, UFM

Burleigh Law, Methodist pilot

Ruby Gray, UFM

John and Elizabeth Arton, UFM
DONOVAN C. WILSON

Heather Arton, UFM
DONOVAN C. WILSON

The Congolese people will not soon forget Dr. Paul Carlson, who in a more peaceful day accepted gifts of eggs, corn, and a chicken after he and his medical assistants gave four hundred polio shots in a village near the Wasolo hospital.

to Timmy, the youngest McMillan, and asked, "What are they doing?"

"They're taking the daddies away," replied Timmy.

And it was difficult at the parting to say whose hearts were filled with greater concern. The women could only imagine the inhumanities that were in store for their husbands. The men were thankful to have their families spared the ordeal of imprisonment, but fully realized they now were prey for an increasingly dangerous and undisciplined rebel army.

8

A Man
for Dinner

During the fall months of rebel occupation Stanleyville became a
camp of contradiction. Growing discontent forced the Simbas to
ease up on the executions at Lumumba Monument (though not
until the victims numbered nearly two thousand and so much
blood had flowed that the torrential rains failed to wash the steps
and sidewalk clean of its stain).

Nevertheless, the killing of Congolese leaders and the literate
continued, now at night on the bridge over the Tshopo, a tributary
of the Congo River that ran through a portion of Stan.

The change in location held advantage. Since the rebels allowed
no burial for their victims, it was no longer necessary to think up
ways to dispose of the annoying mound of dead bodies. Just topple
the bodies into the water; a waterfall below the bridge pushed
them along to the Congo, and there the crocodiles solved the
problem.

This depository for the dead doubled as the hallowed site for
Christian baptism. One Sunday Kinso attended a service at the
Congo River at which one hundred twenty new believers plunged
under the waters, not as victims of violence, but as the fruit of
patient, loving labor.

The size of the baptismal class was indicative of the Church's renewed effort during these bloody days. And sales at the LECO bookshop soared. The new buyers were Simba soldiers.

For the first time many of them heard the jingle of coins in their pockets. They wanted Bibles, some perhaps only for a fetish, some for a symbol of the learning they hoped to acquire under the new regime. One day the wife of General Olenga drove up to the store in her bright red Anglia.

Under the watchful eye of a Simba, this attractive, diminutive woman entered the shop, asked Mary Rutt to show her the line of teaching materials available for her children. Then over tea in the Kinso apartment she asked for and received the promise of a Christian tutor for her four children.

All the while the voice of Radio Stan grew louder in its denunciation of the foreigners. The United States and Belgium raised the greatest ire for having supplied the national government with tools to combat the insensate rebel killing of innocent Congolese. Threats of massacre and cannibalism were vented not only over the air, but in the press as well. The official newspaper of the People's Republic, *Le Martyr*—named in honor of the late Lumumba—was as virulent in its abuse of aliens as the crimson of its headline ink.

The office of this journal joined next to LECO's bookshop. The editor lived above it; he used the stairway the Kinsos and Mary Rutt used, and the same hall led to his apartment as to theirs. But in line with the contradictions of the day, he was a man of mild temper.

"Bonjour, mademoiselle," he would say politely to Mary as he met her in the mornings when both went out to their work.

Bonjour, monsieur," she would reply, wondering what venom would flow from the pen of this well-mannered neighbor today.

The aims of the rebellion drew into sharper focus for the missionaries on their scattered stations. At Bopepe Mary Baker was now joined by her partner, Margaret Hayes, and the two were having fine success in teaching the Bible to scores of village children.

"But we work with urgency," Mary wrote in a secret letter. "Each day here may be our last."

She sensed what appeared as documentary evidence of the trend in rebel policy. One day a fellow cycling with supplies from Kilometer 8 for Mary and Margaret stopped briefly to rest at Banjwadi. The seminary station was halfway between Stan and Bopepe. He called Sonia Grant aside to show her a paper he withdrew from his shoe. He said he had copied it from a document in the dark the night before from friends in Stan.

". . . do away with all missionaries, do away with the Christian religion," read the paper, in French. "Put in their place the worship of Lumumba . . . work upon the weak, use whatever means are necessary."

Was this the manifesto of those who desperately sought for a cause to hold northeast Congo in their grip? On some appropriate day would the crime of being a Belgian or an American extend to being a Christian?

The possibility—indeed, the probability—was forever in the minds of both the missionaries and the Congo church leaders. Yet, the future had to wait upon the present. Nationality alone offered enough for concern. Of this, Kinso was soon to be reminded.

One Saturday morning he heard a pounding on the door at the foot of the outside stairway; he thought perhaps the rebel editor had forgotten his key. But upon descending the steps he saw a Simba soldier stood in the entryway.

"*Bwana,* five of your brothers are over there," the soldier said, pointing to the Central Prison across the street. "They've been there two days with nothing to eat."

"Five of my brothers?" Kinso wondered to whom he could be referring. "Their names . . . what are their names?"

The courier only shrugged his shoulders.

"Well, thank you for telling me," Kinso said. "Now please go find out their names."

The long-legged missionary bounded up the steps two at a time. He burst into the apartment to tell his news to Ma Kinso.

"I don't know who they are, but there are five men in the prison across the street, and they need our help," he exclaimed. "They are starved. We've got to help them."

The German couple, Elsi and Volker Gscheidle, had moved into a spare room on the apartment floor and now Elsi helped Ma Kinso prepare coffee and sandwiches. Kinso kept an eye out for the messenger to return. Soon he saw him leave the prison gate, so went down to the street to meet him.

"Hoyt, Grinwis, Parkes, Hule, Stauffer." He read the names on the paper the soldier handed him. He knew the men to be the members of the American consulate in Stanleyville. They had been in the Central Prison before—at the time Chuck Davis shared their cell. Since the missionary's release the American officials had been moved from place to place. Kinso had not known their location or the conditions of their imprisonment.

In a very few minutes he was on his way to the prison guard-house with a tray of food. The Simbas admitted him to the prison; after they inspected his tray and passed it, the guards brought out the consul, Mike Hoyt, from his cell.

Kinso was astonished to see the condition of the man before him. He was bearded and dirty. He bore signs of ill treatment.

"I'm frightfully sorry," Kinso began. "I didn't know you were here. Had we any idea—had we known you were right across from us, we never would have let you go hungry this way."

"Oh, sir," Hoyt laughed lightly, "we're not so bad off as you think. We arrived here only last night."

To that point the consulate cook had brought food for his employers. But now that they were back in the Central Prison they could hardly expect the fellow to subject himself daily to contact with the unpredictable Simba soldiers. If Hoyt and his men were going to eat, the Kinsos and Mary Rutt and the Gscheidles would have to feed them.

Mary tended the bookshop, so the task of preparing meals for the prisoners fell to Ma Kinso and Elsi Gscheidle. Kinso took charge of delivering them. A boy sometimes came around to carry the trays over, but often Kinso himself went to the prison. Usually this was no problem, for Kinso spoke not only Swahili like an African, but several of the local dialects of the guards as well. One day, however, a surly rebel officer accosted him.

"Why do you foreigners hate us Africans?" he demanded. "Why do you send your fighting men against us to destroy us?"

The Simba had heard that mercenaries were turning back the rebel armies; because of their race, he assumed that these paid South African soldiers were Americans, just as he assumed that Kinso was an American. And he knew that the bullets from the mercenary guns did, after all, kill Simbas instead of turning to water.

"Why do you hate us?"

As the veteran missionary returned to the apartment with the empty dishes, the acccusation burdened his heart. How could one get across the message of Christ's love to these misguided men? What more was needed to show the African that for love the missionary had come to his land to share with him the good news of salvation? What price the proof of love and dedication?

On Friday, October 23, five days before the order went out to arrest all Americans, another messenger from the prison knocked at the apartment door. And once again Kinso answered. The guard handed him a slip of yellowed paper. It bore three names: Al. Dr. Carlson. Mike.

The top name, Al, was Larson's signature. At the request of the prisoners Larson had sent them a message on the outcome of the World Series—"Cards over Yanks, 4-3, Al." Mike Hoyt had made use of the signature to return a message. The "Mike" was, of course, his own name.

But who was this Dr. Carlson?

Upstairs in the apartment the cryptic note produced a conference.

"Who do you suppose has joined our friends across the way?" asked Kinso.

"With a name like that, he is no Belgian," said Ma Kinso.

"Nor German," Gscheidle added.

"An American?" asked Mary Rutt. "The only American doctors

in this part of Congo are missionaries. He must be a missionary."

"Carlson . . . a missionary," pondered Kinso, wrinkling his brow and trying to pull from his wide knowledge of the Congo mission field a clue that would help them. "Carlson . . . Johnson—that's it, MEU."

He referred to the Mission Évangelique d'Ubangi, a work sponsored by the Evangelical Covenant and Evangelical Free Churches of America, both with heavy Scandinavian backgrounds.

"MEU has a Johnson, an Ericson, a Lindquist," Kinso said. "Why not a Carlson?"

"Maybe Dr. Carlson is the new missionary at the Wasolo Hospital," offered Mary Rutt.

Their deduction was confirmed the next afternoon. At four o'clock a knock sounded at the door of the apartment—someone must have left the door below unlocked. And before the knock could be answered, a man walked right in through the open door.

He was a rather handsome fellow—if one could imagine him without his stubby beard and long, scraggy hair, and with twenty or so more pounds to fill out a rawboned frame. The clothes he wore had obviously not been bought to fit him, at least not in his present condition. They were old; the shirt might have come from a missionary barrel.

"I'm Paul Carlson," he announced.

But what a time for a visitor to drop in! An hour before Mary Rutt had turned on the water in the bathroom to fill the heater in preparation for a bath. She then busied herself with other things, remembering the water only when she looked up and saw it streaming across the living-room floor. Thus, everyone was occupied with bucket and mops when Carlson popped in.

Mop in hand, Kinso crossed the room to greet their guest. He noticed a Simba soldier lingering just outside in the hall. Paul Carlson provided the explanation.

"They took me out of the prison this morning," he said. "They

gave me a nice room in the Congo Palace, but of course won't feed
me."

"Didn't you get the food we sent over for you?" asked Ma
Kinso wiping her hands on her apron and approaching the doctor
to make him welcome. "We received the message that you were
there."

"The consul spoke of LECO," Carlson said. "But they separated me from the other prisoners and I spent the night in solitary
—and this morning they took me out altogether."

He said he had asked his guard if he would be allowed to walk
the few blocks to LECO, and to this the guard agreed.

"Oh, you poor dear," said Ma Kinso. "You *are* hungry." She
hurried into the kitchen to prepare him something.

"Would you like a bath?" asked Kinso, with a wink at Mary
Rutt.

"I had a beautiful bath this morning," Carlson replied. "I really
have a nice room at the hotel. But I'm hungry."

Early Sunday morning Radio Stan broadcast that the rebels had
captured an American mercenary . . . a Major Carlson, said the
announcer. He had been brought to Stanleyville and was being well
treated. But the wording of the bulletin left little doubt that his was
a special case, one not to be treated lightly.

Dr. Carlson returned to the Kinso apartment that morning for
breakfast. Ma Kinso fed the Simba guard, which seemed to have
been a part of the agreement between guard and prisoner. No one
spoke of the broadcast. The doctor himself seemed hopeful of
being freed, now that he was finally in Stan. And from other cases,
one might guess that he was taking the route to acquittal—from
prison to house arrest to discharge eventually.

"I'm just a missionary doctor up in a forsaken corner of the
Ubangi. The rebels ought to see that I don't figure in their affairs,"
Carlson said, convinced of his own logic. "Please pass the bread
again. I'm getting my appetite back."

"And well that you should," said Ma Kinso. He had discovered
a bathroom scales in the apartment and to his consternation found
he had lost thirty pounds.

"At times I haven't felt much like eating," he said. He related that the Simbas arrested him in September, took him from his hospital in Wasolo, and confined him first in the crowded jail at Yakoma. Then the local rebel commander lodged him. This man, a lieutenant, treated the doctor decently in private, but abused him verbally in front of the Simba soldiers.

After a few days Carlson and three Catholic priests were ordered into the back of a truck, and the sometimes friendly, sometimes abusive lieutenant beat him severely about the head. They next stopped at the jail in Aketi.

". . . where Bill Scholten died," cut in Kinso.

The doctor shook his head. "I never knew anyone by that name."

"One of our missionaries," explained Kinso. ". . . he died in the Aketi jail before you arrived there."

At Aketi the rebels had Carlson and the priests cutting weeds and cleaning street gutters. The lack of wooden handles on the cutting tools caused their hands to be rubbed raw and bloody. On the road again the Simbas beat Carlson twice more until he thought he would die. Then came Buta, an important town about midway between Wasolo and Stan, and a respite of nearly a month.

At Buta the Simbas actually released Paul Carslon. He lived at a large Catholic mission school, and spoke now of the spiritual kinship he enjoyed with the Flemish priests there.

"These clothes that I have on," he said, sounding as though he boasted of a suit from Bond Street, "my friends at the school gave them to me. And I have some to change into; and I have a suitcase, too. My robed friends found all these things for me."

He spoke of the head father as a young man with whom he carried on many hours of fruitful discussion. The priest loaned him books. One book explaining the Protestant conviction provided the springboard for comparing the fundamentals of their beliefs. Each avowed to the other his faith in Jesus Christ as the Son of God and as the author of his soul's salvation.

"I'm sure each of us had an effect on the other," Carlson said.

He performed hardly any medical service in Buta, though he was now hopeful that in Stan he could get back to being a doctor. In Buta he had had no medical supplies; also, the rebel "doctors" objected to foreigners treating their wounded.

Three times Paul Carlson had tried to return to Wasolo. He asked the Simbas for permission to leave Buta, and since he was in no political affair they said he could go. Three times he caught rides on trucks passing through Buta—and three times the trucks that took him on broke down just outside of town. Each time he retraced the way to the mission school.

Was the Lord preventing him from reaching home? After the third effort he thought so. God evidently had something else in store, though now even here in Stan he did not know what it might be.

That Sunday noon Dr. Carlson returned to the LECO flat for dinner. Peter Rombaut was a guest. The British consul had hurt his leg playing tennis, so the doctor examined it and advised Rombaut how to care for it. Carlson's Simba guard watched closely—he never before had seen an army officer conduct himself like a physician.

On Monday a missionary eating at the Kinso table spoke to Carlson about the accusation with which Radio Stan filled the air each day. "They say you're a major in the mercenary force, doctor —a spy for the American government."

Carlson slumped in his chair.

"Now why did you have to say that!" Kinso said sharply to the one who had spoken. He seldom flushed with anger, but now he did. He had tried to spare their special guest of the news of increasing rebel rancor toward him. To have someone blurt it out inadvertently—well, that was just unfortunate.

The doctor's jaws slackened in dejection. Yet, he did not really register surprise. Perhaps right along he knew more than what Kinso had wanted him to know. He may have been trying to forget the facts that dogged his life. But even in this happy company he could not escape the stormy cloud that was fast settling on him.

"Le mercenaire," he said, sighing. He told them that while he

was at the Catholic school in Buta an important visitor chanced by, one no less a person than Christophe Gbenye, president of the rebel state.

Gbenye and General Olenga had departed Stan on special missions in October, Olenga reportedly to go to neighboring Sudan to purchase arms for the rebel war, the president to tour the northeastern provinces to generate new support for the lagging People's Republic. Before Gbenye quit Stan he promised his followers he would produce for them an American mercenary.

Upon his arrival in Buta the citizens told Gbenye about the American *missionnaire* who had been brought to their town. They wondered what they should do with him.

Gbenye had an answer.

"I'll haul *le mercenaire* off to Stan," he said, grinning widely because his trip into the hinterland had so suddenly worked out well. To his retinue, he cautioned, "Be sure to see that he is protected. We need him in Stan alive."

Le missionnaire, le mercenaire—again the words in French had been twisted. Perhaps this time the interchange was deliberate. Dr. Carlson the missionary was whisked off to Stanleyville as Major Carlson the mercenary. His tape recorder had been brought all the way from Wasolo; termed a *phonee,* it was their evidence against him.

On his return to Stan glib-tongued Gbenye filled the air with convincing speeches. He had his prize by which to rally the malcontents. He even considered exhibiting Carlson in a cage at the Stanleyville Zoo.

Paul Carlson felt he could never pass through a military trial as a paid fighter and a spy and come out alive. He informed the folk at LECO that before leaving Buta he had scribbled out his will and entrusted it to the Flemish priests.

On Tuesday morning, however, his spirits rose somewhat. A Simba who had come to Stan from the Ubangi approached a senior officer to say that *Monganga Paulo*—Dr. Paul—was no mercenary.

"He is a medical missionary," Carlson happily quoted the Simba as saying. "A few months ago he saved my father's life."

On Wednesday of that last week in October the order went out to arrest all Americans. At breakfast time Thursday morning Carlson's guard stopped by the apartment.

"The doctor will not be here for his meals today," he said, beating his head with the palms of his hands. "You see, last midnight they took him back to the prison."

9

Mission to the Detained

Kinso learned that on that same day the Simbas transferred David and Sonia Grant to Stanleyville from Banjwadi. They came in separate trucks, he with Catholic priests, she with nuns.

One of their students, an engaging fellow named Sosthene, rode in the truck with Grant. His arrest resulted from having said "bon voyage" to the Grants as they were being driven away. At a government post en route to Stan, a Simba soldier objected to the treatment given the missionaries.

"They love Jesus and I love Jesus," he said. He swung himself up into the back of the truck to stand with Grant. "If they are going to die, I will die, too."

The trucks crossed the bridge over the Tshopo River in Stanleyville after dark. The apprehensive passengers thought the firing of guns sounded ominously close. In the beam of the headlights David Grant witnessed the shooting of several Congolese; he saw the Simbas toss the limp bodies over the rail to the falls below.

At first the Grants thought they would be imprisoned at Camp Prince Leopold. The trucks stopped at this military installation and a guard said execution of foreign prisoners had begun. But after a while they went on to be interviewed by the corpulent

Colonel Opepe. In gregarious mood, he ordered the whole contingent to be quartered at the Procure, the Catholic administration center.

Kinso took comfort that in an emergency, at least, he could telephone the Grants. Communication with others—with the men across the street in the prison, for example—was less direct. Ma Kinso brought this out by handing her husband a small matchbox.

"What do you suppose this means?" she asked.

"Where did you get it?" he asked. He took the box from her, turned it over, and gave it a close inspection.

"It was on the tray of dinner dishes the boy brought back from across the way," she said.

"Well, I suppose it means that Mike Hoyt is out of matches—" A sharp whistle cut short his speculation. "Look here, Alice. Look closely."

She squinted at the box, which he held so the light from the window made visible some writing in the bottom.

" 'Two Pax,' " she read. She looked up at Kinso, brushed back her thinning hair and shook her head sadly. "The boys from the university are over there."

"They are," he agreed, "the only two Americans still on the campus."

"Pax" was the term by which the two conscientious objectors who worked at Stan's new Protestant university were known. Jon Snyder had come from Oregon in late 1963, Gene Bergman from California a few months later. In their early twenties, congenial, and looking on their required term of service overseas as an opportunity to be useful in a missions program, they had worked around the new campus in all sorts of administrative and maintenance jobs.

"I hate to think of those young boys being thrown into that awful prison," Ma Kinso said, turning away, quietly weeping.

This 28th day of October saw the arrest of many foreigners in Stan. Belgians disappeared right and left from their shops and homes. The Simbas placed a few in the Central Prison. Most, however, they distributed among the several military installations. They viewed dispersion as the best protection against bombing raids which had not come but which they feared someday would.

On the second day following, a Friday, the Simbas slapped the Belgian consul into prison. On Saturday Ma Kinso and Elsi Gscheidle sent food across the street for eleven. That day they also laundered bloodstained clothes for the prisoners, the telltale signs providing a picture of worsening conditions over there. On Sunday —no one in the apartment was able to go out for church—Daniele, the LECO houseboy, sped in from his house on the edge of town to report that he had seen Kinso's Bedford bus go by. Inside it were the five men of Kilometer 8 and some Simba guards.

On Monday morning Bob Latham stopped by the apartment to speak with Kinso.

"I can't find the men of Kilometer 8 anywhere," he said.

"You've checked at the prison?" asked Kinso. He was gratified at Latham's interest in the missionaries, but dismayed at what their disappearance could mean.

"They are not at the prison," Latham said.

"The military camps?"

"They are not there."

Kinso walked over to the telephone. It was again time to get in touch with Peter Rombaut.

The five men from Kilometer 8 were delivered to the Hôtel des Chutes the Sunday on which they were arrested, a disposition unknown to their friends. The Chutes was old, but still in good repair. This tawny plastered establishment of perhaps fifty guest rooms stood a block from the Congo River, near the docks of the storied riverboats that battled the current the thousand miles from Leopoldville. "Des Chutes"—The Falls—referred to the Stanley Falls, the historic series of rapids just above Stanleyville.

The main thing to be said for the Chutes was the two-story layout of verandas that looked on an inner court of flowers and small trees. The missionaries walked through the passage from the street to the lower veranda and there encountered a rebel interrogation center.

The three Americans carried valises (McMillan and McAllister expected to be released before nightfall, so brought none). They set them on the deck, and all five awaited orders. At the far end of the veranda two Simba officers lounged at a table against the wall, behind which ranged the guest rooms. The two advanced to take over the prisoners from the arresting soldiers.

Bob McAllister recognized one of them. He was plumpish and had a round, rather pleasant face. He wore military dress, but was unarmed and bore no Simba markings.

"François is his name," whispered McAllister to Al Larson. "He has visited in our station church."

He had, indeed. Once not long before the rebel siege he said in a testimony meeting that he felt the Church in Congo was lukewarm in its zeal for God; the believers were in need of reviving. McAllister now felt that François recognized him, but the man said nothing to indicate he did. Perhaps he himself had grown spiritually cold since joining the Simba ranks. Or, it may have been that he considered silence the better virtue, considering the plight of those before him.

From remarks they made as they advanced, it appeared that both officers were majors. François' colleague seemed to be a mean fellow. Frowning, he bore down hard on them.

"You're Belgians, aren't you?" he charged.

"No, sir," replied McAllister. By prior arrangement the Americans thought it best if the Irishman among them served as spokesman.

"What country do you come from?" the angry officer demanded.

"I'm Irish; I'm here in Congo on a British passport," McAllister said. The major then called for their identification cards.

An ID was always carried by an individual wherever he went in Congo. It gave the place of birth and other pertinent information about the bearer. Producing the folded blue cards from their pockets, the Americans in particular felt that if being an American were a crime in a Simba's eyes, whatever punishment would fit that crime would not be long in coming. But the antagonistic major did not intend to check their cards. He went to the door nearest the table and rapped.

It was Colonel Joseph Opepe who emerged.

Here was a man whom all the prisoners recognized. Larson, McAllister, and Del Carper had had dealings with him, especially Larson. They had seen him in fine military bearing before, and a few times as he was today—unkempt and slovenly in tattered trousers and shirt, his shoes without laces, his shirt unbuttoned at the waist because it would not reach around his stomach.

Opepe appeared to be in a testy mood. And there was no doubting that he had been drinking.

He paused outside his door and looked the length of the veranda to the prisoners. Suddenly, he pointed a finger at Del Carper.

"What's that man wearing?" he asked.

He had seen Carper's hearing aid. The wire from the earplug ran to Del's shirt pocket, where he carried the battery case. The unfriendly major barked an order for Carper to advance toward the table, where the colonel seated himself.

"Did you see how far away I was when I spotted that thing?" he boasted to his officers. Carper removed the fitting and laid it on the table. François directed him to stand to one side. The colonel was now inspecting the ID cards. He called for Chuck Davis to stand before him.

"Your card says Br— Br—"

"Brooklyn," helped out Davis.

"Brooklyn," said the colonel. He belched noisily. "Brooklyn, where is that?"

"In America," answered Davis. "It is the city where my mission has its office."

"You're a missionary?"

"Yes, sir. A Protestant missionary."

"Stand over there." Opepe indicated a spot next to the wall.

McAllister was next. From previous encounters the colonel

knew he was British. He placed him on the garden side of
the veranda, but not until he first berated him for the planes that
flew over Stan and shot their rockets on the city. His outburst gave
the unfriendly major who stood near Davis the opportunity to
hit Davis on the head with his fist.

Hector McMillan's turn came up. He said he was from Canada.
He could not convince the Simbas that his country was not a part
of the United States.

"Get a map and we'll see," said Opepe. François produced one
from the colonel's room. But to add to the confusion, the United
States and Canada appeared in the same shade of pink.

"See what we told you?" the other major said.

Nevertheless, after much discussion with his men Opepe placed
McMillan next to McAllister, so the lineup was two-to-one. Del
Carper might have joined Davis, but at that point the colonel
decided to test whether the apparatus on his table was a *phonee*.
He inserted the plug into his ear.

"I can hear talking!" he cried. He got up from his chair, walked
a ways down the veranda. Determined to apply the acid test, he
called for his assistants to say something.

"Sure enough!" he shouted. "I can hear through this thing. It
certainly is a *phonee*.

"We should kill him. We should kill all of them right now," the
unhappy major said. He took advantage of Opepe's distraction
to double his fist and strike Davis, then to twist his nose.

The colonel returned to the table. Carper attempted to explain the workings of the hearing aid. But everyone now was
shouting above the other. Over the bedlam Opepe raised his voice.
"You say this man can't hear? Hah! Why then is he talking with
us?"

The one so adept at slipping blows to Davis now tweaked
Carper's nose. "The colonel is no fool," he said.

Al Larson was trying to get Opepe's attention. "We have a
paper, colonel. We have a paper."

"Huh?" asked Opepe, and quiet settled on the veranda.

"We have a paper signed by you that permits Monsieur Carper

to wear his hearing aid," Larson said. He motioned for Carper to produce it. He did, and Opepe examined it.

"This is my signature?" he asked, surprised. He held out the paper to François. "This *is* my signature, isn't it, major?" By the curlicues François said it was. Larson and Carper had visited Opepe's office previously to obtain permission for Carper to wear the device. The authorization was in a gigantic stack of papers that Opepe had been obliged to sign.

But the matter was left pending as the colonel turned to Larson's case. He needed no ID to tell him Larson's nationality. The two had met several times, about the death of Bill Scholten and other matters. For a number of seconds Opepe just stared at Larson. Then he opened the one remaining card, studied it as he had the others. Without a word he folded it again and pointed for Larson to join the two with British passports.

"What's he doing?" Larson asked himself. "He's singled out Chuck because he doesn't know him." The poor guy. He was the only one of them who had already been in prison. Were they going to put him as an American back in custody and let the others go?

His second-guessing did not last long. The two majors began arguing about the hearing aid, whether it was or was not a *phonee*. The one who said so stoutly that it was, turned to the colonel.

"What should I do with this *phonee?* he asked. Preoccupied with other matters now, the colonel looked up in disgust.

"Oh, give me that," he said sharply, snatching up the contrivance. He got up from the table to carry it into his room.

The angry major took advantage of his absence to say to the missionaries that they would all go to prison—immediately.

"Move out," he commanded. Sensing his determination to support his order with his sidearm, if necessary, they started to walk slowly toward the passage by which they had come in from the street.

"Hurry along!" he shouted.

Just as they were to leave the veranda Colonel Opepe stepped from his room.

"Major!" he snapped. "Where are you taking those men?"

"To the Central Prison, sir," the major replied, a bit surprised to be stopped.

"Put them in that room instead," the colonel ordered, motioning to a room three doors down from his and right next to the entry.

Into the room they went. At least it would beat a prison cell.

All day Monday and Tuesday after their arrest Malenza the houseboy searched for the men, and so did Bob Latham—and Peter Rombaut. Kinso dispatched Volker Gscheidle to Kilometer 8 for the welfare of the women and children. Concern was mounting because neither of the non-Americans had shown up.

On that first Wednesday of November Al Larson spoke to one of the Simba soldiers who brought the meager and rather unappetizing rations to their room.

"Wouldn't it be a good thing if you should visit the bookshop across the street from the prison and tell the *bwana* there that we are in the Chutes?" He thought so; he hoped the Simba would. He knew the families at Kilometer 8 would be upset, so wanted to get word to them by Kinso. And he wanted to get a message to Kinso to pass along to Peter Rombaut.

He had no complaints about their treatment at the Chutes. Major François had turned on the air conditioning, saying they need not be uncomfortable during their confinement. The room had a private bath. And by pushing the twin beds together, three could sleep rather well. François rounded up a couple of mattresses to spread on the floor.

But Larson felt it was unjust that McAllister and McMillan were being held. He got an affirmative answer from the Simba about dropping by LECO. Then he was able to suggest that the soldier ought to speak to Kinso about getting on to Rombaut.

It required the rest of the week, but the British consul succeeded in getting McMillan and McAllister set free. He brought them around to Kinso's flat on Sunday noon, a week after their arrest.

"How did you make out? asked Kinso.

"Not bad" said McAllister, "considering that before the week ended additions to our number made us rather crowded."

"Crowded!" put in McMillan, and those present were happy to hear his cackling laugh once again. "Why, I became the world's first missionary in space."

He related how they had pushed the beds together. "Del Carper and Bob slept in the beds," he said. "And I hung in the space between them."

Before the two men left the Chutes, other prisoners joined them in the room. Among them was a Belgian planter edging sixty. M. Bordeaux, a lean man with not much hair, had knocked about in Africa for many years, but had lost none of his European urbanity. The day his Simba captors pushed him into the room, he studied the missionaries a while, deciding finally that Al Larson was their leader. His rigid protocol then called for the exercise of special deference to Larson.

Upon arising each morning he would say nothing to anyone until Larson was awake and dressed, and he could speak to him in impeccable French:

"Bonjour, monsieur le pasteur. Did you sleep well?"

He was even more fastidious in his preparation for a meal. The brown and sometimes moldy rice had to be mounded just so; the spoon, when the guards thought to bring spoons, had to be laid perfectly straight. And before he finished eating he always said to Larson,*"Bon appétit."*

On his part Larson acknowledged the nicety by returning the proper idiom, which meant "the same to you," *"Pareillement."*

The comfortable quarters soon became overcrowded with up to eleven in the room. Two of the prisoners were physicians—one an Italian about thirty years of age, and the other a Hungarian about forty. They came from a large plantation west of Stan where one hundred eighty technicians—including eighteen Malaysians and Indonesians—had died when the rebels cut their throats. The other newcomers were Belgian planters of various ages.

The air conditioner was insufficient to carry away the smoke that accumulated from the Europeans' tobacco. Most of the men

bought beer from the Simbas, and this created a certain unpleas-
antness for the missionaries. But what bore most heavily on them
all was the sense of helpless frustration that settled at times as day
emptied into night and night into another routine day.

The missionaries, being young men and athletically inclined,
tried to keep in physical condition. Del Carper was an ex-subma-
riner, so he most easily adjusted to the small space each one could
call his own. He led them in many a fast hike—all taken while
running in place. Though without his hearing aid he found it very
difficult to hear, he could talk, and by his natural optimism he
encouraged everyone in the room.

Another person who cheered them was a Belgian woman prisoner from the second floor. Mme. Marie Paneff made the rounds of
all the rooms each day to determine if anyone needed medical care.
This one they called their Florence Nightingale was not really a
nurse. She had been a resident of Stan since childhood, and
learned most of what she knew about taking care of sick people
through Girl Scout training in first aid.

As important as the pills she dispensed was the personal sun-
shine she shed. She was a woman in her thirties with brown hair
and bright brown eyes. It seemed she was always smiling. She took
her time in calling at each room; here was a place where people
had time. She would talk to the distraught, encourage the down-
hearted, wrap up the wounds of the injured.

She and her husband, Marcel, owned a shop of beautiful im-
ported gifts. He was being held in one of the army camps. Their
two young daughters stayed with her. Since all of the men in the
room on the first floor were fathers, Mme. Paneff sometimes
brought her girls on her rounds. To talk to them or rumple their
hair seemed to make the day pass more quickly.

How to feed the rising prisoner population of Stan became a
growing concern for those who still had their liberty. The number
in the Central Prison had risen to nearly fifty by this time, so it became a physical impossibility for the LECO missionaries to meet
the need there twice daily, to say nothing of others caring for the
scattered captives.

A Greek dealer in vegetables, a good-humored man named Karichos, called together a number of *commerçants* and members from the professions to deal with the problem. Other Greeks, the Portuguese, the Pakistanis, the Indians—men of many nationalities—quickly volunteered their goods and services for a relief agency they called *Le Central.* They asked the Simbas to let them use the hotel kitchens for cooking the meals. The rebels were very happy to step out of a job that captors rarely performed for their captives in Africa. *Le Central* regularly supplied rice, macaroni, fish, and meat sauces, though sometimes the Simbas stole the sauces for their own rice.

A few of the volunteers were afraid to go near to where the prisoners were being held. But not Karichos. He was a man of great self-confidence. He frequently checked to see that everyone was getting enough. In his nervous, jumpy way, he popped in and out of the men's dormintory at the Chutes four or five times a week.

"We're getting some potatoes in," he said hastily one morning. "And Monsieur Carper, I'll get your hearing aid back. I'll have it by this afternoon."

He was the bearer of perennial good news. "The liberation army is approaching fast. They'll be here in four days."

A Stan physician who started coming in to back up Mme. Paneff's work brought less optimistic reports but more solid pieces of news. He and Al Larson worked out a maneuver that by a handshake they could trade notes under the eye of a Simba guard. The route then for this clandestine mail was to Kinso, to a trusted runner, and finally to anxious wives at Kilometer 8.

Besides meals, *Le Central* supplied clothing, toothbrushes, magazines, even razor blades from the merchants' dwindling stocks. One day Karichos opened the door to the men's dormitory and threw down ten shirts.

"If there's one your size," he called out, "help yourself. And Monsieur Carper, I'll have your hearing aid in a day or so."

The three missionaries in the Hôtel des Chutes, concerned as they were about their families at Kilometer 8 and lonely because of the separation, began nevertheless to view their confinement as perhaps a special mission in their overseas service for the Lord. Shut up with them were men whose lives had been hard and unyielding to the ways of God. Two of the planters in the room had once denied their plantations to the missionaries and to their African brethren for preaching the Gospel. Now they were face to face with the Christian message.

The missionaries took care not to press their beliefs upon a captive audience. But they had brought their own Bibles, and in a few days Larson sent word to Kinso to send in others. Some days one, some days another, joined in the reading of the Scripture and the time of prayer.

Dr. Angelino, the young Italian physician, gratefully received a Bible.

"Thank you so much," he said. "This is the first time, I must confess, that I have ever seen a Bible."

They generally chose to read for their devotional times passages most familiar to the men. Eliciting the greatest interest were the portions that dealt with sin—which the men certainly knew about —and the forgiveness of sin. One or two at times scoffed. One said, "Missions are an absolute failure."

But a fellow by the name of Dubois challenged that statement. He recently had been transferred to Stan from the prison at Banalia.

"With my own eyes I saw something that once I never would have believed," he said. He then began to tell of two foreign women whom the rebels had forced to walk the fourteen miles from their home to the Banalia jail. But they did not walk alone. A Congolese man walked with them.

And when the three arrived at the prison, Dubois had heard and seen the man plead with the rebels that the women be given special consideration.

"They have done so much for our people," the Congolese said. "You ought to give them a mattress to sleep on, instead of the hard concrete floor. They should be entitled to a little privacy."

But all he got for his trouble in their behalf was to be beaten severely and locked up in jail himself.

Dubois spoke of Mary Baker and Margaret Hayes, the missionaries at Bopepe, and of Bo Martin, the faithful pastor.

Larson and Carper, who knew the three well, were not surprised
at Dubois' testimony, though their hearts became heavy to hear
that what they long feared for Mary and Margaret and Bo had
now happened. Bo Martin, who rushed to Mary's defense when
Margaret was still away, had stayed by the two because they were
God's children and they needed his help.

"Why would a man set himself up for the cudgeling that he
got?" Dubois asked, obviously impressed by one who would do
it.

"You saw in Bo Martin the love of Jesus Christ," Larson replied. "Christ loved you so much that He Himself suffered death
that you might stand before God with your sins forgiven."

"Then I should love Christ, shouldn't I?" Dubois said. He read
most of that day in the Bible to learn more about the One meriting
his devotion.

Several times Dr. Angelino asked for assistance in the new experience of reading the Word of God. He said he had always felt
helpless in the face of temptation. "Where can I read of the power
of Christ to make a new man of me?"

Besides the quiet witness to their faith, the missionaries sensed
that they themselves were being shaped for uncertainties ahead.
Del Carper said one day that like the Hebrew children in the fiery
furnace, he felt the presence of another with them—certainly the
Spirit of God was in that room.

Chuck Davis was plumbing deeper into the meaning of the
Apostle Paul's letters to the early churches. He read from the
Book of Philippians:

"I would ye should understand, brethren, that the things which
happened unto me have fallen out rather unto the furtherance of
the gospel."

A few weeks ago he would not have been able to quote that
verse—and mean it himself. But here in the Hôtel des Chutes he
had seen how God moved the mission field in from the jungle into
the confines of four walls. Surely the things that were happening to

the missionaries were in the providence of God.

One Sunday in November Major François entered their room. He requested a private word with Al Larson. He had with him the Bible in Swahili that Kinso had sent in at Larson's request and which Larson had given to the officer a week before.

"Come over here and sit on the edge of the bed," Larson said. They faced the wall to have as much privacy as possible. The young Simba was soon confessing his sins to God.

"My heart is cold and indifferent," he said in a simple but earnest prayer. I need God's strengthening to do what is right when there is so much around me that is wrong."

After his prayer he said he felt he was wrong to be in the Simba army. He asked Larson to read from the Bible.

"I want you to read the account about Daniel," he said.

Larson did. He read how Daniel was thrown to the lions upon his refusal to renounce the God of Heaven, and how God shut the jaws of the hungry creatures and delivered Daniel safely the following morning.

Major François looked squarely at the man who was in reality his prisoner. He spoke as if his was the voice of prophecy.

"*Bwana* Larson," he said, "that story is your story. God is going to deliver you from these hungry lions."

10

A Bad Day for Americans

The rainy season hit its stride as November wore on. And as the clouds widened, the white heat of hatred spread over northeast Congo. Reports found their way into Stanleyville of foreigners losing their lives. Since the day the rebels set up their government in Stan at least six members of the Catholic clergy had been killed.

For example, Father Karl Weber, a German priest at Bokungu, some two hundred miles southwest of Stan, received a mortal wound from a lance thrown by one of his own schoolteachers. A sympathetic young Portuguese buried the priest, but having violated the Simba rule of no burying of victims, he himself was afterward assassinated.

In the opposite direction—it seemed the same whatever road from Stan one might take—the rebels dragged an Italian father, Aquilino Longo, before a people's court at Mambasa. The charge was a familiar one: Possession of a *phonee* by which he sent for planes to bomb them.

The people showed little enthusiasm for condemning; nevertheless, his accusers killed the priest on the spot, first wounding him with a spear, then sending a bullet crashing into his head. The rebels stripped the body and for a full day exposed it for all in the village to gape on.

The slaughter of the Congolese people continued with no letup. The leaders of the Azande tribe in a northern province were killed by hatchet or gunshot. Some time before, this tribe had fled from a hostile situation in Sudan to take shelter in Congo. Now, their chiefs gone, they began a hasty trek back to Sudan.

Witnesses arrived in Stan from many places, their stories much the same. In one hamlet every man who wore trousers instead of a loincloth was killed; mass executions had occurred at local Lumumba monuments in a dozen towns; in Kindu, to the south of Stan, the rebels burned so many bodies before the monument— some said eight hundred—that the sidewalk cracked under the unceasing heat.

At Paulis, to the northeast, observers placed the toll at four thousand. Some died by dismemberment, some by being forced to drink gasoline with fire then touched to their bodies. The Protestant missionary there, Joseph W. (Jay) Tucker, had been in and out of custody. But he rejoiced over the fact that the Christian Congolese at Paulis were standing firm in their commitment to God, and others were glad for faithful Christians at Ibambi and Bunia and Poko and at countless other settlements in the limitless bush.

Surreptitiously, messages came that the folk at Boyulu were now under arrest at nearby Bafwasende, and that Dr. Ian Sharpe and his family of four and the Dennis Parrys and nurse Ruby Gray had joined Mary Baker and Margaret Hayes—and Bo Martin and other Christian Congolese—in the prison at Banalia.

In Stanleyville, the rebel rage against the Belgians and Americans reached a new pitch of intensity. The mild-mannered editor of *Le Martyr* still smiled and spoke politely every morning as he brushed past the Kinsos or Mary Rutt in the apartment building, only to go down to his office to print more inflaming articles. Radio Stan periodically interrupted its programs of American rock and roll to denounce the American imperialists.

One day Christophe Gbenye said in a rage over the air, and *Le Martyr* quoted his speech, "We will make our fetishes with the hearts of the Americans and Belgians, and we will clothe ourselves in the skins of the Belgians and Americans."

In the newspaper the rebel president wrote that "the Americans and Belgians we have in our claws will be massacred in case of bombing attacks."

Kinso discovered how effective the intensifying propaganda was becoming. For some time now he had passed notes to and from the prisoners—he informed the American consul of the outcome of the United States Presidential election the day they obtained the results. But when one of the houseboys of Kilometer 8 was caught by the Simbas as he carried letters for Kinso to take into the Hôtel des Chutes, Kinso as well as the boy ran into serious trouble.

At gunpoint the rebels hustled the missionary off to the police station. To a senior officer Kinso explained that the letters, all in English, were harmless missives about family matters.

"Put this one into our language," the officer ordered Kinso, singling out a letter which Marilyn Carper had written to her father. That particular letter happened to be in verse. Puzzled for the moment as to how he could translate a child's poetry from English into meaningful Swahili, Kinso hesitated, then as the thought suddenly struck him, he shoved the paper under the officer's nose.

"Can't you see that it says 'Dear Daddy?'" he asked sharply. The officer not wishing to appear unlettered, responded with a conforming "Uh-huh."

The officer turned from Kinso to the men under his command and in disgust demanded, "Who brought this man in here? Haven't you anything better to do than bother me with so trivial an affair?"

On the way back to the apartment, which these days he seldom left except to go downstairs to the bookshop, Kinso encountered the sullen glares of persons who would not be so easily dissuaded as the officer was by his vanity. Believing Kinso to be one of the Americans they had been taught to despise, they cursed him as they passed him in the street, turning to call out the now-familiar

"Mateka iko! We'll make butter out of you."

In this charged atmosphere Christophe Gbenye went on the radio to talk about his prize captive.

The rebel president had promised the people a mercenary and he asserted they had one in the American Carlson. He regretted that medical missionaries would turn to the work of a mercenary as this man had done. He could say that about Carlson, for Carlson was so far from his base of operations that few persons in Stan knew enough about him to challenge the statement.

In the midst of his harangue Gbenye paused. He announced that on Monday, November 16, the military would execute "Major" Carlson.

The news flashed around the world. Almost instantly the capitals of the West raised a furor. The American secretary of state vowed that Gbenye would be held personally responsible for the doctor's safety. Even African states in sympathy with the rebels expressed hope that Carlson could be spared.

The Americans and Belgians conducted high-level consultations on how best to rescue their nationals from the grip of the rebels. It had required the serious threat to one good man's life to waken the world to the dire plight of many innocent people caught in the bloody throes of rebel fratricide.

Mercurial Gbenye then postponed the execution. In an issue of *Le Martyr* he described the military trial of the "major." Two Congolese lawyers defended the American with great brilliance, he said, but the truth of his guilt simply could not be overcome. He delayed the execution because the American consul had pleaded so desperately for his countryman.

Carlson knew nothing about a trial or a defense; Mike Hoyt learned of the plea for clemency only by the rebel's colorful account of it.

On November 17 Radio Stan announced that the following day would be a holiday. American fighting men captured in the battle for Kindu, the broadcast claimed, would be paraded through the streets and executed at the monument. As the day's highlight, the American "major" was to be shot.

"Come to Lumumba Square," the announcer shrilled. "Everybody come."

At Kilometer 8, the houseboy Malenza disclosed to Jean Larson that he guessed he would go into town to get a glimpse of the American mercenaries, especially of the "major." She was distressed that so faithful a one as Malenza had been swept up by the incessant propaganda. But this was not the first time.

Around the time of Bill Scholten's death, more than six weeks earlier, the priests imprisoned with him for a night were brought into Stan under the label of *les mercenaires.* Malenza and Fabian went into town to have a look at them. They returned to Kilometer 8, talking about the mercenaries who dressed in the robes of priests.

Jean Larson at that time had tried to convince the houseboys that the priests they saw were priests and not mercenaries disguised as priests. She asked a question that at least made them do some thinking:

"If they were foreign soldiers, how were they able to grow a priest's beard so quickly?"

And today with Paul Carlson the object of their curiosity, she asked another:

"Do you suppose my husband will be paraded to the monument?"

"Oh, no!" Malenza replied. *"Bwana* is a *missionnaire,* not a mercenaire."

"Well," she replied, hoping that he would understand her point, "I thought that if Dr. Carlson was in the group my husband would be, too."

The missionaries at LECO winced each time they heard something new over the radio about the "major." They felt hopeless and defeated when about ten o'clock on Wednesday, the 18th, a tumultuous crowd surged from the monument to the Central Prison opposite their shop.

Mary Rutt, the Gscheidles, and the Kinsos were joined by their African staff of clerks and helpers at the bookstore windows. They watched the scene outside with the air of a person stealing a forbidden glimpse of an evil drama. The unruly mob, packed tightly between LECO and the Central Prison, might have broken the shop windows had not an iron grille kept them at bay. Several waved the flags of Stanleyville's first rebel government. Two men held high a giant portrait of Patrice Lumumba. Men who appeared to be leaders began shouting his name; for a few moments the crowd picked up the magic chant. But in a short while they had forgotten even Lumumba. They raged deliriously for the blood of Americans.

"Kill the American mercenaries!"

"Kill the American major!"

Kill. Kill. Kill. This was now the chant, and it came from one vast speaking chorus. Simbas and civilians—men and hardened old grannies, madcap youths, brazen girls, excited children—the cruelly curious element of Stan made up the disorderly throng. Reluctantly, they opened a path to permit a jeep and a Volkswagen to drive up to the door of the prison. Officers jumped from each vehicle, and ignoring the crowd, went directly into the prison.

"Bring them out," the angry ones called after the officers. "Bring out the Americans! We want to see the Americans die!"

Inside the prison in the cell row across the courtyard eight Americans and the Belgian and Italian consuls who had joined them in their confinement listened to the pandemonium in the street. They tried not to hear too distinctly what the crowd out front was shouting; especially they wanted to shield Paul Carlson.

In the nearly three weeks since his return to the prison, after the few days of respite at the Congo Palace and LECO, Dr. Carlson had suffered much abuse—actual beatings shared with the other prisoners and emotional debilitation that resulted from the threats against his life.

Kinso wrote him a comforting letter. One of the men of the American consulate staff also encouraged him fairly frequently.

"They're simply too fantastic, these charges that you are a spy and a major in the mercenaries," he would say to Carlson. "They can't take seriously something they themselves know is so absurd."

By each new reassurance Carlson picked up new hope. But the continual shifts between hope and despair wore him down drastically. He was hardly ready to face the howlers of hate in the street outside. The hour, however, had arrived.

"The Americans! Give us the Americans!"

The prisoners heard the shouted demands before the swift-moving officers got to their cell. The Simbas burst into the courtyard, screaming commands and countercommands, but leaving no doubt that they meant to take the Americans out into the mob-filled street.

They drew out the consulate staff first. Then they said, ". . . all the Americans."

"Do you mean the missionaries, too?" asked Gene Bergman, one of the two conscientious objectors under arrest. Hoyt and Grinwis his assistant had sometimes been taken out for interrogation, and the young Paxman, the conscientious objector, hoped that such was the objective today.

"All the Americans," an angry Simba replied.

The Simbas did not really know how many Americans they held under lock, nor if they had rounded up all of them. Yet in this time of high emotional pitch they slowed down their action while they carefully made sure that each prisoner signed a paper that said he had left the prison.

One might have expected these several minutes to provide the time to prepare for a dreaded experience ahead. Yet how did a man fortify himself for being dropped into a pit of wild, hungry beasts. Stepping outside from the protection of the prison was akin to that experience. Gene Bergman gasped.

"Jon!" he said to Snyder, his friend. "Can we live through that? Look at those angry faces."

The other Paxman hardly heard him in the noise of the crowd. He thought Gene had asked what could they do. Well, there was nothing any of them could do, except to obey the orders of the Simba officers who formed a cordon around them. Their order now was to get into the cars. The rebels meant to take them somewhere.

Paul Carlson, the two Paxmen, and a member of Hoyt's staff climbed into the rear of the Volkswagen, the others of the consulate staff into the jeep. The guarding officers found places in the front seats of both vehicles. One gave the order to go. But if they were to leave this spot at all, they were not going to get off to a speedy start. The mob pressing in on the cars saw to that.

Slowly, they drove away from the prison. The people surrounding the cars moved along with them. From a turn or two they made, it seemed certain they were heading straight for Lumumba Square.

They arrived there, parking in front of the monument. The Simbas hustled the four in the Volkswagen over to the jeep. While making the change, the prisoners noted the size of the crowd.

"Five . . . six thousand," Bergman mumbled softly to Dr. Carlson. He merely nodded while gazing at the crowd.

People spread out over the traffic roundabout in front of the monument and stretched into the street and on the grassy areas. They peered from the windows of the big post office next to the monument, and crowded the rooftops of the post office, the bank across the square, and other buildings that afforded a line of sight.

Here, however, was not the constriction of the crowd as in the street between the prison and LECO. People had the space in which to move around. An unending procession filed by the jeep to shout profanities at the Americans.

"Dogs! Pigs!"

"The earth's unspeakable scum!"

"Why do your planes fly over to bomb us?"

And why, thought one of the prisoners, don't you know that those planes are manned by exiled Cubans and not by Americans?

The sun blazed its equatorial hottest. The jeep's canvas top provided shade; yet the way the eight of them were packed in the rear of the vehicle they almost wished the top were down to give a better circulation of air. The sides and the back were open. So easy an accessibility only invited further torment.

Members of the *Jeunesse* youth movement walked up to the jeep and shook knives and machetes in front of the men.

"*Attendez!* Just wait!" they would cry, and gesture obscenely toward a part of the body that in due time they would slice from the Americans and eat.

Wait? How long? Did they mean wait five minutes or a week or two days until they attacked with their freshly sharpened knives?

Thoughts of death pulsated in the troubled mind of each man in the jeep. *By what means am I to die? By execution, or by action of the mob? By the suddenness of a firing squad, or by slow dismemberment until the welcome end will finally come?*

The men saw hardly any guns. This motley force was armed with knives and sticks and even pins. Young boys sneaked up to the jeep and with safety pins stuck any arm or leg or neck they could reach. Others burned the prisoners with cigarettes or pulled out fistfuls of hair or beard. Gene Bergman watched a fellow who held a fairly large tin in his arms. He wondered if it contained gasoline. If he threw it on them, the fire from the cigarettes would cook them all.

A nasty-tempered man leaned across the guard at the door of the jeep and swung on the group with a broken ramrod. Donald Parkes, code clerk for the consulate, caught two blows just above the eye.

"Wipe off that blood!" demanded a soldier who seemed upset by the sight of it.

A number of persons came around to ask which of the eight was the "major."

"There is no major here," replied Dr. Carlson in Lingala. He alone of the Americans spoke an African language.

"One of you is the major," retorted a man among the spectators. "We heard about you on the radio."

"We are five consulate staff members and three missionaries," Carlson reiterated. Then in a game to determine which of the eight deserved their greatest anger, the crowd began to guess the identity of the "major." They were certain he was not the one who spoke Lingala. For some unexplainable reason they settled on David

Grinwis, the vice consul. He now received the worst of their abuse.

After about forty minutes a cloud hid the sun and a light rain began. This afforded some relief in what, by their admission to one another, was the hottest, the most frightening, seemingly the longest of any similar span of time in their lives. But the change was to be superseded by another change.

"Line up on the sidewalk!" The command rose over the noise of the crowd. Again there was nothing to do but to obey. The men got out of the jeep. They arranged themselves in no particular order, just in the way they had alighted. The crowd pressed in closer, sensing the morning's climax was about to come. Carlson looked down. He was standing on the bloodstains of those who some earlier day had been led here, as they, and had been made to line up as they now were lined up.

The next order faced them toward Lumumba's portrait.

"Move forward!"

How many had been marched this way before, under the mystical gaze of Lumumba? How many who were as devoted to their land as he, who perhaps held dreams for Congo as close to their breasts as any who claimed to be his heir—how many loyal Congolese had died here under that gaze? How many who sought no more than to live peaceably were caught up in the swelling of evil passion and perished here in awful death? How many "little" people, ignorant tribesmen, ambitious chiefs, promising schoolboys and clerks and teachers had been sacrificed to someone's course toward political rule?

If the eight Americans spilled their blood here today, would others follow after them?

The prisoners advanced to about twenty feet from the monument when behind them they heard the sound of a car driving up. Someone jumped out of it and was hurrying toward them.

"Stop those men!" a voice shouted. Carlson swung his head slightly to see who had arrived. So did Jon Snyder. Then each of the men halted, turned around. They faced General Nicholas Olenga, the top commander of the rebel army.

For half a minute he stared at the men. He eyed one, then another, and finally said for them to get back into the jeep. By the barest of margins he had stayed their march toward Lumumba.

A youth rushed up defiantly to the general. "We want to kill them," he said, enraged. "Let us alone and we'll cut them through with our machetes."

Olenga was not particularly large, but he was strong. He grasped the fellow by the collar of his shirt, picked him up and sent him sprawling to the curb.

"The demonstration here is over," he said. He spoke privately to officers who now gathered around him. When he finished, he got back into his car and drove away.

The Americans, ready to buckle at the knee, clambered back into the jeep. There they sat. The one who had driven the vehicle from the prison was nowhere around. The key was missing from the ignition. At some officer's order, a part of the milling crowd was impressed to push the jeep with its stunned and silent passengers back through the streets to the Central Prison.

At the entrance they sat again, this time to wait until orders on what to do with them came. Finally the driver showed up. A captain jumped in beside him, mumbled his directions.

He half-turned in his seat to speak to the prisoners.

"You can thank Monsieur Gbenye for getting you away in time from the monument," he said. They also learned from him that they were on the way to Gbenye's house near the airport.

To Bergman, to Carlson, perhaps to all of them, it added up that at this time the Americans were worth more alive to the rebel high command than dead. The supposition, however, unfortunately did not extend to the lower echelons. Just what the rebel government had in mind concerning them, perhaps they would learn when they arrived at Gbenye's—if, indeed, they ever got there.

The driver tore along like a madman. With so many in the vehicle they were top heavy. But no matter to the fellow at the wheel; he careened around corners and lay on his horn all the way. He skidded his wheels in the sand to stop before the rebel president's comfortable villa.

Here also a crowd had gathered, though only about half the number as at the monument. Gbenye, in beard and bluejeans, stood at the steps of his house. He spoke into two microphones. The prisoners unscrambled from the rear of the jeep—by this time they were quite adept at evacuating. Again they were lined up. They were to have their pictures taken.

One man who showed talent for public relations placed Parkes, the code clerk, so his cut forehead would not show in the picture. The photography completed, the men were conducted up a walk to the house to stand in front of Gbenye.

He used French in speaking of how wicked were the Americans. He said American soldiers killed innocent Congolese women and children. The American prisoners who had just arrived would be killed, he promised—but not yet.

"Our neighbor Kenyatta asks that we spare them today," he said.

"Kill them now!" the crowd roared back.

"I will kill them, but not yet," he answered.

The crowd would not have it his way. "Kill them right now!"

Sensing that they were getting out of hand, he switched from French to Lingala and began a chant that called for their response. In an aside he directed his aides to throw more guards around the prisoners. Still the people called for blood. He said he would give them blood—if they wished, the blood of Major Carlson.

The game of identifying the "major" began here as it had been played at the monument. This time another of the consulate staff was picked out. Each time Gbenye mentioned Paul Carlson's name a Simba pointed to this staff member. But Gbenye knew his man.

He looked straight at the doctor, coldly and with calculation.

"The major will die," he promised.

All the pessimism that had lain on the shoulders of Paul Carlson in these past days in the Central Prison, the doubt that enveloped him since the day two months before that he left Wasolo, the despair that time after time told him he would never see Lois and the children again—all the brutality of this black night descended on him once more, now with greater heaviness than he had yet known.

From a pocket he drew the New Testament that had been his guide and comfort during his year in Congo. He slipped it into the back pocket of Jon Snyder, who stood just in front of him.

"Give this to my wife," he whispered.

The garrulous Gbenye talked on. The crowd grew more restless. Was this a contest, whether he could promise them Carlson's life to a larger degree than they could demand the lives of all the Americans who waited before them?

"He is a spy," the rebel chief said in apparent contradiction to his try at saving him. "We have his *phonee,* we have papers."

The guards edged the prisoners a few steps closer to the jeep.

"We will execute him," Gbenye continued, ". . . but Kenyatta says wait."

"We won't wait," the crowd hissed back.

Snyder believed the end was perhaps at hand for Carlson, perhaps for them all. The people here showed more intent to have a killing than did those who threatened so vilely at the monument. Among the crowd, standing on some railing or post that elevated him, a foreigner snapped pictures. He obviously was present by invitation, possibly by command, to preserve on film this date of rebel history. Snyder deemed him a likely person to know the conclusion of this drama, if anyone could foretell it. He succeeded in getting the photographer's eye.

Communicating across the mob, which by the minute was falling more out of hand, Snyder asked for a sign that would tell him the outcome. The photographer gave his sign.

Gravely, he shook his head.

11

Bungling the Job

Gbenye fought the menacing crowd with all the moods and measures of oratory he ever knew.

"The Americans are bad people," he acknowledged to his ungovernable audience. "They fight our soldiers and kill our women and children. But we will defeat them!"

To agree with the tenor of their feelings did not produce the control that he had to have. He only incensed them more. For some weeks now the machine of rebel propaganda had cranked out venom and Gbenye himself had on this occasion whetted their appetites for the blood of the Americans who stood before them. Now that it served his purpose to save the captives, to use them alive in his effort to stay the advancing forces of the national government, he had lost his power over the people.

"Lumumba! Lumumba!" he suddenly shouted. He had to sing it out once more before they heard:

"Mai, mai Lumumba!"

Raggedly at first, but in a moment or two in reasonable chorus the crowd echoed, *"Mai, mai* Lumumba!"

"Lumumba, the savior of our land!" he screamed into the microphones. "Lumumba will defeat our enemies!"

"Mai, mai Lumumba!"

He had inserted the magic key. He had them with him now. Once more Christophe Gbenye had proved his ability to head this sometimes tattered, sometimes dissonant, rebel regime.

Quickly and without much show to the crowd he signaled his personal guard to get the prisoners down the walk to the jeep at the curb. While he maintained the chorus at high pitch, the eight Americans repacked themselves in the rear of the vehicle. Their driver, alert this time to what was required of him, threaded his way through the fringe of the gathering.

Another wild ride returned them to the Central Prison, which after the last two harrowing hours became a refuge of comforting familiarity.

Paul Carlson suggested they pray. He led them, and in his petition thanked God for providential care and committed the future to Him. Having passed through so unnerving an experience, they found it difficult this afternoon to settle down. Everyone was eager to talk—to recount their brushes with death, to speculate on their continuing plight, to speak about the things a man must measure up against in what he supposes is his final hour.

Before this there had been little discussion in their cell of things so intimate as those of the spirit. But some matters seemed to pass among them without the articulation of speech. There were qualities in Paul Carlson, for example, that Mike Hoyt admired deeply. One night Hoyt had seen Carlson reading in his New Testament.

"Do you read the Bible every night?" the consul asked.

"Every night, and at other times, too," the doctor replied. He explained that the Word of God was milk and meat to him; he could no more be healthy spiritually without adequate spiritual food than he could keep his body in good shape without the proper physical diet.

He mentioned that the Apostle Paul's letters to the Philippian Church and to young Timothy had sustained him in periods of trial and weakness. *I can do all things through Christ which strengtheneth me.* The power of Christ within—what a difference it made in one's life.

The following day Gbenye himself appeared at the prison to see them. He acted friendly, even smiled. He did not really hold the consulate staff and the missionaries responsible for what he said the Americans were doing to his people.

"You will be moved to different quarters tomorrow," he promised.

The change was to place them in the Résidence Victoria, one of the city's larger hotels and located at the far end of the block from LECO. Somehow, the move was connected with the rebel plan to negotiate the fate of Paul Carlson, and perhaps all of them, in a last-ditch effort to stave off Tshombe's mercenaries. The Paxmen looked upon themselves as tag-alongs with the doctor, certainly the most celebrated of the prisoners, and with the consulate members.

"If they get through this all right, we will, too," Bergman said to his friend Snyder. Both felt a degree of safety now that the United States was fully aroused to the plight of the hostages. They felt the rebels knew that by harming one of the staff men, or Carlson, they would have the might of the United States to deal with. Undoubtedly, this realization produced an official caution. Nothing, however, was really fixed in this rebellion.

The danger, too, lay in accidents, like the vengeance the mob almost brought off the previous day. In recent weeks younger, untrained, undisciplined men had been added to the decimated rebel ranks and with their recruitment the possibility of unplanned incidents grew.

The Simbas transferred the Americans from the prison to the Victoria on the evening of Friday, November 20. This time the streets were calm. They arrived in the midst of an *appel,* a roll call, which had turned into a prolonged assembly for all in the building held under arrest. The ostensible purpose was to check the roll.

The newcomers found the lobby filled with people, mostly Belgians, and what appeared to be entire families were there. The lobby was a large stripped-down polygon room. Dr. Carlson and Gene Bergman took up positions near the plate-glass doors, the others from the prison settling where they could find space to sit or

stretch out. After an hour Carlson remarked that he did not understand why the *appel* was lasting so long. People around him—prisoners and Simba guards both—speculated on a bombing scare.
One of the Simbas said the plan was to shoot all the foreigners and
to dump their bodies into boxes.

For Carlson, however, the immediate problem was not the sub-
jects being speculated on. Passersby in the street were harassing
him. Some seemed to know he was the one Radio Stan discussed
so much. Others recognized him and Bergman as objects in yesterday's clamorings. Not until the two moved to a back hall did they
manage to find an undisturbed place on the floor to get some sleep.

Saturday morning everything seemed to take an upward turn.
The all-night *appel* over, the more recent arrivals were assigned
rooms, the consulate staff on the first floor, Dr. Carlson and the
Paxmen above on the fourth. The missionaries enjoyed their first
bath, with hot water, in three weeks. Then they lay down for a
much-needed rest.

In mid-morning Carlson got up. "There's a man, if he is here, I
want to look up," he said. He went out of the room and down the
stairs and asked people he met for Al Larson.

The foreigners in detention at the Chutes had been transferred
to the Victoria two days before. The three men of Kilometer 8
were lodged in a room on the second floor, the two physicians and
the Belgian planters in scattered sites throughout the building.
Carlson found Larson in his room. He smiled, and stuck out his
hand.

"I'm Paul Carlson," he said.

"It's good to see you, alive and able to get around," Larson
said, returning the doctor's smile and handshake.

"I've heard much about you," said Carlson, "from the Paxmen
with me, from the folk at LECO, from other missionaries."

Under the circumstances Larson thought it best not to bring up
that by means of Radio Stan he had heard much about the doctor.

The two men took an immediate liking to each other. There was
something in Carlson's bearing that impressed people from the
very first time of meeting. Larson's face portrayed his intense sin-

cerity, his alertness to people's needs.

"How about joining in our prayer meetings?" asked Larson. He explained there were other missionaries in the building with whom they had already met.

"Miss Rine—Phyllis Rine—a young woman of the African Christian Mission, is one," he added. "And the Schaub family . . . we meet in their room because of the children."

The doctor said he would attend. He then asked what medical needs Larson or anyone else had. In answer, Larson said they were well set for the present. He had vitamin pills and medication for dysentery. "You'll have to meet our Florence Nightingale," he said.

That noon *Le Central* served lunch. Then the Simbas circulated the order for all men to shave and everyone to put on his best clothing. No one explained why they should look their best. It was understood, however, that Jomo Kenyatta was expected from Kenya, and the rebels wanted their treatment of the prisoners to create a good impression.

To his roommates Del Carper and Chuck Davis, Al Larson said with a laugh, "I'll put on my best clothes. With only one set that won't be hard to do."

Just before three o'clock, the hour the missionaries planned to meet, Paul Carlson opened the door to Larson's room.

"They've called another *appel*," he said. "We're all to report downstairs immediately."

As the hostages filed from their rooms—reluctant to face another long stay in the corridors or lobby—they received the command to go right outside. There were no speeches this time, no harangues, no checks to see that all were present. Just a scurrying to get everyone outside.

The rebel guards appeared to be very nervous. And in this condition they posed a greater threat than when things went well for them and they could afford to treat their captives with equanimity.

Larson was one of the first to get to the outdoors. He saw

parked in front of the hotel a brown bus, one he figured had outlived its usefulness as a schoolbus in the United States and had been shipped to Africa for retirement duty.

"Onto the bus," a Simba ordered him.

The bus was built to hold forty persons, but by the time the rebel soldiers stopped pushing in "just one more" nearly a hundred persons had been crammed aboard.

"Like the tins of sardines at Kilometer 8," called Larson to Del Carper across the aisle.

When not another person could be squeezed on the bus, the rebels started loading up a truck with prisoners. This accommodated about fifty persons. Someone gave the signal; the truck and then the bus started moving away from the hotel. About forty prisoners remained behind, there being no way for them to travel.

The sun beat down unmercifully with all its equatorial heat. Even with every window open, the bus was devoid of circulating air.

"We'll not go far in this heat and overcrowding without a lot of us fainting," someone predicted.

Just how far were they going? And where? Larson looked out the window, detailed their progress to those around him whose vision was blocked.

"We've just passed LECO," he said. "It looks like we're heading for the Tshopo Bridge."

His guess stirred a number of groans. The Tshopo Bridge— currently the site favored by the rebels for the execution of their enemies. To be mowed down by a Sten gun as they left the bus and their bodies then tossed into the falls below—was this the rebel answer to the steadily advancing mercenary column of Major Mike Hoare?

But neither the truck nor the bus stopped at the bridge. They lurched onward, passed the native shanty towns, and headed for the country.

There was a military post on this road. Perhaps that would be their destination. The rebels may have thought the hotel was too

fine an accommodation for prisoners, so were transferring them to
something less auspicious. But drawing even with the camp, they
failed to stop there, either.

"Banalia," several said, naming as the objective the ferry crossing on the Aruwimi River that Henry M. Stanley described in his
explorations journal. It was in the Banalia jail that the planter
Dubois had seen Bo Martin beaten because of his pleas for Mary
Baker and Margaret Hayes. It was there that the latest news
placed twelve of the UFM mission family.

Larson was acquainted with the river at Banalia. It could swallow up as many bodies as the Tshopo. With one hundred fifty
"problems" suddenly handed to the rebel force at Banalia, the
river, he thought, might well provide the simplest solution.

Even if the Simbas did not plan to kill them outright, there was
great danger in being taken from Stan. The farther removed from
the rebel high command, the more likely that "accidents" would
happen. Should the prisoners be divided into small groups and
dispersed throughout the bush, that meant exposure to the whims
of Simbas who knew little and cared less about the official policies.

And speculation on their destination aside, to be moved from
Stan meant to be placed beyond the reach of a possible rescue
force. The mercenaries of Major Hoare would arrive in Stan any
day now. Were they so near that their imminent attack was the
cause of the Simbas' frayed nerves? Perhaps there was substance
to the rumors at the Victoria that six hundred Belgian paratroopers were poised on Ascension Island out in the Atlantic opposite Africa's coast.

Whether by ground or by air, the attempt to snatch the hostages
from their rebel captors would utterly fail if the Simbas succeeded
in dispersing the foreigners from Stan.

A half hour after the departure from the Victoria the motor of
the bus coughed and quit. The truck up ahead was stopped. Simba
officers in charge of the journey conferred on what to do.

The vehicles sat in the full blaze of the afternoon sun. Men on
the bus peeled off their shirts. Nearly everyone was wringing with
perspiration. Some who stood in the aisle doubted they could take

much more. Larson spoke to those jammed tightly around him:

"Hey, everybody. Those of us who have seats—let's trade for a while with the ones who have had to stand."

Most of those seated were willing to trade, though a few suddenly found something outside the bus that riveted their attention and they pretended not to hear. Not long after the breakdown a number of Congolese from nearby homes gathered around the bus.

"Bring us water," someone in the bus called.

A woman went to her house and returned with a basin. She handed it through a window.

"What do you think, doctor?" several asked Paul Carlson. "Should we drink it?"

Now back in the role of physician, rather than just another prisoner, he bore the weight of protecting the health of many persons around him. He knew they suffered from the heat, and that a drink of water would bring relief. Yet one did not drink just any water in Congo because of the prevalence of parasites.

"Just moisten your lips," he advised. And reaching over to pound on the side of the bus to gain attention of the guards, he said:

"Can't you let a few of the people out? If you don't you'll soon have large numbers collapsing."

Some, then, were allowed to leave the bus. Those who still had money bought bananas and papayas from the local citizens.

"I got a nice one," said Del Carper. "I'll save it for after a while."

In no way had anyone's thirst been quenched. Well-meaning women from the houses pushed their water onto the parched people. Someone among the prisoners took a drink. Others followed, then seemingly just about everybody. Al Larson couldn't hold out. After gulping down too much even had it been pure, he refused to look in the doctor's direction. Not so much that he was embarrassed; he wanted to give Carlson a chance to drink, too.

Those outside were pressed into the task of pushing the bus. The truck also pushed for a distance and the bus started up, but after a quarter of a mile the motor died again.

The driver tried to repair it. The Simbas called for a mechanic among the prisoners. None volunteered. Again they called. Still no one wanted to put the bus in operation so it could continue to take them away from Stan.

Finally a Belgian man, Marco Paneff, the brother-in-law of "Florence Nightingale," said he'd have a try at fixing it. He asked for a screw driver, and one was found.

"There is a leak in the gas line," Paneff said to the Simba in charge. This diagnosis meant nothing to the officer.

"Fix it," he said, and by that he meant to bang on the motor. This Paneff began to do. At a joint in the line he hit and gouged and scraped and finally threw up his hands.

"I can't stop the leak," he moaned.

Of course he couldn't, not by aggravating the condition. He had, in fact, bunged the fuel line so that nothing short of a new part would put the bus in commission again. And where in this jungle was an engine part to be found?

By six thirty darkness was falling fast. The Simbas had to do something quickly if they were to prevent a mass escape by their prisoners. The house of a Congolese stood near, not a large one, perhaps twelve feet by fifteen or eighteen feet. It was a mud house, with leaf roof, and it contained a single room. The rebels herded all the prisoners on the bus and the truck into this house. By the time all were inside, the house was as packed as the bus had been.

For two hours most of the hostages stayed cramped up in the house, though a few were permitted back on the bus. From time to time one or another mentioned the recent statement of Gbenye that the Simbas would place barrels of gasoline at the doors of foreign houses and at the appropriate moment ignite the barrels. They had no assurance that this would not happen.

The heat abated, yet there was danger of suffocation in the overcrowded house. One man lapsed into unconsciousness; Dr. Carlson diagnosed his case as a heart attack.

Relief arrived when officers drove out from Stan. The prisoners should have been gotten ready for dispersal, they said to the guards, but someone had panicked and sent the group off without orders. The growing tendency of the Simbas to panic worried Al Larson.

Next a cattle truck from Stan arrived. In this, in the original truck, and in a third that had been commandeered on the road, the whole group rode back to the city.

Al Larson and Del Carper were in the back of the cattle truck, Carper still hanging onto his papaya. About midnight and just about a mile from the Victoria the truck ran out of gas. It happened at a roadblock. While they waited for refueling the weary prisoners had another annoyance to contend with.

Simba soldiers from the guard point began hitting the sides of the truck with pipes and sticks, causing the prisoners to pull their hands in. The rebels climbed up the sides of the truck to ask what kind of cargo it contained.

"Pigs," said the driver, and he laughed long and loud at his joke. "Just pigs."

The prisoners, too, could laugh at mere words. What difference did it make what one was called?

"La peau, la peau," the Belgians on the truck were saying. Not one's pride, but one's skin was what mattered.

12

Nothing Strange at Kilometer 8

Hector McMillan sometimes would say with a mischievous gleam in his eye, "I know English, French, Swahili, and a little Portuguese."

The "little" Portuguese was a half-pint barber whom his customers called Poncho. On Monday following the rebel attempt to disperse the hostages, Poncho called at Kilometer 8.

"I've just cut *Bwana* Larson's hair at the Victoria," he said prosaically.

"You've what?" exclaimed McMillan, who met the barber in the driveway.

"I've just cut—"

He did not finish. McMillan grabbed the little fellow and held him in a bear hug. The families at Kilometer 8 had heard that the rebels emptied Stan of its prisoners Saturday night. This was the first news that they were back in the hotel, alive and safe.

"Come in," invited McMillan. "Come in and have some tea, and tell us about our men."

Poncho was only one of several visitors that day at Kilometer 8. The Simbas came to confiscate Del Carper's truck. A rebel demanded the vehicle at the point of his gun.

"You're afraid of my gun, aren't you?" he asked Bob McAllister.

"Give me that gun and let me point it at you," returned the Irishman. "Let me see if you're afraid."

The rebel refused. He too had learned that bullets on impact did not turn to water.

Before permitting the Simbas to leave with the truck, McAllister said they must first pray. The soldier who had climbed to the driver's seat called out, his voice choked with emotion, "If you're going to pray, pray for me. Pray that I'll get back safe from battle."

Like so many others, he was to be thrown into the defense of Stan against Major Hoare's steadily advancing mercenary column. And like all the Simbas now in and around Stan, he was uneasy about his chances of surviving.

Carper's truck was the last of the vehicles at Kilometer 8. On the previous Saturday the rebels pulled away an old mission car with no radiator. Now several of the missionaries remarked that loss of the truck was hard to accept.

They had not driven the cars for three months for fear of confiscation. But finally to lose them all meant that should an emergency arise they would be immobile. Bob Latham could no longer help them, of course, since the rebels had taken the truck of the United Nations man; he now usually stayed home up a road from Kilometer 8.

In their bent to self-pity over the truck Ione McMillan reminded her colleagues of the "think-it-not-strange" verse in Peter's first epistle. Again and again she quoted it; each time it ushered in a quiet submission to circumstances that at present they could do nothing about changing, but had to accept as the will of God.

The rest of the day produced no excitement. The children went back to their lessons, Jean Larson thought up still another way to serve sardines, Ione McMillan reflected on the book she had finished reading the day before—the life story of Adoniram Judson.

From time to time that day she reflected on the great sorrow that overtook Judson when his beloved wife died. He would visit her grave every day to mourn and to puzzle over the separation of the soul from the body. How could he endure the loss of his wife's body to the elements of the earth? The torments of his mind nearly drove him insane.

In her musing Ione acknowledged that the book had given her a valuable lesson.

"If a member of my family is ever taken in death," she said to herself, "by God's help I am not going to waste time and the energies He gave me worrying over a body of clay."

After all, wasn't the important thing the soul that must answer to God? She decided quietly in her heart that it was.

Most of that Monday was calm. Yet there never really was a settled feeling at the mission compound. The wives and children of the Americans felt keenly the absence of the menfolk under arrest in town. The weekend news over the BBC had been so much about Jomo Kenyatta's talks of negotiation in Kenya. But from the morning news this day they learned that the rebel representative had failed to show up in Nairobi Sunday. Later broadcasts emphasized the immediacy of a drop on Stan by paratroopers should those negotiations break down.

Bob McAllister expressed the feeling of dread that pervaded the crowded house. "Deliverance is bound to come, either by air or land force," he said. "But before it does, some of us may suffer."

Various ones spoke hopefully of liberation, but they could only surmise what the Simbas might do in their attempt to prevent it.

"Hector," Ione McMillan said to her husband after one of the news broadcasts. "I've laid out some clothes that you ought to pack in your suitcase. When rescue comes, we want to be ready."

He mumbled an acknowledgment, but she noticed he was hardly aware of what she had said. She asked him to help the children sort out their toys and other belongings and to store in the attic the things they would be leaving behind. This he did, but he ignored completely his own preparation.

More and more she was finding Hector a little hard to understand. Responsibilities that he used to assume with the boys he now left to her. It almost seemed he was prying himself away from his sons. Tonight, for example, at the boys' bedtime he made no move to go over to "the hangar" to read the Bible and to pray with them, something he always enjoyed and very seldom missed. After vainly waiting for him for several minutes Ione decided she would have to go in his place.

Hector sat with Bob and Alma McAllister and other missionaries around one of the dining tables. In the smoky glow of the kerosene lantern they discussed the final wretched days of their colleague, Bill Scholten, in the Aketi prison.

"What do you think, Hector?" McAllister asked. "Did Bill die in the permissive will or the perfect will of God?" Ione paused just before going out the back door. She wanted to hear her husband's answer.

"Why," said Hector without hesitation, "I believe with all my heart that his death was in the perfect will of God."

As she crossed between the main house and "the hangar" in the darkness, Ione was glad that her husband answered as he did. How good it was to be assured that though their troubles mounted God was still working out to His satisfaction the course that the lives of His children took.

Their faith was all that any of them had to rely on, especially after hearing what Radio Stan had screamed tonight.

"Sharpen your knives!" blasted out the command. "Sharpen your machetes! Sharpen you spears! If the paras drop from the sky, kill the foreigners, all the foreigners. Do not wait for orders. You have your orders now: Kill, kill, kill!"

Tuesday morning, November 24, Kilometer 8 awoke to the noise of several planes overhead. From the main house, from "the hangar," from the small house in the rear, the missionaries and their children scurried into the backyard to see what was up. Were the planes carrying paratroopers? Were they bombers? Or were they a reconnaisance outfit for the army column moving up from the south? Kilometer 8, five miles from the center of Stan and farther still from the airport, was too far away from where the planes seemed to be circling to allow them to form any accurate judgment.

"Let's get out of the yard," McAllister said anxiously. "First thing you know we'll attract some carload of Simbas going by."

No houseboy showed up to prepare breakfast. Someone saw Malenza and Fabian and their families go into the forest, no doubt to sit out the danger they were sure would come with the planes. So several of the women pitched in to help Jean Larson cook the wheat cereal and slice the papayas for the meal.

The children were of course excited, but with the aid of the grown-ups they fairly well held in their fidgeting. Ordinarily, Bible reading and prayers followed breakfast, but on occasion there was not enough time if they were to listen to the BBC news at eight. Thus, devotions would be delayed until the broadcast was over.

It was this way today. The women began to clear the tables and the children to play either inside the house or just off the veranda in back of the house. Someone walked into the living room to snap off the radio when another person quite casually announced:

"There are some Simbas in the backyard."

McAllister and McMillan went out to meet them.

"What motor is that which you have running?" demanded one of three rebels who darted around the yard, seeking the source of a whirring sound. Of all the many Simbas who had called at Kilometer 8 none seemed so agitated as these were now. The missionary men believed the trio to be high on hemp. They wore khaki pants and were stripped to the waist, an indication they were ready for battle. Two were armed; one carried a rifle, the other an automatic pistol.

"Show us where your generator is," one of them said, betraying his nervousness.

"You must give us the *phonee* you used to call the planes this morning," another insisted.

"The motor you hear is not a generator running a *phonee*," McMillan replied. "We have a pump that lifts water from the well to a tank on our roof. Come, I'll show you."

He led one rebel to the far side of "the hangar" to show him the motor they heard. McMillan shut it off. This did not satisfy the Simba.

"We want your *phonee,*" he said.

Another of the three stormed into the main house to order the women and children out to the yard. Cursing because they did not clear the rooms as quickly as he wished, he knocked over the table on the back veranda, breaking a water bottle.

"Get out!" he shrieked.

Muriel Davis, who held her baby daughter Beth, stood nearest him. He pushed her. She stumbled but did not fall. Had that occurred a few weeks earlier, what tears of resentment might have welled to blind her, just as she had resented being pushed that night in August from the car into the empty but frightening street of Stan in front of LECO. She was certainly frightened now, but her measure of Christian grace had grown. Perhaps God had sent her to Congo at this particular time not to serve as she had always thought of serving, but to learn spiritual lessons in a most difficult school.

Without a word, she moved out into the yard with the others.

There was nothing to do out there, except to stand anxiously around and wait for the Simba inside to search the house. Before he finished, one of the rebels standing guard over the group directed the women and children to go back in. This they did. They seated themselves around the living room and in some of the chairs pulled up to the table almost under the archway between the living and dining rooms.

Quietly but tensely they waited out the rebel visit. Mothers held the youngest on their laps; six persons crowded the couch; the McMillan boys, having found no place in the living room, occupied the chairs near the archway, Kenneth, the eldest, actually sitting in the dining room. In a few minutes the remaining Simbas and the two missionary men entered the house.

The rebels began to turn the rooms topsy-turvy. They discovered among other things a hall cupboard containing food. Jean

Larson heard the *clunk* of tins as a Simba dropped sardines into a container. This one stepped to the dining room, a filled cloth bag in one hand and his drawn pistol in the other.

Those seated so they saw him noted how fierce was the look on his face. Waiting for his cohorts to complete their inspection, he paced between the tables nervously, muttering threats. Ione McMillan said to herself that the term "Simba" fit this rebel precisely; he was behaving just like a caged lion.

Suddenly, a fourth Simba burst into the house through the rear door. His mood matched that of the ugliest of the three already present. He swore that a *phonee* existed somewhere in the house, and was determined to find it.

He searched the bedrooms, but found none. He looked through the hall cupboards. He walked back into the dining room and moved toward the front of the house. His eye settled on the portable radio in the living room and he lunged for it.

"So, you have no *phonee?*" he asked mockingly. Hugging the prize to his naked chest, he bore toward the back door.

"The men will go with us," he said, motioning the others to bring McMillan and McAllister as they followed him out.

"It's the prison for you," those in the front room heard as the captors went out with their captives.

One Simba remained in the house, the one with the bag of sardines and the drawn gun and who was unstrung so that he could not stand still. He bolted for the door, but just before reaching it turned back, ran almost to the archway. In face of the roomful of watching women and children he raised his gun straight at them. Without warning he fired wildly into the seated group.

In a moment he fired again. Then a third time. And a fourth. Perhaps he shot twice more. No one really knew, for by this time who was counting the deadly blasts?

Meanwhile, outside, Bob McAllister walked a way in front of Hector McMillan as the rebels herded them up the driveway toward the road. McAllister had covered perhaps two thirds of the distance to the rebel car, but McMillan had got only to the mango tree at the front corner of the house when suddenly the sickening sound of shots broke the silence of the cloudy, dew-filled morning. McMillan paused, as if perhaps to turn around. That was a mistake. At nearly point-blank range the Simba with the rifle shot him in the leg, then in a moment or two in the side below the arm. Grotesquely, McMillan lurched back and fell full length at the feet of his assailant.

McAllister swung around. He saw the blood streaming hopelessly from McMillan's body.

"You've shot my best friend!" he cried in anguish.

The one who fired at McMillan then aimed his rifle at McAllister. His bullet, however, grazed the Irishman's forehead and spun him around dizzily. He threw himself hard to the ground.

He lay motionless, crumpled in the position in which he fell. To display any sign of life would be to invite another shot. And the next time the gunman would make doubly sure that his effort to kill did not fail.

The Simbas, believing their deeds done, hurried up the drive to the car. From where he lay McAllister heard them drive off in the direction of Bob Latham's home.

"Oh, not to kill Bob Latham!" he cried under his breath, in a desperate prayer for the United Nations man. In rapid succession his mind filled with the horror of Hector's bleeding wounds, with his own miraculous miss, and then with the terrible certainty that faced the one who had befriended the missionaries by his transport and by many willing ways.

This thin, stooped fellow almost seemed to belong to their group at Kilometer 8. How much he changed after adversity threw them together. Once a scoffer toward God, in recent weeks he talked as if he not only had met God, but had become God's friend.

There was the time, for example, just a few days before, that Alma McAllister and Mina Erskine risked their lives to go to Latham's place to deliver an African woman who lived on his property of a son. At the delivery Alma said she had no medicine for her patient, only the Lord's undertaking.

"Isn't that enough?" Latham asked sincerely.

One day he passed along to the woman a supply of clothing the missionaries had sent with him for the children. She thanked him.

"Don't thank me," he said. "You have God to thank for this."

Had Bob Latham become a believer in Christ after his years of indifference? Fearing the worst of mortal fates for this kind friend, McAllister prayed that if never before, Latham would in these last minutes left to him recognize the Lord to be his one eternal hope.

As McAllister lay in the driveway, not yet daring to move, a second car containing Simba soldiers stopped on the road at the entrance to the compound. By their voices he could tell they were angry—angry in a defeat they had suffered in Stan. By some means they had been pushed out of the city, and in their retreat they were determined to take vengeance on all foreigners in their path.

"There are foreigners living here we can kill," McAllister heard one of them say.

The men headed for the house. But one exhibiting great surprise stopped the advance toward the prone McAllister.

"Look!" the rebel cried. "The foreigners there in the driveway —they're dead already!"

"Yes," agreed another, voicing disappointment that they were too late. "They're dead already. Let's go on."

Before the last Simba left the house, before he shot into the group of women and children, Ione McMillan thought the purpose of his running toward them was to frighten them. When he fired the first time she saw the flash and then the smoke that streamed from the gun barrel, and she said to herself, "That's a blank. He's trying to scare us, just as the rebels have done right along in shooting off their guns."

From where she sat in a chair opposite the big archway she lifted her gaze from the gun to the face of the one who held it.

"He's smiling like a cat because he knows he has frightened us," she thought in the fraction of time that followed the discharge. Then once again the barrel flashed and smoked, and somehow she lay on the floor with the others, attempting to cover the youngsters and feigning death as Al Larson in his practical school of survival had taught them.

How many times he fired, Ione did not know; but in the blackness behind her tightly closed eyelids she heard other shots. They had a different sound, farther away, more muffled—but not much. They filtered through the walls from outside, from out where Hector her husband and Bob were.

Olive Bjerkseth lay where she could see out a window.

"That Simba shot Hector in the leg!" she gasped. She turned from the window. She could not bear to see what further violence might be done.

The small children began to cry—whether from their own experience of just moments before or from the shots that were ringing outside, no one could tell. The older children and the women began to pray, and among them Viola Walker intoned a Psalm . . . *God is our refuge and strength, a very present help in trouble . . .*

The crying and the praying were not much more than low mumblings, and in a few brief seconds became inaudible. Then in the stillness that seemed akin to death Alma McAllister, who had raised herself from the floor so she could peer through the bamboo blind covering the front door called in a hoarse whisper:

"They've shot both the men!"

No one dared say more or move. The four Simbas were still in the driveway; if they learned their job of killing was not yet done, they would return to finish it.

The short while that the beat of one's heart was all that intruded in the void of sound seemed to last an hour, yet was actually only three or four minutes. Sixteen-year-old Paul McMillan opened his eyes and under the table where he had dropped saw his older brother, his face contorted from pain.

"Kenny's been shot," Paul said. He felt a trickle on his own cheek, brushed it with his hand, and discovered that he, too, had been hit. A quick but nearly silent inventory determined that the two boys were the only victims of the Simba's point-blank shooting.

Paul's wound was slight. Alma McAllister, having crept to him, probed it superfically and could not tell if he had been struck by shrapnel or by a splinter from a table through which one of the bullets had gone. Kenneth's injury was more serious. He had been struck in the hip by a bullet, and was losing blood.

He suffered in silence as Alma stopped the flow and others in the house carried the cushion from the couch to make him a bed in the hall, a place considered safer should the rebels return and begin shooting again.

After the second car of Simbas drove away, Alma McAllister and Thelma Southard went out the back door to check on the men. In the meantime, Ione McMillan had gone to the front door to look out.

"I see Bobby," she said, and noted that McAllister did not move. "He's lying face down in the dirt."

"Maybe he's faking," ventured one of her younger sons.

"I don't see Hector," Ione said. Then she spotted him. "Oh, here he is. Here's Hector, right close to the porch. He's lying on his back with his face up and his face is as white as a ghost's."

The two who had gone out the back now approached Hector. Ione watched anxiously to see whether there was a stir of life as they would speak to him. Alma called him by name. He did not move. Ione felt a quick stab of pain. There was no question about it. Her husband was dead.

The women went on to Bob McAllister. Would there be another widow to share the shock of Ione's loss?

"Bobby," Alma said as she approached her husband. "Bobby, are you all right?"

Cautiously, he raised to his hands and knees, then stood up, very much alive.

"Bobby!" Alma cried, and ran to her husband. She saw the line of welts that the grazing bullet had raised across his forehead. By only the fraction of an inch her husband's life had been spared.

McAllister and the two women carried McMillan's body into the house. They laid their burden on Al Larson's bed in a room just beyond where Kenneth rested in the hall.

Ione looked with searching eyes at Alma. "Is there anything we can do to revive him?" she asked.

"Nothing," Alma replied. The second shot had killed him instantly.

Alma slipped out, leaving Ione alone. Ione, feeling her loss deeply, yet with no hint of a sob in her voice, called her five younger sons to her.

"Come in here, boys," she said. "I want you to see your father."

Stevie, the second youngest, entered the room crying. But soon he dried his tears. This mother who now had six sons to raise without a father's help smiled softly at them all and said:

"You can cry if you want. I don't think I will. After all, we know Daddy lived in the will of God, and God doesn't make any mistakes . . . You can be proud that your Daddy was counted worthy to give his life in the service of Jesus."

In a few minutes Bob McAllister went in search of someone to help him build a coffin in which to bury Hector. No one was around, however, except an old Congolese couple whom Hector had tried to counsel when some years before the McMillans centered their work at Kilometer 8.

Old Nduli and Telese his wife braved the chance of being caught in the presence of foreigners on this day when quite apparently the rebels would not countenance such a fraternization. They entered the house to see for the last time the one who had befriended them.

Ione recalled so vividly how Hector used to mediate their constant squabbles. Both wizened and toothless, they would stand on either side of him and hurl their accusations at one another. And always at least once in these domestic sessions Telese managed to sneak her hand past Hector and smack her old husband on the face.

Well, here they were, within the hour of his death, hugging Ione and assuring her that the Lord did care.

The persons in the house sensed danger not only to this couple who out of kindness had come, but to themselves. If it was fact that the paratroopers had landed in Stan, or that Major Hoare had arrived in the city and the rebels were being pushed out, they could certainly expect more to stop by to carry out a bitter revenge.

Hastily, they decided that the mothers should take their small children into the forest for protection. Lunches were made and bottles filled with water. All but a few of the women and children then went down the path to the jungle.

Kenneth could not go, of course, so the McMillans remained in the house. Bob McAllister worked on the coffin, though he was unable to nail the boards together for fear that the pounding would attract any rebels going past out on the road. Viola Walker stayed, too. She made them tea, for which Ione was especially grateful.

In the quiet of the hallway Ione sat on the edge of the long cushion on which her wounded son lay. It was a time for sharing intimate thoughts.

"Mother," Kenneth said.

"Yes, Kenny?"

"Mother, if somehow we escape, will you come back?"

"Yes, son," she said. "I'll come back."

"Mother."

"What is it, Kenny?"

"Mother, I think that Jesus someday may call me to be a missionary to Congo. Maybe I'll get the chance to tell the love of Jesus to the men who shot Daddy."

Her heart lightened as she listened to Kenneth express his inmost feelings. Was this not what she had said to Malenza the houseboy one day—that if the Simbas should require the lives of the missionaries, perhaps she would have sons who would return to take up the work?

Would the call of her children to the mission field be akin to her own call? How strange that she should have caught the vision of working for Christ on a faraway foreign field from John and Betty Stam, the martyrs of China, and now her own dear partner in the work was himself a martyr. Yet, she was not to think it strange. To lay down one's life in the preaching of the Gospel had never in the history of Christendom been a strange thing.

Had she and Hector not known this when they volunteered to forsake the shelter of home and go to Congo years before? Someone had once said, "Go far for God," and this they had been willing to do. They had gone far in distance. Who could have told, however, that Hector would have had to go so far as to surrender his life to an assassin's bullet, and that she would have had to give him up without a rankling bitterness?

To go far for the Lord, just as far as He required them to go—this had been at the heart of their missionary commitment. To accept the perfect will of God—this was her present task.

There was the very real chance that the day's violence was not yet over. It was still only mid-morning. From the sound of gunfire in the distance they could tell that something was happening in Stan that should warn them to be ready for any eventuality.

Ten-year-old Timmy, the youngest of Ione's sons, came into the hall and dropped to the floor beside Kenneth and his mother. Looking up with a confident face that reflected hers, he began reciting in his small but steady voice a Psalm he memorized during these past days of confinement:

" 'If it had not been the Lord who was on our side, when men rose up against us . . .' "

13

Massacre in a Side Street

The dispersal of Stan's foreign hostages now halted by the break-down of a bus and the prisoners once again returned to their rooms, a strained calm settled on Résidence Victoria. It was broken mainly by the whirlwind visit of Karichos, the Greek who put together *Le Central.*

"Get enough to eat this morning?" he asked, poking his head into the room of Larson, Carper, and Davis on Sunday, the 22nd. "After being out on the road the way you were last night—oh, Carper, about your hearing aid. I'll have it by tonight for sure."

Then he was gone.

Sunday and Monday the missionaries met several times for prayer and Bible study. Al Larson led the meditation once, as did Chuck Davis. On Monday when it happened to be his turn Dr. Paul Carlson said how much he enjoyed the time of their fellowship, especially the singing of hymns. Then he focused their thoughts on a passage in II Timothy which had come to mean much to him in his long period of affliction.

The Lord stood with me, and strengthened me . . . this was his personal testimony . . . *that by me the preaching might be fully known, and that all the Gentiles might hear . . .* this was the

158

purpose of his experience . . . *and I was delivered out of the mouth of the lion. And the Lord shall deliver me from every evil work, and will preserve me unto his heavenly kingdom* . . . this was to be his future.

Afterward Larson said to Carlson, "By you the Gospel has become known, all right."

Carlson looked at him, waiting for an explanation.

"Well," Larson said, "from what we hear from outside, the testimony as well as the plight of Paul Carlson has gone around the world."

"I'm no different from you fellows—"

"But the rebels singled you out," Larson said.

"Not until they announced that you would be executed did anyone get excited about the rest of us," added one of the Paxmen.

"If we get out, it will be because of you," Davis said.

But Paul Carlson could hardly picture himself a world figure.

"Why," Chuck Davis continued, "we hear by the grapevine that the greatest nation on earth is negotiating for your release."

Carlson shrugged, saying merely he hoped the whole thing would have a good ending. Larson sensed the gloom that was beginning to gather. Trying to inject a bit of humor, he said:

"When you get to Washington, Paul, and go up to see the President, remember to take us along as your bodyguards."

Carlson laughed quietly, then shook his head in seriousness.

"I don't think I'll get out of this," he said, sighing. "They've said too much about me to let me go."

By his pessimistic appraisal he did not mean to disavow the Scripture he had just read. Despite the blackness of his own feeling, he expressed confidence that God would not abandon him. Somehow, unknown to him at this juncture, God would work things out. Perhaps the fact that he ran a malarial fever today had lowered his spirits.

Dr. Carlson went back to his room on the fourth floor; he tried not to let his emotions get in the way of the work there was to do. By the ingenuity of Mme. Paneff, and the foreign colony's *Le Central,* a fairly large supply of medicines and some examining equipment had been assembled in his room. He was happy once more to be a physician; he forgot his own discomforts as much as he could to tend to the ills of those about him.

At the same time, the other missionaries were finding in these quiet days opportunities to serve their fellow prisoners. By a sturdiness of character they encouraged many who almost gave up to despair. Though housed separately at the Victoria, Larson and his roommates maintained contact with the Belgian planters and the European physicians who had shared their quarters at the Hôtel des Chutes. Each of these men was now reading in the Bible daily; even those who before had scoffed at such a thing as faith were finding a solace they never knew existed.

A few of them sought out Al Larson and asked to have regular times of prayer with him. Showing considerable change in his life was the planter Dubois, through whose tough old hide the Gospel first penetrated by way of Bo Martin's heroic stand for the missionary women at the Banalia jail.

"I've read this Bible you gave me," he said to Larson. "I've read it a lot, and God has changed me."

He was a man who had always drunk excessively. But indicative of the change that came over him was his refusal of the beer the Simbas brought to the hotel.

"Here's beer," the fastidiously proper Bordeaux would say in urging him to drink. But each time Dubois would refuse. Some new men were placed in his room at the Victoria. They let their antagonism to all religion be known, but this did not deter Dubois from his avid reading.

Dr. Angelino, who saw his first Bible during confinement at the Chutes, could hardly wait for the calling of each session for prayer and Bible study.

"To think," he said, utterly amazed, "I had to be imprisoned to get to know God."

The quiet waiting afforded a time to reflect. Who could not now see the unfolding of recent history? At first the rebels gave the assurance of "business as usual," and no doubt they meant it as long as it served their cause. But then to rally the people around a faltering regime the Simba leaders launched their hate campaign against the Americans and Belgians. The assistance the two nations gave the Congo government to put down the rebellion fed the flames, of course. And now the vendetta threatened to overtake all the non-Africans under the rebel hand.

If Tshombe's national troops, led by mercenaries, succeeded in storming Stan, the foreigners would meet certain death. If paratroopers dropped on the city, the chance of rescue would improve, but by no means was deliverance assured.

So as the planes flew over the city on Tuesday, November 24, hostages were routed from the Victoria and into the street by wildly nervous Simbas, not only were the lives of the Americans and Belgians at stake; the life of every foreigner in northeast Congo—perhaps some two thousand in number—hung by a tenuous thread.

Gunfire rumbled in the distance as two hundred fifty prisoners of Résidence Victoria marched under Simba prodding down Avenue Sergeant Ketele about seven o'clock in the morning.

The street was wide; a few houses opened onto it. From where he stood as the column halted, Al Larson noticed particularly one such house, a small one with a walled veranda, across the street, perhaps twenty yards away. Clearly it was abandoned. The Belgian owners may have been imprisoned, and in their absence the Simbas plundered the house of everything of value.

On the near side of the street, at a corner around which the column bent, the land was open. Just beyond, on the farther street, ranged a series of commercial buildings. On the open corner, in a grassy patch, a crew worked feverishly to ready a machine gun. Behind them on the diagonal between the front and rear of the bent column walked Colonel Joseph Opepe.

Despite his enormous paunch, he was neat and soldierly this morning. He wore blue-gray gabardines, and his rifle was slung correctly on a shoulder. This rebel officer who had befriended his prisoners on several occasions eyed the wondering hostages as he paced back and forth.

"Sit down!" he barked. They sat. Simba soldiers who wore mostly rags paraded nervously around them, checking now and then their automatic guns or rifles. The firing in the distance became more distinct.

"More than rebel weapons are being shot off down the street," Larson said to his missionary colleagues. During the past months he had learned the reports of the various rebel guns, and some of what they were hearing was too heavy to have come from weapons the Simbas possessed.

"How long until the paras can get here?" asked one of the Paxmen. The airport was a mile and a quarter away, in the direction of the firing, but no one knew when the paratroopers had started on their march toward the city center, if, indeed, they had.

"Don't crowd up, don't crowd up," Larson cautioned those around him. Flanking each other were Del Carper, Paul Carlson, Larson, and Jon Snyder, in that order. Gene Bergman sat just behind them toward the curb, and Chuck Davis in front, a little more out in the street. On the right were the bulk of the Belgian prisoners, whole families among them. Near the corner where the column turned sat other Americans, the Schaubs and Phyllis Rine, and also Marcel and Marie Paneff with their two small daughters, and Paneff's brother Marco, who crippled the bus engine so hopelessly Friday night.

"Inch yourselves apart," Larson said. "You never know when you may need the room to maneuver in."

Colonel Opepe walked to where Larson and the others sat. For a moment he stood over them. Larson felt the colonel's staring eyes to be on him, but he did not look up. If Opepe was not sure about the nationality of others, he certainly knew that Larson was American. How many times this had been established, Al did not know; nevertheless, he did not want to create an opportunity for the colonel to make an issue in this explosive setting.

"Some of you understand Lingala," Opepe said. "You translate for the others." He was shouting, and that was unlike his usual manner, but he evidently wanted all in the seated group to hear him.

"Your friends are coming," he said. "You will be happy to see them."

Your friends . . . happy to see them. Colonel Opepe was saying to them that the paratroopers were on their way. Good old Opepe! If he could just keep talking long enough—

Without his hearing aid Del Carper heard little of what the colonel said. So Larson and Dr. Carlson were the only ones in their immediate area to understand Opepe. They provided a running translation for the others.

"Haven't I been your friend?" Opepe asked. "Haven't I protected you?"

He spoke under restrained emotion; his hearers detected a note of sadness in his voice. He had protected them. The mistreatment that some received had come in spite of Opepe, usually when he was away drinking or in his room sleeping.

"Nothing has happened to you. I have taken the responsibility for your lives. Well, I can no longer be responsible. I cannot tell what will happen."

That sounded ominous. Larson quickly surveyed the surrounding area to pick out a place to run to if it should become necessary. He settled on an open area behind the machine gun, but his plan was quickly shattered by the approach through that area of four armed Simbas.

"Kill them! Kill them all!" shrieked one of the four who ran to Colonel Opepe and waved his gun in the colonel's face. Opepe turned his back.

"Kill them now!" the Simba demanded. Opepe paid him no heed. The rebel then turned to the guards standing near the colonel.

"Kill these people!" he commanded them. Opepe, however, quickly swung around and countercommanded the order.

"All right," said the Simba in disgust. "If you won't kill them, we'll kill you."

From the other direction, along the way the prisoners had come from the Victoria, a truck bore down on the people seated in the street. The missionaries thought it would run them down, so braced themselves to leap out of its path. For a split second Larson felt that the rebels had decided to crush the people under the truck wheels as their method of extermination. But just in time the vehicle swerved and came to a screeching halt near Opepe. Out of the cab jumped a bearded fellow whom nearly everyone recognized as Major Bubu, the deaf-mute bodyguard of defense minister Soumialot.

A driver sat behind the wheel, and a half-dozen Simbas occupied the bed of the truck. The men in the rear worked over a machine gun that was larger than the gun on the grass at the corner. Now they interrupted their endeavor to join Major Bubu in his gesticulations to Colonel Opepe.

The deaf-mute Simba could do no more than utter gurgling sounds in his extreme agitation. He pointed his Sten gun at the crowd and shook his fist. It was not difficult to understand his intentions.

Colonel Opepe, however, managed to back the major into the truck cab and to order the driver to move on, which he did by roaring off toward the ever-nearing gunfire. It was a relief to have that menace gone.

A relief, yes. But to men who had been through months of peril, relief was an elusive thing. Al Larson knew what it was to live one's possible last moment, to have a gun stuck into the stomach by the nervous hand of a man bent on doing an evil deed, and then, surviving that, to deal day after day with capricious rebel soldiers who could at any time decide to strike with all their vengeance. Chuck Davis, too, had walked the brink of death before, as had the Paxmen and Paul Carlson.

To watch as one's faithful nurses were shot down in the very place they served, to be beaten about the head and the body until it seemed impossible for death not to come, to be singled out for the sentence of public execution, to be the object of a mob's leashed violence—Paul Carlson certainly knew there could be no relaxing as long as the Simbas held the power to kill.

And these veterans were right; relief was only momentary. The truck sped back from the way it had gone. The Simbas who rode in the rear were now given completely to panic.

"The paras are coming! The paras are coming!" they shrieked in terror. The guards in the street took up the cry. Some ran to Colonel Opepe with this information.

The paras are coming! Was not this what they in the Victoria had hoped all weekend would happen? Since the planes awoke them at dawn, had they not counted on the paratroopers to be their means of liberation? But now that rescue was almost here, their liberators somewhere just around the corner, Larson, for one—Carlson, for another—could not forget the words of Opepe which they had translated for the others:

"Haven't I protected you? . . . I can no longer be responsible."

This is it. The next hour should tell the story. Larson spoke thus when he first saw the planes from his window. Well, this *was* it, and the next five minutes, maybe two, would now tell the story.

Major Bubu was out of the truck again. Colonel Opepe was doing his best to restrain the bearded mute, but it was plain to see he was making no headway. In passionate anger Bubu leveled his gun at the prisoners as he had done before and grunted with articulate meaning that those in the street should be shot during the fraction of time that remained.

Fear, malignant intent—these emotions prevailed. The foreigners sat silently in the street, each of them disabled by some degree of paralysis. They could only view the scene before them, not play a part in it; they were spectators, not actors, and they wondered what next would happen. If the Simbas chose to open fire there was nothing the hostages, nothing that Opepe, could do to stop them.

The crew on the grass at the corner had readied the machine gun there. They hovered impulsively over the treacherous weapon, waiting for the order to cut loose. The heavier gun in the back of the truck was not yet workable. One or two soldiers who had not lost all nerve in face of the coming paratroopers still sought to correct what may have been a jamming from the last time the gun was used.

Larson thought about attempting to break away at an opportune moment. Where would they run to? To the small house across the street? To the open lot behind the machine gun? Or shouldn't they run at all, but wait for the paras to arrive and hope that rescue would come off?

The deep crackle of automatic rifles sounded astonishingly close. A sudden burst of shooting, and off flew the corner of a concrete building just beyond the open lot. And then from a spot there in the street, some rebel sent a bullet crashing into the seated crowd. The thin cord of restraint now snapped instantly; another Simba fired; then all at once a score of rebels were emptying their guns at two hundred fifty human targets.

From the grassy corner the machine gun spewed an arc of bullets upon the stunned prisoners.

Then in the immediate reaction screams of terror and shrieks of sudden pain filled the street. Horribly bewildered persons stood up, some to run, some to stand as easier targets simply because in the awful confusion their minds refused to function.

"Hit the ground!" shouted Al Larson. "Dig! Dig!" The spacing of themselves now paid off. The missionaries, unable to do anything but hug the pavement and watch, saw parents fall on top of their children to stop the rebel bullets with their own bodies, and mothers try to run with children in their arms, only to be dropped by the shots of Simbas who dashed crazily after them.

All around lay the dead, and the wounded and bleeding, many of whom would die.

"Don't run, not yet," Larson called to those near him. They should wait until the machine gun ran through its belt of ammunition—there! Larson sprang to his knees. "While they reload . . . that house across the street."

With a calmness he did not know he possessed, he ran bent over, low to the ground. *Rat-tat-tat-tat-tat-tat!* The machine gunning started again. He threw himself to the ground, just beyond the curb. Another body plunged beside him. It was Chuck Davis; he, too, had broken for cover.

Others streaking for trees or houses or other possible places of shelter hit the ground. For some, the fall was no part of their effort to escape. If not struck by a rebel bullet, they sank simply because their legs collapsed, as in a frightening dream. A woman being chased by a Simba with a smoking gun found herself in the worst of dreams. She fell; she could not get up, could not move. Helplessly, she watched as her assailant stood over her and curiously drew a fatal bead.

The burst from a Sten gun cut a Belgian child in half. A young American woman—the missionary Phyllis Rine—ran toward a building. She, too, flopped to the ground and blood from her wound soon stained the street.

Mme. Marie Paneff slumped near a curb, a bullet having torn through her thigh. This woman who had cared for the wounds of others so faithfully in the recent past now needed assistance herself. But who in this fiendish nightmare could give it?

The lull came again. Once more Larson ran for the house as a hundred others sprinted in a dozen different directions. Davis ran again. Jon Snyder also decided the house was safer than the open street, especially if the Simbas succeeded in getting that big-caliber machine gun going.

Not everyone moved. Del Carper lay as though dead, his faulty hearing a blessing in this crushing noise of guns. The other Paxman, Gene Bergman, also stayed still. Paul Carlson still lay in the street; finally, convinced that in the house lay the better chance for survival, he got up and ran toward it also.

Larson was now among several men lying prone at the base of the wall of the house's front veranda. The wall, of solid masonry, probably would reach to his chin if he stood up. The steps to the veranda were around the corner from where they lay and in the line of fire. If one were to get onto the veranda and into the house, one would have to scale this side wall.

"There are too many of us here," Larson said to the Belgians who lay alongside him at the wall. "We're ducks for any Simba who may see us."

But to get over the wall he would have to stand up, and any poor fellow who stood in one spot for just a second became an irresistible target for the Simbas. Larson raised up enough to look over the situation. There was no rebel gunner who was not chasing after a fleeing prisoner. He leaped to his feet and almost in a single motion grasped the top of the wall and swung himself over.

Jon Snyder ran to the wall, but decided to find safety by running around a fence that stretched out from the house. Paul Carlson followed Snyder, and he, too, disappeared behind the fence.

Marcel and Marie Paneff, both of them now wounded, exerted more effort than could be reasonably believed in pulling their two small daughters to the wall.

"Monsieur Larson went over," gasped Mme. Paneff. "I saw him go over. Our daughters will be safe with him."

With tremendous effort the parents lifted the five-year-old to the top.

"Au revoir, ma petite," sobbed the mother as they dropped the younger girl on the other side. "Good-by my Isabelle."

They tried to lift the other girl, who was two years older than her sister. They could not. Their strength had almost played out. So taking Brigette between them, they hobbled away as best they could toward a grove of palm trees.

A Simba saw them trying to escape. He ran after them. He had no gun, only a spear. Drawing back his powerful arm, he sent it flying through the air with all his might.

The lance, however, passed clean between the couple. It barely cleared the head of Brigette. But miss them all it did, and fell harmlessly to the ground in front of them.

At that instant Dr. Carlson came back from the way he had run. Chuck Davis had not yet gone over the wall. By a wave of his hand Carlson indicated that Davis should get over first. There was no time to argue priorities; Davis sprang for the wall. He climbed and wriggled and slithered until he was on the other side.

Carlson, already winded and weak, placed his hands on the rim of the wall; by the sheerest of efforts he hoisted himself off the ground.

For him there could be no athletic spring of a Larson or a Davis, no quick kick of the leg to pivot the body up and over. The soreness from his beatings frustrated the drive within him that said escape from the mad fire of the Simbas was now or not at all. When he needed it more than in any other time of his life, his strength was diminished, dissipated by the loss of much weight. And at this critical hour his body throbbed from the feverish ache of malaria.

In spite of these handicaps, he exhibited an amazing will to get away, to gain the protection of the veranda wall, to find somehow a way to live in that house beyond the realm of Simba bullets. He planted his elbows on top of the wall, and managed to draw up a knee and to plant a foot on top of the wall. From the other side a hand reached up—it was Chuck Davis' hand—to grasp his. One last exertion and he would be over, behind the wall in safety.

As he hung thus exposed a Simba gunner rounded the end of the fence, the way the doctor had just come. Perhaps Carlson had seen him somewhere back there and for this reason had turned around in his flight. The rebel stood directly behind the luckless figure on the wall. He carried a Sten gun. He raised it, took careful aim. The first bullet slammed into the doctor's head.

Paul Carlson's hand slipped from Davis' grasp. Silently, effortlessly, almost gracefully he slipped from the wall to the ground. The good Dr. Paul was dead.

Before moving on to other fair game the rebel emptied his gun into the lifeless body. Paul Carlson had fallen a victim to the ruthless pursuit of men who had chosen to make themselves his enemy, not by the execution that they once had set for him and postponed, but by the murderous bullet of a cruel and messy war.

Evil men in their grasp for power had stopped his ministry at the sprawling cement-block hospital at Wasolo. They cut short his service to the people of the Ubangi by hauling him away a despised prisoner. But by singling him out for a special display of their venom they had given him a witness to the whole world. By their scheme to make him a *mercenaire* when in truth he was a *missionnaire,* they gained for his witness to Christ his Lord a hearing by untold millions.

In the fraction of a minute he would have dropped behind the wall. Within a minute or two deliverance would have come by the paratroopers. The first of the Belgian airborne force was now running at top speed into the street where the massacre was still going on.

The paratroopers arrived in time to save many lives—but too late to rescue Paul Carlson. Heaven itself had snatched him out of the lion's hungry jaws and transported him to the eternal safety of the Lord's kingdom.

But by thwarting rebel vengeance, the daring rescue of Stan's hostages unwittingly spread the danger. The lion had been wounded, but was far from dead. Goaded now, it threatened greater harm to more people than before. What had happened in Stan, or worse, could happen throughout northeast Congo where the Simba still slashed with a vicious claw.

14

Tuck in Your Head!

Al Larson dared not stand where he had dropped behind the wall, on a concrete veranda three feet off the ground. Crouching low, he surveyed the scene quickly. Three Belgian men were on the veranda also. Perhaps they sailed over the wall with him, or mounted the steps at the front of the house between sprays of the machine-gun fire which raked that simpler entrance.

At any rate, keeping low behind the wall afforded them protection. Bullets were striking the other side, and each time they hit, bits of the wall exploded in powdery clouds. There was protection here, but for how long? Likely some Simba saw Larson or the Belgians go over the wall or the Belgians make their way up the steps. The rebel gunmen would surely not leave them here alone for long.

The Belgians knelt at the door to the house; they reached up to pick at the lock. On hands and knees Larson scrambled to where they worked.

"You gotta get that door open and not play with it!" he said. "Stand aside."

It was a double door, the kind which swings shut upon itself. Larson forced his foot against one panel and pushed until he could

171

grasp the molding of the other with his fingers. This he pulled. The opposing pressures snapped the lock; the door sprang open. The Belgians scurried inside.

Larson looked back to where he had dropped from the wall. From somewhere a child had appeared; Chuck Davis also stooped there. Larson cocked his head at Davis, pointed to the child.

"The Paneffs' youngest—"

But Davis hardly saw the child. With anxious attention, he riveted his eyes on his empty hand, a hand that until this moment had grasped the hand of someone fighting desperately to get over the wall, but who in a sickening burst of gunfire slipped away and fell—on the wrong side of the wall.

"Come, *petite!*" Larson said, running to the child and sweeping her up in his arms. Bent over, he fled to the open door. Just as he entered the room one of the Paxmen crashed through a window in the rear of the house.

"Oh, brother! Am I glad to get away from him," Jon Snyder said, panting as he picked himself up from the floor. "I tried to work around the house, and ran straight into a Simba."

The house was stripped of furnishings. Beer bottles lay strewn over the floor. Not much place to hide here—except for a closet that extended from one of the sidewalls and divided the house into two rooms. Larson dropped next to the closet in what may have been the dining room. He picked up a bottle, swung it by the neck.

"Arm yourselves, fellows," he said. "There are enough of us to overpower anyone who comes in after us. That is, if we take them by surprise."

The Belgians, however, were peering into the closet through a door glass that ran from about waist high to the top. They opened the door, entered the closet. Snyder followed them.

"Maybe you're right," said Larson. "If we can just stay out of the Simbas' sight until the paras arrive . . ."

The Belgians pushed to the back of the closet, which was already crowded with several cases of empty bottles. Snyder stretched out on the floor as much as room allowed. Larson placed the Paneff child on top of him, then crawled in himself, taking care to brace himself to keep from crushing the girl.

Another joined them. It was Chuck Davis; he ran to the closet, climbed in on top of the others. He lay just below the bottom of the glass. He reached out and pulled the door shut.

Outside, the shooting continued. One shot crackled as if it were fired from the veranda. Then as he was in position to look through the glass Chuck Davis saw a man rush into the house.

He watched the fellow, his rifle at the ready, pause just inside the doorway, then walk cautiously into the room. Davis exhaled; he tried to keep from breathing, and by the inch or two of lung deflation, to sink farther below the exposing panel of glass. But he could not control his convulsive breaths or the shaking that had seized him. His trembling telegraphed to those under him that an armed Simba stalked them in the room.

Having heard but not seen the intruder, Larson tensed for a possible spring. His thought was to take the fellow by surprise. But before they in the closet could act, they first would have to unstack themselves. A mere rattling of the handle of the door would be enough to reveal their presence to the Simba, who, one could guess, had pursued them with murder his intent. If by outside chance they could disarm him, how many others following him might there be to contend with? Sheer folly, that notion. They would have to sweat it out, to wait to be discovered or overlooked.

Davis now entertained a hopeful thought: Was the rebel soldier seeking a place of refuge, as they had sought, from the death out there in the street? Davis looked for a sign in the man's action. But he did not look long. The Simba walked to the rear of the house, turned, and strode toward the closet. To avoid the blatant challenge of a confrontation, Davis buried his face deep between Larson's shoulder blades.

A step, two steps—somewhere—beyond the closet door the Simba halted. Nothing now but silence. Had he seen them through the window? Was he taking his aim to send a bullet shattering through the glass and into their defenseless bodies? In the suspense the single form of a prayer ascended from the closet, "Thy will be done."

Then sound again, footsteps, going away now, in full and rapid retreat through the doorway and onto the veranda. He was gone! Who could say whether he had seen them. If he saw them why did he leave so suddenly? What matter, why? The important thing, he had gone, and all were still alive.

Even so, there was no assurance of safety. Outside, the guns still blasted. Not the machine gun on the grass; this deadly weapon seemed itself to have died. From the noise of the exchange, the lighter, more familiar guns of the rebels were falling back, and heavier weapons, bazookas perhaps, dominated. But for those in the house there was nothing to do but wait, for how long and for what end, they could not tell.

In the closeness of the closet and in the tenseness of the moment Al Larson rehearsed the terror of that morning in the street. Who besides these here with him had lived through the attack? The Paneffs—their younger child was in the closet protected by his body, but what about the parents? Paul Carlson and Del Carper and Gene Bergman the Paxman—the last he had noticed they lay in the street. On further thought, though, did he see the doctor get up and run?

Mike Hoyt, and the consular staff, where were they? And the Schaubs and Miss Rine? M. Bordeaux and the plantation doctors, and Dubois? In this time of peril, had Dubois found a sustaining in the promises of God?

Larson breathed a prayer of thanks that the women and children remained at Kilometer 8 on that day the men were arrested. Yet, how safe were they? If the rebels were retreating, how soon in their rout before they would fall on places like Kilometer 8 to avenge their defeat in Stan?

And where was Kinso? What was happening to the Grants and the Gscheidles and Mary Rutt and other folk in the city? He chafed to get out of the closet and run to their aid, to warn them to beware of the wounded lion, to gather them up from their various locations and bring them to a center that soon would be safe. But that time was not yet, not until more of the rebel guns were silenced.

The boots of a soldier again scraped across the threshold.

"Petite fille. Petite fille." A voice called for the little girl. She tried to move. Larson put his fingers to her lips.

"Shh, shh," he whispered. Had a Simba seen her parents drop the child over the wall and now was in search of her to kill her as they had killed women and children in the street?

"Petite fille. Petite fille," the person called again. His voice was tender—yet how was one to be sure? At so close a range even Davis did not dare to lift his head to have a look.

Whoever the caller, he quickly went out. In seemingly a minute, however, the boots returned. Others entered with him. Voices spoke a language that was not the French of Congo; Larson thought it somewhat familiar.

"Flemish?" he whispered to Snyder underneath him, vaguely recalling his year of language study in Belgium long before.

"Yes, Flemish—I think, " said Snyder quietly.

The next voice they heard spoke in English. "They're in here. I know I saw them go over the wall."

Fingers touched the handle of the closet door and swung it wide open. Exposed now, the men inside scrabbled out to startle Gene Bergman and two Belgians with him in combat uniform.

This was it! Truly, the paras had come! After nearly four months the prisoners of the Simbas stood face to face with their liberators. They were free! Yet, this hardly seemed the time to celebrate.

"There are others . . ." Larson stammered before the blood had time to flow back into his whitened face.

Outside the sun shone with tropical brilliance, highlighting the details of the carnage before them.

"Twenty-eight dead—a preliminary count," someone said somberly. The wounded would exceed that number.

Larson ran from the veranda to where the six in their missionary group had sat in the street. Five men lay in ugly sprawls near the spot. He searched for his friend Del Carper, and was relieved that he was not among them.

"If anyone here is alive and conscious," he said, "lift your hand." Only one did. Larson carried him to a collection point from which the paratroopers were starting to evacuate the wounded to the airport.

He then looked toward the veranda wall for Carper. Neither did he find him there, but at the base of the wall he noted a figure who was familiar, yet one whose face had lost the intense character that Larson had known in it.

"Paul Carlson!" he exclaimed, and only half choked back a sob. "They killed Paul Carlson!"

Gene Bergman approached Larson as he stood over the doctor's riddled body, unbelieving. "I picked up his New Testament," the Paxman said. He took it from a pocket to show Larson. "I knew he wanted his wife to have this."

Stunned and silent, mostly too grief-stricken for conversation, Larson moved over the street where the hostages had sat; he made an accounting of the dead. There was Phyllis Rine, the American missionary, dead from the loss of blood. Another was Marco Paneff; he had saved their lives by "fixing" the bus Saturday night, but now he was dead. Larson saw an entire Belgian family— mother, father, and child—clasped in a final embrace, and all tragically dead.

There was yet another among the dead who in retrospect Larson would have to count as a friend. Colonel Joseph Opepe had fallen in the massacre, as much a victim of cruel hate and nervous trigger fingers as any of his prisoners. This man who had tried to protect the hostages, who even orated to kill time rather than people while the paras fought their way into town, he who was a soldier first and perhaps a poor Simba second—this rebel officer with the soldierly bearing despite his unsoldierly physique had been shot in the back by his own men.

"When the shooting broke loose, Opepe fired," an eye-witness related to Larson. "But he never killed anyone. He couldn't. He was shooting off to one side and into the ground."

Most of the heavy firing was now over, though not all rebel snipers had been routed from their shelters in nearby buildings.

Once Larson and Chuck Davis crashed through a shop window to escape a sudden shower of ricocheting bullets. And once in carrying wounded to the collection station they passed the heavy machine gun on the back of Major Bubu's truck. The Simbas had not been able to make it work. And fortunate that they could not. Had they gotten it going before the paratroopers came, there likely would have been no survivor.

Larson rode to the airport on the rear of a three-wheel airborne vehicle. There he pleaded with Belgian officers for a small task force to run out to Kilometer 8.

"Sorry," a commander told him. "We have no transport until the mercenaries arrive."

"The Procure—"

"That's in town," the officer said of the Catholic administrative center. "We'll get to that—and to your folk in the apartment."

During the anxious wait for Major Mike Hoare to pull in from the south, Larson encountered Del Carper.

"Del," he cried, hugging his friend in relief. Carper had come through the massacre unscathed. He lay in the street all the time, pretending to be dead. Here he was, perfectly whole. He even carried with him the valise he brought out from the Victoria early this morning.

Chuck Davis arrived at the airport. Larson arranged for him to be flown out to Leopoldville on one of the early planes.

"My family is at Kilometer 8," Davis objected.

"Never mind," snapped Larson. "I'll get them. I want you out of here alive."

That he was alive seemed more than a miracle to Chuck Davis. It was the result of a choice—Paul Carlson's choice.

"You get over the wall first," the doctor had indicated as at the same time they came to the base of the wall. Davis spoke of the deep feeling his experience had left him.

"Only one of us could go, and I was that one," he said. "Paul might have gone first, and I second. Then I would have been stuck there on the wall, a target for the rebel soldier. Paul is gone; I'm alive."

Reflecting in his speech the weight he now felt, Davis said that for the rest of his life he as a minister of Christ carried a double responsibility—"Paul Carlson's and mine."

Larson again pledged to bring Muriel and the children from Kilometer 8, so Davis obeyed the order; he boarded one of the huge American transport planes that waited to evacuate the rescued foreigners. Larson turned to Carper. He spoke closely in his ear about putting together a rescue team to drive to Kilometer 8.

"Every minute we wait, the chances grow thinner for our families," he said. "The rebels are furious in their defeat. They'll kill every foreigner they can find."

By ten o'clock Hoare's men began to arrive. Larson saw the first section while it was still on the road. He dashed out the airport entrance and flailed his arms to stop the column. First in line of a dozen vehicles was an armored car. A Belgian volunteer stood in the open turret.

"There are twenty-five Europeans and Americans eight kilometers to the north," Larson shouted. "I need your help to go out and get them."

"In this?" the mercenary asked and chuckled. "How many could I carry?"

Larson might have been inclined to argue, but next came a jeep, pulling a two-wheel trailer loaded to its sides with boxes of ammunition and jerry cans of gasoline. As this vehicle slowed to turn into the airport, Larson accosted the one he believed was in charge.

"I need help," he called in English, not knowing which language to use.

"What can we do for you, buddy?" the officer replied in perfectly good American idiom and accent. He was of dark complexion, as were the three others in the jeep (one was a Negro) and a half-dozen men in a small truck behind the jeep. All had beards and dark wool caps, the kind that stevedores wear. Their leader appeared to be about fifty; he was tall, quite evidently strong, just about the soldier of fortune that one would expect to see in an army of mercenaries. Yet Larson thought he detected in him a broad streak of kindness.

"You can do plenty," replied Larson. His eyes blazing with intentness, he quickly informed them about the families at Kilometer 8.

The officer turned to his men and spoke in what Larson thought was Spanish. And though that was a language which Larson had not learned, he needed no one to translate the exchange:

"What about it, boys?"

"What about it? Let's go!"

Larson climbed into the jeep. The officer held out his hand.

"Name's Carlos."

"Larson's mine."

They shook on their new acquaintance. Carlos said they were a Cuban outfit—"not Castro Cubans. I know what you're thinking." He said until they could fight Castro they would fight for the things they believed in, in any part of the world. "Where you from, Larson?"

"Brooklyn."

"Well, I've spent time in Texas, myself."

They pulled up to a mercenary assembly point at the airport, where Carlos said he would have to report to the brigade commander before making the trip to Kilometer 8. There Larson came across Del Carper again, who insisted on going along.

"No, Del," Larson said emphatically. "The Simbas may sock us in on the way out. So if we're not back in an hour or so, you lead a party to bail us out. You're the only one around who knows the way."

Before the jeep and the truck pulled away from the airport, a mercenary officer thrust a heavy rifle into Larson's hands.

"You may need this," he said.

"I'm a missionary," Larson protested. "We don't use guns."

"This is different—"

"No—"

The officer placed the rifle next to Larson, who sat between the

driver and Carlos, just behind the gear box and at the elbow of the
Negro Cuban who manned a .30-caliber machine that stuck out
over the hood. As they started, Larson cautioned Carlos that without doubt they would encounter many Simbas en route to Kilometer 8.

"We may draw a lot of fire," he said.

"Well, now. What do you think of that?" Carlos laughed. He
looked back at his men who perched on the sides of both the jeep
and the truck and who were armed with automatic rifles or submachine guns. "So we'll draw fire? Just what kind of a journey
do you think we've had all the way up from Kindu?"

They had to cross through Stan. About halfway between the
airport and the central part of the city they began to meet foreign
refugees who streamed toward the one place of safety. Larson
stood in the jeep. Among the hundreds they were passing were
many persons he knew—Greeks and Cypriots, Pakistanis and Portuguese, merchants and professional men, their wives and children
—forsaking everything that life had held for them, glad for the
opportunity to flee for their lives. The Belgians—and most, of
course, were Belgians—he could almost hear saying, *"La peau. La
peau."* They were getting out with their skins.

In the lead of one large group of white-robed priests and nuns
he saw a familiar Congolese face. He looked a second time to
make sure that he was right. It was Major François, the Christian
who had wanted to get out of the Simbas. It was François who had
sought spiritual guidance from Larson and prophesied that God
would deliver Larson from the lion's den. François was dressed as
a civilian. If it had been anyone else, this switch might have appeared opportunistic. But François had not taken part in Simba
rituals, nor inhaled the hypnotic *bangi,* nor even worn the insignia
of leopard skin. With intervention at hand, today was the first time
he could press for his release.

"I hope he makes it," Larson said, addressing no one in particular. Yet he knew the chances were thin that the national army
would permit him to live.

"Al! Al Larson!"

The calling of his name tore him from the dubious future of Major François. It was David Grant who called. He and Sonia were in the midst of the group of priests and nuns led by François. That meant the overpopulated Catholic Procure had been liberated.

"Stop a minute," Larson said to Carlos. He then informed Grant they were on their way to Kilometer 8. "Do you want to go along?"

Grant did. He left his wife to walk on to the airport without him. He clambered aboard the pick-up truck behind the jeep. That was best; if the vehicles got separated, each would have a guide.

Farther along Larson hailed Ma Kinso and Mary Rutt and the German couple, Volker and Elsi Gscheidle. They trudged toward the airport, each with a few possessions.

"Where's Kinso?" Larson called out. Again, he asked Carlos to stop. He leaned in front of the officer to speak with his friends.

"Where is he?" Larson was worried that something had happened to Kinso.

"He wouldn't come," replied Ma Kinso. "He said he won't leave Stan until those at Kilometer 8 are rescued."

Well, there was Kinso for you. The pioneer missionary, captain for so many years, just like the captain of a ship. As long as the crew was in danger, the captain refused to budge.

"Good old Kinso," Larson said to himself. What did not occur to him was that he himself was now the captain, and that in inheriting Kinso's job he had inherited many of Kinso's traits of leadership. Talk about not abandoning ship—

"Don't worry," Larson said to those along the road as he gestured for his band of Cubans to move on. "We'll get the ones at Kilometer 8—and Kinso, too."

They stopped by the LECO apartment, but a paratrooper standing guard near the capitulated prison said a man of Kinso's description had left the building a few minutes before—apparently at the insistence of the military—and moved off in the direction of the airport. So after conducting a quick inspection to see that the

paratrooper was right, Larson waved the rescue party on to Kilometer 8.

Trouble started at the end of the macadam paving. Two hundred yards beyond stood Camp Prince Leopold, where the rebels
had concentrated their forces. As expected, the rescue patrol drew
heavy firing from the camp. The mercenaries returned shot for
shot, not from as many guns of course, but their weapons were
superior. Whether the rebels suffered casualties, Larson did not
know. The jeep received two slugs, which did not slow it, and one
of the Cubans was nicked in the back pocket. He hardly thought it
worth mentioning. Larson himself came close to being shot. A
bullet whistled by his elbow, and he felt its warmth.

"They've built a roadblock about a half mile ahead," Larson
called over the noise of the shooting to Carlos. The officer nodded
that he had heard. Roadblocks were nothing new to these men.
The fellow in the front seat sprayed his machine gun into the
grassy ditches. By the time the vehicles arrived at the barrier, the
Simba guards had heard enough noise to imagine that Tshombe's
whole army was on its way. For this reason they had fled, and the
roadblock now belonged to the mercenaries.

The gunners in the vehicles spattered the area with lead while
one of their number slithered along the ground to unhook the steel
bar and push it out of place. This combat team had perfected
the maneuver. The next barrier was only a bamboo pole. The
jeep sent it splintering to the ground as the hail of bullets dispatched its guards for cover.

"No more roadblocks," Larson said to Carlos. But up ahead
was a car, traveling in the same direction.

"Hold your fire," Larson pleaded.

"Why?" drawled Carlos. "It's standard procedure to rip up anything in the road."

"There may be innocent civilians in it," Larson replied, knowing
this was unlikely since the Simbas had garnered everything that
moved on wheels. But at his urging, the Cubans permitted the car
to speed up and get away without suffering harm. Then above the
general firing that never really ceased Larson said they were ap-

proaching the mission home. Could they put up their guns before arriving?

"Okay," said Carlos, and permitted his men one last ear-splitting burst.

At Kilometer 8 about three hours after Hector died, Ione McMillan still sat in the hall with her wounded son. Most of the women and children had gone to the forest; it was feared that after committing their evil deed at Bob Latham's the Simbas would return to see whether their massacre here were complete.

"And if the rebels are pushed out of Stan," warned Bob McAllister, "you can expect large numbers to flee in our direction."

Because of these forbidding probabilities the little group that remained in the house had nearly been drained of confidence. A child, however, reminded them of a source of help yet available.

In the Kilometer 8 kindergarten, Ruthie, the four-year-old daughter of Bob and Alma McAllister, became acquainted with a few characters of *Pilgrim's Progress*. She and the other small children wore grown-up sun helmets and swung wooden swords in fighting the terrible Apollyon; but when they tiptoed through the Valley of the Shadow of Death their only weapon was prayer. And now that a trip through this dread Valley seemed imminent, even to a child, it was the weapon of prayer that Ruthie employed. Midway through this fearful morning her father searched for the girl. He found her behind the bathroom door, kneeling, her face lifted toward Heaven, and her tiny hands folded trustingly in prayer.

As the morning wore on, the feeling of helplessness grew heavy. Where two might meet in the hall they would stop to pray. At one point Bob McAllister voiced a desperate plea:

"We're shattered, Lord, completely shattered. Won't you give us deliverance—*right now?*"

The impromptu prayer was cut short by a terrifying burst of gunfire on the road leading from Stan. The few who wandered aimlessly in other parts of the house hurried into the hall, the safest spot against any random shooting that might occur outside. Because they were in the hall none heard the mercenary vehicles pull into the yard nor Al Larson's frantic calling.

Before the jeep stopped, Larson was out of it and running toward the house.

"Careful," said Carlos. "Who's to say that house is not full of Simbas?"

"Don't shoot into it," Larson called over his shoulder. He saw the soldiers dismounting. They encircled the vehicles, ready to shoot at anything that moved.

"Bob! Bob!" Larson called as he ran the length of the driveway. "It's Al!"

He saw no movement in the house, not at the windows, not at the bamboo blind that hung in the front door.

"Jean! Can you hear me?"

He began to imagine the worst. Perhaps the rebels had already been here and everyone inside was dead.

"What about it, Larson? What about it?" Carlos had moved in behind him and was demanding an immediate response. "Do we fill it full of lead, or do we scram outta here as the best way to save our necks?"

"Wait a minute," begged Larson. "Hold your fire. There's got to be somebody around."

He called again. This time he gained a response. Around from the rear of the house stepped Bob McAllister.

"Bobby! You're here!"

"Yes, Al," McAllister said. "We're here. There are no Simbas here—now."

The two men hurried toward each other.

"Now—" What did Bobby mean by that?

"They were here," McAllister said. "They shot Hector."

"You mean—he's dead?" asked Larson. He did not have to ask. All he had to do was to look at the usually bounding McAllister; he saw in him a broken man. He grasped the Irishman's strong shoulder and lay his head on the backs of his hands. Hector McMillan dead! A missionary's missionary. The servant of the servant of God. The man everybody depended upon—to fix a broken pump, to tell a funny story just when they needed to laugh, to stir the heart with a challenge from the Word of God.

Larson raised his head. McAllister pointed to a scuffed place under one of the mango trees in the driveway.

"Kenny and Paul—they're inside with wounds," said McAllister. "They'll live. The Simbas almost got me." He pointed to his forehead. Red welts still showed the line of grazing.

Dave Grant talked with them now. McAllister explained that some had fled into the forest.

"Tell the folk to get ready to go," Larson said quietly. "I'll get those in the forest." He was not one to be numbed long by shock, especially when something needed doing. There were people to gather up now and to remove from this danger spot before the rebel army arrived in force. He ran behind the houses and down the path to the jungle's edge. He began his calling all over again.

Marilyn Carper came out first. Del's girl grasped him as if he were her father. She clung to him; he had to pry loose her hands.

"Your daddy's all right," he assured her. "But let go of me. There are others I have to get out."

He called for Jean his wife, for Muriel Davis, for the single women, for others who would have gone with the small children. Jean emerged with their Carol. How overjoyed he was to see them unharmed. Yet, there was not time to speak of all that had happened, to tell one another about their days of loneliness and concern.

He called, and Jean called, and a few at a time they came out. Some had run fairly deep into the forest, but his cries were so loud and so filled with urgency that everyone heard him, even Olive Bjerkseth, who had gone in farther than the others to find them a more secure place.

"An hour later," one of the women said, "we would have been in the forest too far to have heard you."

On the way to the house Jean said to Al that when the group in the jungle heard the mercenary guns on the road, they thought Simbas had returned and killed everyone remaining in the house.

"But the children were sweet," she said. "They tried to tell us that we weren't hearing guns. They said what we were hearing was the noise of falling trees."

Larson hurried into the house to see Hector's body. Then at
Carlos' insistence he began to prod everyone into the vehicles. The
injured Kenneth was assisted to the truck. His mother would ride
with him. The others would have to scramble for places in the
truck or the jeep.

"Where do we put our suitcases?" someone asked.

"No baggage," said Carlos.

No baggage? Not room enough to take it? No room except for
people—living people? Larson stole a glance at Ione. He believed
he read her thoughts. *How would they carry Hector's body, since
there had been no time yet for a burial?* He looked at Carlos and
then at the two small vehicles, which were even too small to take
all the living safely. His eyes swept back to Ione, and in their deep
expression they said as they caught and held hers for just a
moment, "I'm sorry."

There were tears in his eyes, but hers were dry. Didn't she
understand that they would not be allowed to take Hector with
them? He noticed she was finding her place near Kenneth in the
truck, so certainly she understood. But if she knew, perhaps she
did not realize that to leave her husband's body in this place might
mean never to give him a burial. And then he saw the faintest
smile brighten her face and heard her confident voice speak a word
of encouragement to her wounded son, and he knew that she knew
—and somehow with her it seemed not to matter.

What he himself did not know was that only the day before she
had come to the place of deciding that it is not the body—not even
the body of a dear one—that counts in death.

What did she say yesterday? *If a member of my family is ever
taken in death, by God's help I am not going to waste time and the
energies He gave me worrying over a body of clay.* Why this
decision just yesterday? Why had she read so recently about
Adoniram Judson's bitter experience? Why had someone once
bought this book, perhaps to put it aside, only for her to pick it up
years later? Why had the great missionary struggled through his
grievous vale?

It was all a part of God's plan—God's perfect will—for her at this precise moment.

Five years before, perhaps five weeks before, she could not have gone away and left poor Hector's body there in the house alone, knowing how quickly it would yield to the elements of the tropics. But now Hector's own words comforted her as they rang so clearly in her memory:

Someday, I'm going to give this old body, with all its troubles and limitations, back to the elements. Someday, I'm going to claim a new body from the Lord.

She hadn't wanted Hector to talk that way when he said it, but today his words seemed so right. Yes, when she could share the feelings of her heart with others she would reveal to them that before her crisis came, God prepared her to meet it. She could face that which was required of her in this hour because from the God who called her to serve and to suffer she had received an abundant and timely measure of His special grace.

Everyone had found a place to ride. The mercenaries had handled their charges gently. Their main concern seemed to be that the missionaries not take them for Castro Cubans.

The commander Carlos had a word of caution for them.

"We came out through serious gunfire," he said, "and on the way in there will be more of the same. I just want to warn you about what to expect."

Al Larson had one final thing to say before they set off for the dash to the airport. It was an order, and it was specific, right out of his school of survival.

"You're riding in open vehicles, fully exposed to Simba fire," he said. "So bottoms up! Tuck your head between your legs. You can take a bullet better in your seat than you can in your brain."

La peau! the Belgians would have said. He had the skins of many to worry about. Not just those in the vehicles here, but people whose lives were at stake throughout the whole of northeast Congo.

15

The Answer Comes Hard

"Cuba, *si*. That's us," said the big Negro fellow a couple of times in the intervals between bursts from his machine gun.

"But Castro—he's not our boss," explained the driver of the jeep. He turned his face from the rain-rutted road to make sure his passengers understood that their crew were political exiles.

"Castro . . ." rejoined a gunner from the rear. He shot at a pig roaming near the road. ". . . someday, we do that."

Jean Larson, sitting next to the driver and holding daughter Carol on her lap, pressed her head down on the gearshift. Had she not been frightened by all the heavy shooting she would have smiled. Their lives, too, were at stake, these burly mercenaries, but here in this blazing no-man's land they worried about their image.

The truck led; from the truck bed behind the driver's window Dave Grant directed their return routing. The Simbas at Camp Prince Leopold had lain in wait for them, so they experienced some anxious and very dangerous moments during the furious exchange of gunfire there. But they got past without casualty. They arrived unscathed at the airport as people from all over Stan converged on this tumultuous scene.

Kinso had arrived. But Del Carper was not there. Apprehensive when Larson's party failed to return as soon as he thought they should, Carper rounded up a truck and with a few mercenaries drove to Kilometer 8. Somehow, the two groups did not pass each other on the way.

At the mission compound his calls raised no response. Noting his own truck was gone, and not realizing it was Simbas who took it, Carper supposed that all had driven to Stan. He did not go into the house, so did not then learn of Hector McMillan's death. He picked up a few bags that had been brought to the front yard and abandoned. He then returned to the airport, where he met the others.

Larson had pleaded before with officers at the airport, and with Carlos at Kilometer 8, to make a run to Bob Latham's place. Now he hounded the mercenaries again.

"Eleven kilometers is a long way out through a forest road," a captain replied, shaking his head. "And we just don't have the force to deploy as we would wish."

What he meant was that for so much risk involved, there was little chance of finding the United Nations man alive.

For a while Larson worried about Peter Rombaut's safety. But this debonair diplomat was quite capable of fending for himself, and Larson learned that he would stay in Stan for a few days until the evacuation of foreigners was more complete.

". . . the university people," Larson said. "We can't go without them." The Loewens, a Canadian family, and the Lampes, a German family, remained on the campus at the edge of the city. Larson wanted to get Carlos and go after them. Major Hoare, however, pledged to lead a patrol to the campus. Then there was the matter of the other missionaries scattered throughout northeast Congo.

Larson called his men together. They agreed to send their families on to Leopoldville; they themselves would stay around Stan to push out on the jungle roads with any rescue squads.

Their decision ran counter to official plans. A Belgian colonel attached to the Congolese army informed them that attempts at rescuing hostages would be done by the military. The missionaries were not to stay in Stan. The best they could do was supply him with names and probable locations and maps of how to reach the captives.

The entire group of missionaries then boarded a crowded plane for Leopoldville. As they walked up the ramp of the cavernous American transport they were thankful to be alive. But their relief was tempered. Beyond the tiny cordon of reclaimed area in Stan were beloved colleagues and thousands of dear Christians who had not their fortune to escape the clawing lions of Congo.

There was one bright spot, however. Al spoke to Jean about a long-time burden lifting from his shoulders.

"Remember the decision we faced about evacuating our Stanleyville people last August, the time the plane arrived to take out American personnel?" he asked.

"The consul offered you nineteen seats," she replied.

"And I turned him down, saying we would all stay," he said.

"While you were in Stan making that decision we women at Kilometer 8 made the same decision," Jean added. "We said among ourselves that we would stay."

"I can hardly believe it mere coincidence that every one of our people who could have left Stan that day has come safely through these four months."

"Hector—"

"He was at Boyulu, far beyond reach."

"And Kenny and Paul, the only ones to be wounded," she added. "They were with their father."

"I'm sure God kept us in Stan for a purpose," he said. "Maybe as much to teach us lessons of patience and trust as for anything else. When we have an opportunity to start our work again, we'll have a pretty good idea, knowing the situation firsthand, of what the job will require."

Their defeat in Stan infuriated the rebels. But they did not give up the city easily. They fell back only as the superiority of paratroopers and mercenary fighters and weapons pushed them along a block at a time; as they retreated they rained vengeance on anyone handy, African or foreigner. Rombaut tried to get out to Kilometer 8 to bury Hector McMillan, but intense fighting prevented him from approaching the place. He later said to Al Larson that had rescue not come for the folk there when it did, Kilometer 8 would no doubt have experienced a massacre almost as bloody as the one in Avenue Sergeant Ketele.

The rescue operation in Stan was to breed widespread repercussion for long distances in every direction.

A large number of foreigners lived at Paulis about three hundred fifty miles northeast of Stan. Since late August when the rebels overran the area the foreign population had been in and out of prison, and life to them was a series of harassments. In early November the rebels arrested seventy-two men, including the only American man in the area, the Rev. Joseph W. Tucker.

"Jay" Tucker was a farm boy whose love and concern for his neighbor went far past his home town of Lamar, Arkansas. After high school he worked his way through Southwestern Bible College in Oklahoma, and entered the ministry of the Assemblies of God. One hot summer night in New Orleans, in a smothering room over the rescue mission where he worked, Jay was not able to sleep. It was on that night that he told the Lord he would become a missionary to Africa.

In 1939 he sailed for Congo. On the voyage he struck up an acquaintance with Angeline Pierce, a dark-haired, dark-eyed recruit assigned to his missionary party. She had opened her heart to the love of Christ in a small Canadian town north of Spokane, Washington, and within weeks felt the call to missionary service in Africa. A year and a half after they met on their way to the field Angeline and Jay were married.

For twenty-five years they preached, baptized, helped establish churches and schools, dispensed medicines, and, having developed a proficiency in language, translated many books into Swahili. He became his mission's director in Congo, but still inked his fingers in the Assemblies print shop in Paulis and trekked through the bush to aid Congolese pastors with their flocks.

Nearly everyone around Paulis was acquainted with this tall,

well-built, gray-haired, outgoing man. Seldom was it possible for
him to walk down the street without being stopped by someone
who had a problem or project to share. The Africans thought
highly of him—busy as he was, he always had time to listen to
them, and he could see their point of view.

But local standing carried little weight with the Simbas, especially with those who descended on Paulis from other regions of
Congo. In the general roundup of Belgians and Americans that at
Stan had denied Kilometer 8 its men, the Simbas arrested Jay
Tucker. They imprisoned him and other foreign men in a new
boarding school for European children which the Dominican owners had had no chance yet of using.

There they did not lack for comfort. Individual rooms opened
off a central court. Each room was equipped with a cot, and each
cot with a mattress and mosquito net. The Catholic sisters who
remained at the school prepared meals for the prisoners. Despite
all the amenities, they found their confinement harsh. The Simbas
frequently beat the prisoners.

During the early part of November about half of the men were
freed. It became clear that those remaining in custody were being
held as hostages against the day that the national government
might try to recapture Paulis. The rebel leaders sensed that day
was at hand when on the morning of November 24 Radio Stan
went suddenly dead.

An uneasiness hung over Paulis all that day, for news of the
drop of paratroopers on Stan reached into the hinterlands by
means other than radio. Even the prisoners at the Catholic school
heard about the liberation.

By evening all seemed peaceful again. At eight thirty a nun at
the school telephoned Angeline Tucker at her home to say that Jay
was concerned about his family; he wondered if developments at
Stan had caused them any trouble.

"Everything is calm here," Mrs. Tucker said. They had just
finished supper and she and the three children were settling down
for the night.

"All is quiet at our place, too," the sister said.

Ninety minutes after the nun hung up the telephone drunken Simba soldiers, crazed by the smoke of hemp, rushed on the school. They waved a list of names of prisoners, which officers retreating from battle areas had selected to bear the brunt of an angry retaliation. Second from the top of the list of thirteen was the name of Jay Tucker.

"We want the missionary!" shouted the Simba who held the paper containing the names. In the flickering light of the pitchy torch they bore, the rebels burst into room after room until they found the one they sought. They shoved Tucker into the courtyard.

"We are going to kill all the missionaries tonight," the leader of the group said bruskly. Their vehemence now transcended nationality; they directed it at religion.

From other rooms tumbled other prisoners—four priests and an assortment of Belgian businessmen. Two Simbas knocked Tucker to the ground, then trussed him up by tying his feet and hands together behind his back. In the uncertain light of the torch the missionary glimpsed what was happening to an Italian priest.

He, too, had been tied. A rebel then shot him, as he would shoot a fettered pig. But the priest still lived. So another Simba rushed at him with a machete and cut off both his hands. This was too much for even one so hardy; the priest soon bled to death.

Jay Tucker's turn came up next.

In the near-darkness someone swung a bottle across the missionary's face. With a dull thump the bottle broke; blood covered the face that in agony turned to grovel in the dirt. In the glassy-eyed glee that their hemp afforded, the Simbas began to whoop as they searched for sticks to finish the job. Those finding sticks made use of them, others their rifle butts. They took turns at hitting the missionary. Starting at the neck, they worked slowly down his back, striking again each time their victim squirmed.

At Wamba, between Paulis and Stanleyville, the rebels had sealed off the region when the People's Republic gained control. Within the perimeter the missionaries were allowed to work, but of course not without interruption and restriction. In the general roundup—here on October 30—the work of the missionaries of the Worldwide Evangelization Crusade ended. The six WEC missionaries at the central station of Ibambi were herded with other foreigners into a truck and driven off to Paulis.

Among the forty-four carted to Paulis was a bachelor missionary of twenty-eight, a man of small stature—five foot two, one hundred ten pounds—a small bundle of dedicated energy, William P. McChesney. He had come from Phoenix, Arizona, to Congo in 1960, so had worked amid only uncertainty and upheaval. But Bill McChesney gave himself unstintingly to the twin tasks of auto mechanics and evangelism.

The commander at Paulis had received no orders from Stan, so refused to accept the consignment of prisoners. Returned to Ibambi, the missionaries discovered how they stood with the African Church.

The Christians saw them arrive back about five in the afternoon. A large group soon gathered. They went wild with joy. Hadn't they prayed for many hours that the missionaries would be released? God had answered their prayers. Yet they knew that their foreign friends were not free from trouble; they openly pledged their support.

"If the Simbas try to make you deny the Lord," one old deacon said, "we are ready to die with you for Christ's sake."

Their attitude augured well for the future of the Congo Church.

The next weeks were indeed difficult. The rebels threatened to kill the missionaries. They convened public trials frequently, and in them accused the missionaries of varied and grievous crimes. Being American, Bill McChesney was singled out for particular abuse.

On November 14, when he was ill with malaria, the Simbas sent McChesney to the WEC station in the town of Wamba to join four other missionaries under house arrest. One man was among the four—James Rodger, a forty-two-year-old staid Scot who twice had been rejected for service in Congo, but who on his third application was accepted because the mission so desperately needed teachers.

"He's too theoretical-minded," the mission examiners had said of Rodger. "The Africans will never respect him."

But in five years of service he did adjust to another culture and established himself in the esteem of his students.

During their days in Wamba together McChesney and Rodger became staunch friends. The rebels permitted them considerable freedom. So the two sometimes hiked the nearby paths; often they discussed the Christian fellowship of suffering, agreeing that at no previous time was their faith ever so refreshed.

"I've never known the Lord to be so much a part of me," Rodger said one day. "What possibly can He have in store for my life?"

He was to find out very quickly. On the tenth night after Mc-Chesney joined Rodger the Simbas defeated by the paratrooper drop on Stan swept into Wamba.

"Why does the American stay free?" a raging rebel asked on his arrival. He shook his fist in the face of a local cadre. "Prison! Throw him in the prison!"

Though they came only for McChesney, Jim Rodger climbed into the truck to be with Bill. In the short drive the arresting soldiers beat the young American severely. Already weak from sickness, he was unable to stand up under the punishment. Rodger carried his small, frail friend into the prison. They both were shoved into a tiny, filthy cell already crowded with forty prisoners. They found breathing all but impossible.

The Simbas had torn the clothes from McChesney's back. Priests in the cell gave up their garments to keep him warm through the chill night; they could not, however, stave off the scorn that the rebels poured upon this one they despised.

In the morning a baleful colonel pulled the prisoners out of the cell to the prison courtyard. There the local population, whipped into frenzy by the newly arrived rebels, urged violence. The colonel seemed slow and deliberate in his actions. He first called out the local Catholic sisters to witness the executions he said would occur. Then he separated the prisoners according to nationality.

Some he determined to be Dutch civilians, others Spanish. Eight bearded Belgian priests were easy to classify, though one of them, the Wamba bishop, had been so disfigured that not even the nuns were positive of his identity.

The colonel moved next on McChesney.

"American?" he asked, snarling bitterly as he spoke the word.

McChesney could only nod as a reply. The colonel then turned to Rodger. "And you?"

"British."

The Simba officer ordered McChesney to stand apart from the others. From signs he made to his men it seemed certain his next command would be to kill the American. But Bill McChesney did not move to the designated spot. He couldn't.

Jim Rodger stepped to his side. He said quite stoically to this young friend who had helped him find a new fellowship with God:

"If you have to die, I'll die with you."

"That man is no American," called out one of the priests to the colonel upon seeing what Rodger had done. "He's an Englishman."

The colonel walked a few paces to confront Rodger.

"What *is* your nationality?" he demanded.

Rodger said nothing. So the colonel spoke for him:

"American, British—they're the same."

The straining spectators would no longer be held back. They had picked out the prime targets for their passion. No one could delay their striking.

Some with clubs fell hard upon the two missionaries. Bill McChesney died almost at the first blow. Jim Rodger caught the small, battered body and gently laid his friend upon the ground. Then he himself was knocked to the ground. The mob of madmen trampled on him until he died.

For several minutes they continued their vengeful dance, then with the brute of jungle beasts they killed the bishop, seven other priests, and sixteen foreign civilians before they vented their lust.

Men of cooler passions gathered the bodies in roadcarts to haul them to the Wamba River. For McChesney and Rodger the Wamba might have been a Jordan. It was as though these friends and fellow servants of Christ were on one of their walks, and arriving at the river decided to cross over to the other side.

The paratroopers jumped again. Two days after the drop on Stan, two days after it was too late to snatch Jay Tucker from his tormentors, the Belgians floated their silks down on Paulis to rescue foreign residents.

Angeline Tucker and her three children were among those flown out to Leopoldville by the American transport planes. Smoothly, they flew above the clouds; for the first time in many weeks they were safe. Mrs. Tucker leaned back against the ribbing of the plane and realized that God had done everything He once had promised her He would do.

Jay and Angeline and the children—John, eighteen; Carol Lynne, thirteen; and Crickey, eleven—had returned to Congo in August from a year's furlough in the United States. They were aware that the interior provinces threatened trouble; friends in the United States, in fact, advised them not to return to Congo. But Tucker remonstrated, "If we don't go back, our African Christians will think we are afraid to live among them." They also eagerly anticipated their fifth term on the field. For one thing, they were anxious to put into service a new bookmobile, for which a church in Arkansas had donated five thousand dollars.

As far as a rebellion, they did not believe that Paulis would offer more than the usual annoying incidents to which they had grown accustomed before their furlough. They knew nothing of the apparent infiltration the rebels were using to capture Paulis some-day. They did not know that the rebels called themselves lions.

But to be prudent they decided in their layover in Leo that they would fly to Paulis only if they could obtain a regular commercial flight.

In his quiet way when deciding something important, Jay said to his wife, "We certainly won't go in if the only flights are to evacuate people."

Stan was of course closed to travel, as by this time in August the rebels had taken over that city. So the children jumped and

clapped in wild delight when their father returned to the hotel
where they were staying and said he had procured seats on a direct
flight to Paulis. To the children, to the parents, Paulis was home,
and they were going there!

The night before their scheduled flight Angeline Tucker found
sleep impossible. She got out of bed and walked into the room
where the children slept. She stood by their beds. She prayed silently.

"Lord," she said, "you know Jay and I want to go back. Paulis
is our home, our work. You've called us to serve you there. But
these children—what about them? How can I take them into so
unsettled an area?"

In the light that shone in from the street she surveyed each sleeping child, and her heart began to be comforted. It seemed that God
was speaking directly to her.

Don't forget—the voice was still and small—*I love these children even more than you do. I promise you I will deliver them out
of the den of the lions.*

How strange! What did this mean? Her mind harkened back to
Daniel's deliverance from the den of Darius' hungry beasts. And as
with Daniel, the promise was deliverance *out of,* not avoidance of,
the lion's lair.

This thought held no real meaning for her this night; but trusting
that God knew, even though she did not, she returned to her bed
and slept soundly.

On the flight the following day the Tuckers traveled with a few
Belgians and several Congolese. Midway the captain of the plane
strode back from the cockpit to ask:

"Why are you folk going with us to Paulis?"

"Why?" asked Tucker. "Why, because Paulis is our home."

"But, sir," the pilot countered, "we're flying a mission of evacuation. We are en route to Paulis to pick up persons who are fleeing
before the rebels arrive."

The startling information contradicted what Jay had been told
twice the previous day. But the plane would not of course turn
back; and at Paulis there were more persons demanding seats on

the return flight than there were seats available.

There was nothing they could do but go on to Paulis, to establish their home again on the outskirts of the town, and to wait to see what might happen.

On August 19 the troops guarding Paulis capitulated, and the Simbas came in full force at two in the afternoon. The sudden blasts of their guns chilled the Tuckers. After the firing diminished and the rebels fanned throughout the town, a group swarmed around the missionary house.

"Simba! Simba! Simba!" they chanted.

Angeline Tucker's heart jumped to her throat. Here in this excited utterance she now understood the promise God had given her that night in Leopoldville. Now she realized that it was from these Swahili lions that the Lord had said He would deliver the children. With the frightening appearance not only of their leopard skin, their feathers, and their weirdly daubed paint, but of their glassy stares and their dope-crazed actions, she was completely thrown back on God and would have to trust Him to make good on His promise.

After the initial shock wore off she still felt a clutch of terror in her breast. She had taken for granted that Jay was included in that promise from the Lord; but now she feared he wasn't.

Well, they certainly were in a lion's den. And the lions were attacking, mauling, devouring people all around them day and night. They killed the town's telephone operator, so for several days the system closed down; they gathered in tribal chiefs from the bush villages to mow them down by automatic fire; they executed officials of the deposed government; they shot into crowds of ordinary people in the streets.

Simba! Simba! Kill! Kill! Kill!

Their battle cry sounded all over the town.

One day Jay Tucker was ordered to walk uptown to report to the rebel authorities at the police station.

"This is the day you are going to die," the commander raved. He shoved his pistol in Tucker's face; the missionary filled with fright. Then he looked straight in the eyes of the officer. From that moment every ounce of fear left him. The commander lowered his gun, walked away, and became as polite as anyone could ever be.

Upon his return home, his face blanched not from his experience at the police station but from the sights and smells along the way, Jay spoke sadly of the death that was overtaking their community. For several days they thought only of wanting to get away. They prayed only for deliverance. One day Jay broached the subject to Angeline.

"We've not had one day of peace," he said. "And as children of God, this ought not be so. Are we praying for the wrong thing?"

She agreed that perhaps they were.

"Shouldn't we open our hearts to whatever work the Spirit of God wants to perform?" he asked.

"Yes, Jay," she answered. And they did. Beginning that day, they spent hours in prayer and Bible study. New Testament passages that she had said were meant exclusively for the Early Church—because it had undergone so much suffering—she now was willing to accept for their own situation.

"You know, Angeline," Jay said one night after that, "I believe God placed us here in Paulis to stimulate people at home to pray for Congo in these trying days."

He explained that if the missionaries were not there, most Christians at home would be praying little for Congo, simply because their missionaries were out. But as long as they remained, great volumes of prayer would go up, and somehow he felt that prayer would be the force to turn the tide so the Congo Church would not be destroyed.

Many of the Christians at Paulis risked their lives to keep the missionaries in provisions. The Tuckers warned the believers to stay away; continued contact with foreigners would sooner or later arouse the suspicion of the rebel government, and the Congolese could then expect dire consequence. But still they came; they said they needed the fellowship—and the missionaries acknowledged they needed theirs.

Thus, through the fall months the missionaries felt the undulating control of the rebels on all they did. The Simbas placed a guard at their house, a fellow named Andre who seemed friendly enough. But Andre soon wearied of guard duty; he recruited two young boys to stand in for him. The Tuckers called Andre their "big guard" and the boys their "little guards."

The boys, indeed, were little. One was twelve years of age, the other eleven. At times they were like any boy, anxious to tell all they knew. For Crickey, the younger Tucker son, they detailed the Simba rites; the cuttings of the forehead; the *dawa,* or spiritual medicine, which they said made them go wild. They revealed that promotion in rank depended on the amount of killing a Simba did. The younger of the two boasted that he had killed a government official with a spear during a public execution.

The boys had been instructed by Andre to sleep outdoors, but when night fell they always became afraid. They pestered Mrs. Tucker until she finally made them beds in the dining room.

Some days other, meaner rebels would call at the house to press their inspections. They often raised guns to the heads of the Tucker children. Several times Jay went to jail. Twice John, the teen-age son, was arrested. At these times Angeline Tucker had to fight off waves of doubt that God would—or could—deliver her son out of this den of death.

Once when Jay was gone she thought she simply could not stay alone. But she recalled a verse of Scripture that Jay had memorized early after their return to Paulis.

" 'I will both lay me down in peace, and sleep,' " she recited as Jay did every night on retiring, " 'for thou, Lord, only makest me dwell in safety.' "

After her husband's latest arrest she received a reminder of his desire that only the Lord's will be accomplished in their tribulations. She sent a birthday card to him at the Catholic school that was now his prison. He managed to slip it back to her with a brief, penned note. It said:

"God first. Family second. Dad."

How she was to need his perspective on that morning of November 25! She went to the old desk in the office of their home and picked up the telephone to call the Catholic sisters.

"How are things out there today?" she asked the mother superior.

"*Comme si, comme ça.* Just so-so," the nun answered.

"How is my husband?"

"Your husband"—the nun sounded strangely hesitant—"your husband is in Heaven."

Angeline reeled under the shock. She fell against the desk and gasped, "Oh, God, I can't go on! This is the end of everything!"

Then she finally managed to stammer into the telephone, "When —when did it happen?"

But the connection was broken.

The children heard the alarm in their mother's voice. They ran into the room to see her holding desperately onto the phone.

"Mother, what's the matter?" asked John.

"Well—Daddy," she began, not knowing how to tell them. ". . . I think they've killed Daddy."

"Daddy? They've killed Daddy?" The children began to sob. Crickey the youngest screeched his grief. Mrs. Tucker placed the call to the nuns' residence again.

"Were there others?" she asked, and then discerned that the mother superior was hardly able to speak.

"There were others," the nun said softly. "Yes, there were others; as far as we know there were thirteen."

"Are you sure my husband was among them?" Angeline asked, grasping at the one last hope that somehow there was mistaken identity.

"Yes, we are sure. He was one of them."

John comforted his mother, but how was one able to assuage the anguish of young children? Yet they must stop their crying. A friendly watchman of the house next door where several Simba officers lived hurried over to give warning that the rebels must not hear the children.

"If the young ones cry for their daddy, the Simbas are sure to kill them, too," he said kindly, but firmly.

She finally got them quiet. And in the silence she had her own feeling of emptiness to face. This was emphasized when about noon one of the Christians who worked for the Government Hygiene dropped by the house. Just prior to midnight he had been routed from his bed to gather up the bodies in the school courtyard to take them in his truck to the Bomokandi River. There under orders of the ones he now worked for, he threw the bodies one by one into the river as food for the crocodiles.

"Two years ago," this man now said to Angeline Tucker, "your husband helped me to find my way to God. I am sorry I was not able to befriend him."

He said he had something of Jay's to give her. She extended her hand to his, and when he drew away there lay her husband's wedding ring.

He explained that in cutting the cords with which the bodies were tied, he was able to slip the ring from *bwana's* finger, even though the Simbas were watching him.

"I don't know the custom in your land," he said, and tears welled in his eyes, "but I thought you might like to have it."

After he had gone, after their houseboy had forsaken them out of fear, after the friendly watchman next door had fled, Angeline Tucker felt very much alone. She was alone with the thoughts that crowded into her mind. Again and again those thoughts melted down to one word:

Why?

"Why, Lord, why did he have to die?"

And then like a wind tugging at a loose shutter the Spirit of God seemed to be trying hard to pry her loose from her torturing bewilderment.

The first draft was somewhat shocking to her.

Except a corn of wheat fall into the ground and die, it abideth alone; but if it die, it bringeth forth much fruit.

"But, Lord," she protested, "why Jay? Why one who gave his best years to Congo? And if it had to be Jay, why so cruelly? Couldn't death have come more gently?"

That afternoon she felt impressed to read the eleventh chapter of the New Testament epistle to the Hebrew Christians. She went

to her bedroom, closed the door, and began to read slowly and
with deliberation.

Now faith is the substance of things hoped for . . .

Faith. Yes, that is what she needed in this troubled hour. Seeking the key to fulfillment of her need, she read on. She read of
victories that Old Testament heroes had achieved by faith, of the
deliverance from Pharaoh's wrath that the Israelites experienced,
of faith that subdued kingdoms and wrought righteousness and
obtained promises and stopped the mouths of lions and quenched
the violence of fire and escaped the edge of the sword . . .

"But, Lord," she cried in desperation, "these were all victories,
all deliverances."

Keep on reading, God seemed to say.

. . . women received their dead raised to life again . . .

"But, God, that's still victory."

Keep on reading.

*. . . others were tortured, not accepting deliverance; that they
might obtain a better resurrection . . .*

Was that it? Jay had not accepted deliverance because it had not
been offered. *A better resurrection.* Yes, she thought, that was it.

Now that God's refreshing breeze had blown away the doubts,
the fears, the self-pity, now that in their place there was this thing
she hoped for, a faith that was beginning to fill her soul, she
understood why God had allowed them to fly into the death trap
that Paulis was last August. She could hope with a hope that
sprung from confident faith that Jay's entrance into the presence of
his Heavenly Father was a glorious event.

A better resurrection. If for Jay, why not also for Congo? There
was a resurrection of the just and another of the unjust. By his
years of faithful service, how many in Congo had moved from the
line that led to the resurrection of doom to that which led to the
resurrection of unending life with God?

Because of his life, hundreds—even thousands—in Congo had
believed. And now that his life had become a corn of wheat, a seed
that death had planted, who could say how extensive the fruit of
resurrection might someday be?

16

Left Bank Countdown

"You boys look hungry," Angeline Tucker said to the "little guards" who had been away since early morning, but who returned to the house about eight o'clock that evening.

"We haven't eaten a bite all day," the eleven-year-old said.

"We heard how *bwana* died," added the older one. "How could we eat on a day like this?"

As they spoke of the death of the *bwana* of "their" house they both began to cry. Mrs. Tucker smiled warmly at them and patted the smaller fellow on the head.

"Well, you come and eat now," she said. "I've got a big bowl of manioc greens. Wouldn't you like to have it?"

Just being near this kind woman made them feel better, so they regained their ravenous appetites and fell to eating.

"Where's Andre?" she asked, inquiring about the "big guard."

"Oh," said the older boy, "there is bad fighting near Buta. The officers have sent a lot of the big Simbas there."

She was relieved to know that Andre was not around tonight. While he had been friendly toward the Tuckers at first, lately he had said things and had exhibited attitudes that made Mrs. Tucker distrust him. Throughout the day the feeling had grown that the

Simbas might cause all the foreigners in Paulis much trouble. A rumor was going around that on the next day the whole foreign population would be killed. Mrs. Tucker did not know whether to believe it or not. But she had found anything but comforting the fact that Simbas occupied the house on either side of her and the one across the street. Especially was she afraid for her eighteen-year-old son.

"Johnny," she said to him earlier in the day, "don't you dare set foot outside the house."

He did not have to be told why. The day that his father was arrested for the last time three Simbas acting on their own and not on orders haled him before the military authorities. They said he was one not to be considered as a boy, but as a potential fighter against them. The officers let John go back home. But now, realizing to what lengths the fury of the rebels could go, Angeline Tucker feared most for her son, though she wondered several times during that long day whether any moment might be the last for all of them.

It helped that two Assemblies women missionaries who lived over the print shop in Paulis came out to spend the night with the Tuckers. Yet this move almost proved disastrous for the women and for the Tuckers.

The following day, November 26, was the American Thanksgiving. Angeline Tucker awoke about six. Before getting out of bed she sighed heavily and asked herself:

"How can we get up this morning and face another day of not knowing what will happen? This living in fear and dread—how are we going to do it?"

Then in less than ten minutes planes roared overhead!

Angeline Tucker sprang out of bed and hurriedly crossed to the window. The morning fog hung very low out where they lived at the edge of the forest.

"Rescue planes!" shouted John from his room.

"Do we go home today?" asked Crickey as he bolted to his mother.

Soon all in the house were up. In great excitement they clung to the windows, straining to see what was going on in the sky over-head. Through the tiniest of clearings in the clouds they now and then glimpsed a plane. From the sound they could tell the planes were circling.

"Maybe they'll drop paratroopers as they did in Stan," said Johnny hopefully.

"Too bad we're not at our apartment in town," one of the visiting women said. "From our windows we can see the airport very clearly."

Soon they heard the loud crack of gunfire. Not long after it started Simbas began running behind their house into the forest.

"Pull the curtain," Mrs. Tucker said to her daughter, Carol. "It's not safe to be seen by a Simba today." The front of the house was nearly all window; because of this she said they should stay in the more-protected rear rooms.

The younger children were extremely worked up over what they believed would be immediate rescue. Their mother insisted that they calm down long enough to eat a piece of bread and a helping of pineapple. She quickly gathered together her Bible, the notes that Jay had written and sent to her from his prison, and a few other things of value.

"You be responsible for your father's briefcase," she instructed John. "All our papers are in it."

But an hour passed, and no one showed up to escort them to the airport. A second hour ticked away, and the shooting and other noise slackened. There was no longer any sound of planes.

"I'm afraid they've gone off and forgotten us," Mrs. Tucker said.

"But remember, Angeline," one of the women missionaries said, "the Lord promised He would deliver these children out of the lion's den. He's not going to leave us here."

"Well," Mrs. Tucker replied, "it is kind of hard to hold to that promise with all that has happened." She fully knew what would happen if rescue planes did come and go and they were left behind. Even a high-flying plane enraged the Simbas, so sure were they that all planes carried bombs. One did not have to go to great lengths to imagine what the result would be of missing out on the one chance to escape.

"But you are right," she said to the one who had brought up the promise that God gave her in August. "The Lord *will* see us through."

In a very few minutes Crickey pulled back a curtain at the front of the house to look out.

"Mama!" he called. "European soldiers!"

Everyone dashed to the front windows. Sure enough, seven paratroopers walked down the street toward the center of town and the airport. In passing by the Tucker place they had called for all foreigners to come out, but no one in the house heard them.

Rescue had come. The missionaries gathered a few belongings. Under protection of the Belgians, they walked to the airport. No plane was there. Already it had taken off with one hundred fifty Belgian women and children. But, assured the paratroopers guarding the field, the plane would return; there would be rescue for all.

There wouldn't be, of course, for Jay, nor for twenty others executed since his death, nor for a Belgian woman who this very morning had been killed by her Simba guard as soon as he heard the planes. But God's promise to Angeline Tucker had held.

The big plane returned to Paulis. A few minutes after landing it took off again. This time Mrs. Tucker, her children, and the young women associated in the work were securely aboard. As the plane shuddered in the race down the dirt runway and the nose lifted into the untroubled skies, Angeline prayed silently on this Thanksgiving Day.

"I wouldn't have done it that way, Father," she said. "But I thank you that your way is always best."

The drop of paratroopers on Paulis was the second and last in the Congo rescue operation. About two thousand foreigners and hundreds of Congolese were airlifted to safety. But throughout northeast Congo the number of hostages remained large—among them the survivors of the Wamba affair, and as far as could be determined the UFM missionaries now gathered at Banalia north of Stan and at Bafwasende, to the east, just beyond the large Boyulu station. Nevertheless, Belgium withdrew the mercy angels and the United States the planes that had spilled them from the heavens. From this point on, ground troops would have to fight their way from village to village over rutted and ambushed jungle roads if any more rescue was to be accomplished. Mike Hoare and his mercenaries would have to probe deep in rebel territory if more hostages were to be found and liberated.

How tragic that the relief forces knew nothing of the depravity that palled a part of Stanleyville itself, directly across the Congo River in the Left Bank section called Rive Gauche.

In the month preceding these events Père Charles Schuster motored regularly to the forest villages at the end of the roads out of Ponthierville, seventy-odd miles south of Stan. This cargo-transfer point at the head of Stanley Falls served as his headquarters. For twenty-four years he penetrated the bush to minister to his scattered flock. He liked the jungle and its people. On their part, they welcomed this gray-haired man with long beard and white robe into their mud-wall houses.

At times he compared the tropical forest here to the lovely wooded hills of his tiny homeland of Luxembourg. He imagined how peaceful it must be there in the crossroads settlement of Dellen. There a day's activity resolved into a farmer's gathering in of his sheep or a housewife's putting a shine on the windowpanes of her home.

It was not always peaceful around Dellen; men fought two massive wars in the fields just over the ridges. And here in Congo, which once was peaceful, the spiteful acts of bitter men now inflamed even the remote settlements that made up Schuster's parish.

The Simbas overran Ponthierville about the time they captured Stan in August. In the weeks that followed the local commandant convened frequent "people's courts" to try both Congolese and Europeans on charges of crime against the People's Republic. Sometimes the sessions lasted all day. Père Schuster's fellow priest from Luxembourg, Jean Trausch, suffered gravely in these military tribunals.

Trausch described to Schuster the manner in which the Simba major would place his desk outside the government building and the importance in which the assembled townspeople held him as he opened the dossier of the accused before him. How many times the accused had been Père Trausch, neither Trausch nor Schuster could remember.

"By your *phonee* you have called the Americans to send their planes overhead to bomb us," the commanding major would charge. Never once did the priest answer. Rebuttal or silence by any prisoner produced the same effect. Bruises from court-administered beatings covered Père Trausch from head to foot.

Père Charles Schuster spent most of his time in the bush; for this reason he escaped the wrath of the Simbas in Ponthierville. But early in November the rebels extended their courts to the jungle hamlets. Père Schuster soon became a regular defendant.

At first the trials were ridiculous affairs. The Simba in charge would ask the villagers, "This father who visits among you, is he a good fellow or bad?"

"Good," they would answer. The perfunctory procedure then over, the Simba would allow the priest to say Mass or to catechize the village children, and to move on.

By mid-November, however, attitudes began to change. Behind his back the Simbas kindled the people against Père Schuster. The verdicts of "good" were harder to come by, and failure to achieve favor drew him blows. After a few days of this it was not safe for him to venture out of Ponthierville.

Yet, neither was it safe there. The rebels said they could not prevent the harm the townsfolk wanted to inflict on the priests, and on the sisters who served with them in the Mission of the Sacred Heart. On Sunday, November 22, the Simbas prepared for travel a car on the railroad which bypassed the river rapids to Stanleyville. They ordered the priests and nuns aboard.

Was the move to be, as the rebels said, for the protection of the clergy? Père Schuster doubted the benevolence of their aims. For as he mounted the plain wooden coach he saw that already it contained a man, his wife and four children, and two older women; he noted that each of them, including two very young daughters, bore severe cuts and bruises.

Whoever the assailant, he had struck only moments before; the blood still ran from their wounds.

Even prior to this day Cyril Taylor and his family and the two older women had learned painfully the means by which the rebels carried out their malevolence. At first the fact of being missionaries stood them in well; after a while neither religion nor nationality nor a long record of devotion to the Congolese protected them from maltreatment.

All served under Worldwide Evangelization Crusade. Cyril Taylor and his wife Joy, a couple now in their middle forties, arrived in Congo in 1942 from their home in New Zealand. A nearly bald man with flashing eyes and heavy brows, he impressed one with his earnestness. He was a gifted linguist. In 1962 he and Joy settled in Lowa, two hundred miles upstream from Stanleyville, to open a Bible School for training future Congolese pastors.

The two older women were WEC pioneers. The seventy-year-old Mary Harrison was the widow of C. T. Studd's successor. After Jack Harrison died some years back, she carried on, sometimes alone, sometimes as partner with Muriel Harman. Miss Harman's age made her eligible for retirement, but her heart kept her in Congo. In thirty-seven years on the field she visited her home in Canada only three times.

Muriel Harman was a nurse and a teacher. Once she went to tend a sick missionary at another station. As her African helper set up her camp cot, he asked where her sheets were.

"Sheets?" she said. "Do I have any sheets? You have to put something on the sores of lepers."

The plight of this little mission group became desperate. The authorities at Leopoldville learned of it, and dispatched two helicopters to bring them out. The missionaries, however, were not at their station when help arrived. They had been removed to across the river and imprisoned. The futile flight by the helicopters only resulted in further ill treatment of the prisoners.

By someone's order the Taylor party was transported by river launch from Lowa to Ponthierville, arriving there November 22. At Ponthierville Joy Taylor received head wounds and with the others underwent abuses little short of death itself. That same day the Simbas placed them aboard the train to ship them on; before long both Protestant and Catholic missionaries journeyed under strict guard to Stan.

The following day they alighted at the rail terminal at Rive Gauche, a section of Stan consisting mostly of marshaling yards, docks, and government installations. The Simbas thrust them into a dark dungeon underneath the headquarters of the Military Police.

This cellar, which measured about thirteen feet square, was already occupied by other prisoners, the majority of them priests or nuns. The new folk arriving from the south swelled the total in that lightless, airless, torrid hole to near forty.

Across the river from the main part of Stan, only a mile more or less from the Résidence Victoria, where on this same night the hostages spoke with keen hope of liberation soon—in the same city, yet they might as well be five hundred miles away. In their cellar the Rive Gauche prisoners knew nothing of the events on the other side; and over there, none was even aware that in Rive Gauche there were people in desperate need of immediate help.

That Monday night terrible things went on in the cellar; the indignities, the cruelties, the inhumanities plumbed new depths. Then on Tuesday the Simbas permitted Joy Taylor and her two small daughters to occupy a room on ground level in a building on the military compound. Never without an armed guard, she hung back in a corner because in the room also were about twenty young rebels, the *Jeunesse*. They milled about idly, threatening and taking delight in their ability to strike terror in the hearts of those within their power.

All the time she was in the room Mrs. Taylor heard the popping of gunfire across the river in the main section of Stan. She of course did not know that paratroopers and mercenary forces engaged the rebels in a fight for the city. Nor could she anticipate that someone among the national troops across the river would nearly bring about her death through the casual firing of a mortar shell on Rive Gauche.

A thundering blast shook the building. In the cloud of dirt and dust that choked the room she saw that some of the rebel youths had been killed; others were injured. And in the confused melee she watched in frozen terror as a Simba guard grabbed up a machete and sprang wildly at her and the children.

He swung and slashed as he cursed her for the direct hit on the building. The older girl, six-year-old Colleen, dropped to the floor. Blood flowed from a long gash across her forehead. Pauline, half the age of her sister, slumped in a heap, her head cut open in two places. The enraged rebel then aimed a swipe at Joy Taylor's heart. By instinct she threw up an arm as protection.

Her arm caught the force of his mighty swing. By the time his fury abated, she had received several slashes and her arm was broken in two places. Through tears of fright and pain, Joy Taylor gathered up the bleeding girls in her own bleeding arms and staggered with them outdoors. There she lay under a palm tree. Pauline sobbed hysterically.

Cyril Taylor heard his daughter's cries. He rushed past the cellar guards to run up the steps to his battered loved ones. He got them to the basement. There Muriel Harman and the nuns did what they could to patch up the wounds, but had no proper means of treating the victims.

An uneasy truce between the jailed and their jailers endured throughout the next day. That evening the Simbas routed out the occupants of the cellar, except for Mrs. Taylor and the two girls, who were very ill from their injuries, and Mrs. Harrison, who in all the goings-on had broken her hip. The others the rebels forced one by one to walk up the stairs to an area outdoors in front of the building. There they administered beatings and sent the group back

down into the dungeon. Ten minutes later an angry voice called
down the dark steps:

"Everyone must come out!"

Soldiers hurried down to get the people out. Again they permitted Mrs. Taylor and the girls to stay. Seeing that Mrs. Harrison
was unable to walk, two Simbas tried to carry her. She was too
heavy, however, so in their anxiousness to get up to where the
others were they dropped her on the stairs and ran outside. There
was too great a promise of excitement to be bothered with an old
woman.

The guards led the prisoners to a house on the Military Police
compound. In the beleagured company were Taylor and his two
sons, Murray, fifteen, and Barry, twelve; Miss Harman; Péres
Schuster and Trausch from Ponthierville; nuns and other priests;
and three Belgian civilians. Because night had fallen, two rebels
carried a large candle and an oil lamp to light the way.

The Simbas thrust the prisoners into the house, which contained
two rooms joined by a wide archway. The light bearers planted
their candle and lamp on the floor of the larger room. Here the
soldiers forced the men to line up. They shoved the women into
the other chamber. If the sinister setting in the dim light was not
unnerving enough, certainly the entrance of a sergeant and two
men with submachine guns overwhelmed the captive group with
the feeling of doom. By the flickering dance of the candle, stuck
down near the door, the prisoners saw that the new arrivals had
come from a fresh bout with smoking hemp.

"You call yourselves men of God," the sergeant spat out at the
men who stood before him. He cursed. "You are not men of God.
You are liars. All of you. You say you do not call the bombers by
your *phonees,* yet the bombs fall. They fall because you want them
to fall. Liars! Liars!"

The candle and the oil lamp cast weird shadows on the wall.
Long beards and robes took on grotesque shapes and sizes. Père
Schuster recalled the shadow pictures he had made as a boy
against the church wall in Luxembourg, and how fat old Père
Kinsch, his village priest, would get between the candles and the

wall and make the funniest picture of all. But reverie was to be brief.

The sudden burst from a gun shattered the murky air.

Cyril Taylor slumped to the floor. In the adjoining room the women screamed. Then as if they recognized that all in the house stood directly in the face of death and that somehow screaming was not appropriate for the occasion, their shrieks ceased, and were replaced by the scarcely audible mutterings of fervent prayer.

The one who had shot the Protestant missionary turned slightly. He fired again, at the next man in line. His spray cut a priest almost in half.

Schuster took quick stock. How many ranked between the dead and himself?

"*Trois, quatre, cinq*—three, four, five," the priest counted. Number three crumpled to the floor. Schuster himself was number twelve—no, number ten; the sons of the Protestant pastor had slipped from the line and hugged the wall behind the archway. Out of the corner of his eye he saw they pretended they were dead.

Why not try that? At the next burst why not fall as though shot and crawl to where the boys lay? But why prolong the agony when there was no question that the Simbas intended to kill them all? The second gun was now in use. And number six had fallen, with not even time to gasp. The women looking on through the archway sobbed quietly for him.

Number seven. Number eight; several shots were required to stifle him.

Number nine, a Catholic brother next to Schuster, fell bleeding, but was not yet dead. Both guns were empty. Would Charles Schuster, the good priest of the bush, escape death for lack of ammunition?

No such smiling fortune, evidently. A soldier brought a new supply of cartridges. Hastily, the nervous gunner inserted another clip. He took aim at his next target, Number ten—Père Schuster. He squeezed the trigger . . .

The first three bullets raced past the priest and lodged in the wall behind him. The next two struck him in the chest. He fell beside the wounded brother. He would now lose consciousness, he dazedly said to himself in a queer sort of dialogue. *You will never know when the last bullet strikes.*

But an unconscious man does not feel the *whish* of a bullet past his head, which Schuster did. He does not feel the creeping process as his own and his neighbor's blood soaks into his garments. He is not aware of the sweat that wets his beard. But Charles Schuster retained the senses that told him all this was happening. Motionless, he watched as the heartless rebels now pushed the women into place at the feet of the fallen men.

Once again the gunners started their routine. Muriel Harman fell first, then one by one the nuns. Now there was not even the mumbling of prayers. Except for the report of the guns, all was eerily still.

Two nuns fell on his legs. Since the beatings in the cellar and in the yard his ankles had swollen and they pained him. How heavy these emaciated sisters lay on his legs. He tried to draw away.

"Make as if dead," whispered one who had not yet expired. Then she herself was gone.

With the fixedness of pleading the brother stared at the priest.

"I give you absolution," Père Schuster said in a throaty whisper. The brother's eyes then rolled back and froze in emptiness.

From somewhere down the line a voice began to shout in delirium. Schuster recognized it as that of a young priest from Holland. "Father . . . Father . . ." He spoke the name of his village pastor. Then he called for Heaven's help . . . and in a line of sight that Schuster discovered he had, he saw the muscles of the pained face relax as the Hollander slipped into a merciful coma.

The Simbas were not fooled by the Taylor boys, but went along with the attempt at deception and allowed them to escape. Murray and Barry hurried back to their mother and sisters and Mrs. Harrison in the cellar.

"Mummy," Murray said, fighting back the tears as he sank down beside her in the near blackness of the dungeon. "Mummy, Dad has gone to be with Jesus."

The man of his family now, Murray quietly commanded, "Let's pray." He began by offering thanks. Thanks? After the horror he had just come through?

"Thank you, dear God, for taking Dad out of all this misery."

But the expression of gratitude did not finish his prayer. He had a petition.

"And, dear Father," he prayed, speaking out with the firmness of conviction, "forgive the man who shot him, and forgive the other Simbas. They don't know what they're doing."

Now his prayer was completed. He spoke reassuring words to his mother.

"I'll take care of you. Barry and I will," he said. "We'll get food somehow for you and the girls and for Mrs. Harrison."

"But, if they come back down here—"

"They've gone. I don't think they'll come. And if they do, I'll still take care of you."

Younger Simbas did return, the profligate *Jeunesse*. Shortly after the sergeant led away the killers two young men entered the house to carry the bodies outside to a terrace. They grasped one corpse then another, dragged each through the doorway and threw it onto a heap that likely they would burn.

Several were carried out. Then they approached Père Schuster. Weakened and unable to flee the room where so many of his comrades had fallen—twenty-eight were dead, he thought as he had lain there—he now moved no muscle. The youths grasped him firmly under the arms and conveyed him to the pile.

"Heave!" one said. "The stack is getting high."

The next to be carried out was the young Dutch priest. A faint spark of life still burned in him. This startled the pair and caused an interruption in the macabre task.

"No one is allowed to live!" sang out one. His partner then pulled a large double edged knife from a rag girdling his middle. He cut the poor fellow's wrists first, then his throat.

"A deed for Patrice Lumumba!" the knifer shouted, and the other quite agreed.

In the course of moving the bodies they discovered another who squirmed. They planted the knife in him, then randomly in several others. But business before their sordid pleasure . . . they returned to the house for another cadaver.

In their absence Père Schuster mustered more strength than was his due; he slid off the pile of bodies and stole away into the darkness.

He first found refuge in what seemed to be an abandoned hut. But he calculated that no building was really safe. Before dawn broke he dragged himself to a manioc patch, holding a handkerchief to his wounds to stop the bleeding. The grossly overgrown plot, a tangled jungle of bushes, vines, and weeds, would provide good cover. He settled down here—for how long, or what should he do next, he did not know.

The morning came, and after an interminable time the sun stood overhead. The afternoon passed just as slowly. Sometimes he slept. Sometimes he thought of the years he had spent in Congo, of what he had tried to accomplish here. Occasionally, he permitted himself to dream of the pine forests that covered the hills of Luxembourg, of good Père Kinsch, the buoyant priest who had taught him as a boy about God.

He thought about God and the priest. Whom would he encounter first?

Just how close he lay to danger he did not find out until the following morning, Friday, November 27. At that time the mercenary army holding the main section of Stan decided to cross the river and reclaim Rive Gauche for the national government. On that morning the priest in his hiding place heard the usual noises of rebel shooting and drunken conduct. Then he thought he heard sounds that were different—the reports of different guns, different voices, a different speech. He hazarded to peek from his place of concealment. There near a tall nest of termites he spotted Belgian soldiers.

The boys of Pastor Taylor talked with the soldiers. Rescue had come!

Père Schuster stood up from his hiding place in the manioc patch. And no more than six yards away, five Simba soldiers rose up from where they had been hiding. Glancing at the rebels he recognized as having had a part in the horrors of the other night, and who he chillingly realized had lain so near him during these days and nights of waiting, he ran into the arms of the soldiers.

The Simbas ran, too. They sped off the other way.

17

"That Your Name Be Honored"

Near downtown Leopoldville stands a venerable hostel whose appetizing table and wide, breeze-swept verandas have long been favorites of missionaries traveling in Congo. This establishment, Union Mission House, became the haven for people displaced from the rebel zones.

Al and Jean Larson, Ione McMillan and her boys, the Del Carpers, the Bob McAllisters, and others from Stanleyville took up temporary residence there. Next door, Mary Rutt shared an apartment over LECO's main Congo headquarters. Kinso and Ma Kinso stayed across the street with the British Baptists.

Some folk scattered over the city; the Tucker family and Chuck and Muriel Davis lived at the American Baptist compound across town, the Paxmen in quarters that Stan's new university had borrowed in order to carry on its work "in exile."

At one time or another they all gathered at the hostel. In the dining room at mealtimes or on the upper veranda after breakfast or dinner they turned the old place into a sort of spiritual command post; here they prayed, they planned, they compared experiences, and they swapped scraps of information on the struggle that waged for the minds, the hearts, the very life breath of Congo.

220

Newsmen from the world's press dropped in at all hours to interview the refugees.

"How did people react to rebel pressure?" a correspondent asked one of the missionaries.

"Do you want to meet a brave man?" the missionary rejoined. The reporter nodded. "Do you see that man over there?" The missionary pointed to Al Larson at the far end of the veranda; Larson was helping his little daughter color a picture book. "There sits the bravest man in Congo."

He then related how Larson had exposed himself to Simba wrath time after time to safeguard the missionaries under his leadership, capping his account by telling how Larson had organized and led the rescue team to Kilometer 8.

Larson was at his best as in these tense days he gathered the people to pray for the fifty or so missionaries still held captive by the rebels, and attended to a dozen matters a day that fell on him as field leader of his mission.

The day after the Stanleyville massacre and rescue Larson gained a valued helper. Ralph Odman, general director of Unevangelized Fields Mission, realized that a rescue attempt was soon to be made so rushed from headquarters near Philadelphia to Congo; he wanted to be there to greet all who emerged from captivity—and to weep with the ones whom the day would leave weeping.

Larson drove to Leopoldville's airport in a car he had ordered from America months before but which had not yet been shipped from Leo to Stan. On the way back into the city he said to Odman, "I'm afraid we have to report the loss of all our vehicles—except the one we are in."

"Who cares about equipment!" exploded Odman. He said that what mattered was that so many of them had escaped.

"The Belgians have a word—*la peau*," Larson quipped. "One's skin, *la peau*, that's what matters."

He had not lost his sense of humor. Yet deep inside he knew that the skin, the body, life itself, had actually ceased to be the all-important thing.

A few of the Belgian paratroopers shed tears when they were ordered home before the rescue of foreign hostages was completed. They received a hero's welcome in Brussels, but from some quarters of the world strong criticism rained on Belgium and the United States for the drops on Stan and Paulis. On the other hand, some voices spoke out that liberation of hostages should have been carried off with no cock of the ear to world opinion.

Nevertheless, the governments that planned the mercy drops were determined to prove to the critics that their objective was humanitarian, not military—a dash into Congo for a quick rescue of two concentrated groups of foreigners, and then an immediate withdrawal. This was international diplomacy, and it had to be accepted.

But the missionaries feared that apathy would once again set in; and their colleagues behind rebel lines were now in greater danger than before the intervention. The rebels stirred with new vengeance.

So they redoubled their prayer efforts. And being practical men, Larson, Odman, and Dick Sigg, who had arrived from Uganda, sallied forth every morning from Union Mission House to the American, Belgian, and British embassies. They went there to remind those officials that folk in the interior still needed rescuing, and please, please not to forget it.

There were limitations on how fast the mercenary-led Congolese army could penetrate into rebel territory. The road to Bafwasende, where several persons were imprisoned, was red dust on dry days and deep mud on wet days. North of Stan, on the road to Banalia, where Mary Baker, Margaret Hayes, Dr. Sharpe, and others were being held, the bridges had been destroyed. Besides poor road conditions leading to these centers, progress was impeded also by the fact that it was taking longer than expected to subdue the rebels in Stanleyville.

In the prayer sessions, none beseeched the Lord more fervently than Ione McMillian. Her prayers were for others, not for herself, though she was faced with the prospect of rearing her six boys alone. The periods of Bible reading and prayer with her sons reminded her that Hector always used to take the lead in this. One day she spoke to a friend of the change that came over Hector shortly before he died.

"Those times toward the last that he shifted responsibility to me," she said, "perhaps he was aware of what he was doing, perhaps he wasn't. But I see now that in it God was preparing me to do what I now have to do without my husband."

None at the hostel seemed stronger in faith than Ione McMillan. One day she replied to the question of a newsman who interviewed her:

"No, I don't think it strange—not strange at all—what we have had to go through. When we give our lives to Christ, we say that He knows best—and we mean it. He doesn't expect us to be foolhardy, but hardy; and if we suffer in serving, well, others before us have suffered."

Some who heard her speak recalled that in his last letter home, which the world was now reading, Dr. Paul Carlson had called this the century of the Christian martyr.

In the prayer sessions Ione McMillan led out in her clear, even voice, and as she prayed there seemed to be a radiance both in her speech and on her gentle face.

"Dear Father," she said one day in praying for the missing missionaries, and one might have amost thought she was conversing with Hector, "help Jean Sweet to keep her glasses. She has very poor vision without them. She would have a hard time getting about if the rebels took them from her.

"And let kind hands minister to the needs of Nora Parry; she's a gentle person, and people of that nature don't thrive well under harshness. She's frail of health, and she and Dennis have two children with them to care for."

She prayed for Margaret Hayes, the English nurse who in the last few years had been Mary Baker's partner at Bopepe. It was Margaret who visited at the seminary station of Banjwadi when the Davis family was arrested early in August. She heard that Mary Baker suffered at the hands of the Simbas, so caught a ride on a truck back to Bopepe to share Mary's burdens.

"You know about Margaret," Ione prayed. "She has a speech difficulty. She's an unusual person to have come to the mission field with such a handicap. I'm concerned, dear Father, that should she speak to a Simba with her impediment and he cannot understand what she says, he may get very angry and mistreat her."

Chester Burk, held at Bafwasende, was one who had been physically weak, and Dolena, his wife, suffered from an eye disease. She asked the Lord to be their strength.

"And give dear Mary Baker the patience she needs."

Mary had a certain kind of patience that never wore out; by it, she stuck to a job, no matter how tedious or lasting, until it was completed. But there were some persons and some ways they did things that were a great trial to Mary. She liked to see things done properly. The Simbas could not be depended on for doing things as right as Mary thought they should be done.

"So, Lord, give her a special measure of patience toward them."

There was another to be remembered in her prayer. "Those folk out there in the forest—they need someone to buoy up their spirits. Maybe, dear God, Laurel McCallum is the person for that. She's a very brave soul, and just as Bob and Alma McAllister wouldn't let us get down in the dumps at Kilometer 8, perhaps You will use Laurel to cheer up those who must not lose hope in their dark days of captivity.

"And another thing, Lord, You know what wonderful fellowship Laurel has with the Congolese people. She has such a winning way about her that it would break down the heart of even a lion."

Others in the circle of bowed heads and burdened hearts prayed for Dr. Sharpe and his family being held prisoner at Banalia, and for nurse Ruby Gray and the John Artons with their daughter Heather.

"This schoolgirl is so vulnerable to the evil intentions of some of the Simbas," said Jean Larson. Before they left Kilometer 8, the missionaries had received reports that Heather's vacation from her school in England was not all misfortune. During this trying time she was a great comfort to her parents, although they wished that for her safety she had not come to visit them. The native tongue that she learned as a girl on various Congo stations quickly returned to her, and she took an active role in evangelism work among the Conglese youth.

The missionaries felt they could not just pray that their colleagues would be delivered. They hoped they would be, and they reminded the Lord that He had once delivered Daniel from a hopeless den. But many had died. The death of Hector McMillan, for example, must have been in the will of God just as clearly as the escape of Ione and his sons had also been in His will.

"We ask, our Father," Al Larson prayed one day, "that whether by life or by death of Your suffering servants that Your name will be honored in Congo."

They petitioned God's blessing on the members of other missions who still had not been freed or even heard from. And they made the Congolese Christians a particular object of their praying. Often they spoke of the love and faithfulness of their Congolese brethren.

To those who hadn't heard the story Bob McAllister said that one day he had been sitting at tea with the Kinsos at the apartment over LECO in Stan. Through the window he saw a Congolese man carrying a suitcase up the street.

"That's my case!" McAllister exclaimed. It was a piece of luggage that had remained at their station at Ponthierville when they left on a trip in July, but he recognized the bag as his own. He ran down the apartment stairs, reaching the sidewalk just as the man walked by. Close enough now to see who carried the suitcase, he recognized the man as well.

The fellow had worked for the McAllisters at Ponthierville. McAllister called his name.

"*Bwana,* it's you!" the carrier said excitedly. "I've brought clothes for your little girl and food for you. I thought you would need these things."

All the way up that dangerous road—a seventy-mile hike just to supply the missionary with some items he might need!

"*Bwana,* I asked God to help me find you in the city, and here you come to meet me on the street!"

Everyone stopping at Union Mission House soon heard of the faithfulness of Bo Martin, who had gone to prison at Banalia rather than abandon Mary Baker and Margaret Hayes to the pitilessness of the Simbas. But Bo was not the only Congolese to accompany a missionary to prison.

At Ian Sharpe's jungle hospital the rebels one day arrested Masini Philippe, pastor of the village where the hospital was situated. Masini held membership in the political party that opposed the People's Republic. Dr. Sharpe intervened for the pastor and got him released. Later when the Simbas arrested Dr. Sharpe and his family, Masini Philippe and his son Mbongo Samuele stood by the missionaries.

Every refugee around the big table at the hostel spoke of the firmness that African believers displayed under intense pressure. Teachers carried on though government salaries failed to arrive. Those who had a little shared with those who had nothing. Pastors and flocks alike met to worship God at times when prudence said they should not venture out of their homes.

One day on the front veranda of the mission hostel a Congolese pastor conversed seriously with Ione McMillan. He said he had heard that her husband was killed by the rebels and two of her sons were wounded.

"Yes," she said, and smiled in appreciation of his sympathy. "And many Congolese have lost their lives."

"I am struck with great force," he said, "on how high is the price of bringing the Gospel of Christ to Congo."

In her presence he dedicated himself anew to his Christian calling.

"I'm a different man because of seeing you," he said, and there seemed to be a glow about his face, centering in the light of his eyes. "Through the suffering we have seen our foreign friends endure, and which we ourselves have endured, the cold, stony soul of God's church in Congo is melting."

He was sure that with their hearts contrite, the Lord was going to perform miracles through the refining fires.

Asani was constantly on everyone's mind. It appeared that the president of the Evangelical Church of Upper Congo had been shunted aside when he barely escaped across the Uganda border during the earliest days of the Simba regime. Now with the picture having come into better focus, no one doubted that what seemed to be happenstance was actually God's way of preserving this stalwart leader for another day of service.

How many Congolese died under the hand of the rebels was anyone's guess. Some said forty thousand; others believed a hundred thousand would be a fairer estimate. In so many instances the victims were the very hope of Congo. Had Asani and Yokana Jean, director of UFM's schools, been caught by the rebels, these two men in all likelihood would have suffered the fate of so many other leaders.

"In village after village the work of the last twenty-five years is gone," a veteran missionary said to Al Larson. And what promise did the next generation hold? It was also anyone's guess as to how many ten year olds had been given a gun and taught to murder in order to gain advancement in the Simba ranks.

What lay ahead for missions in northeast Congo was simply pioneering labor. Needed would be stalwarts willing to face challenges which most of the world did not know existed.

Around the temporary missionary quarters in Leopoldville one question predominated:

"When can we get back to our work?"

There was no bitterness, just an eagerness to return to schools and dispensaries and bookshops and churches. But some of course would not be going back. The ranks of Protestant missionaries thus far in the year had been depleted by eleven. One afternoon a second McMillan son joined his older brother in saying he believed that someday he would return to Congo to teach his father's killers about the love of Jesus.

For the time, no missionary would be able to work in that vast area still dominated by the rebels. The burden of starting over would fall squarely on the shoulders of the Congolese Church. When the way opened Asani and Yokana Jean and their counterparts in other church groupings would go back to their villages; they would till the parched and hardened ground and plant the early seed.

The blood of the martyrs would provide the irrigation.

The missionaries spent almost as much time at the Leopoldville airport as they did at Union Mission House. Every plane bringing refugees from the troubled zone was a plane to meet. Dick Sigg and Ralph Odman skipped hardly one, always hoping that some of their missing missionaries would be on board.

Countless reunions—some joyous, some tragic—occurred whenever a giant American transport dropped open its rear section to reveal a hundred bloody or unkempt and distraught survivors of Simba violence, and relatives or friends surged to the ramp to claim their own. Some evacuees emerged weeping hysterically; some walked out speechless, disbelieving that no longer were they crammed into a damp, fetid cell in Bondo or Yakusu or Bambili or some other town in northeast Congo. Always on every landing ambulances backed up to the plane to receive the sick and wounded.

Often Al Larson and Del Carper haled friends who had come in from Stan. One day they met Karichos and other merchants who put together *Le Central* for benefit of the prisoners.

"Oh, Monsieur Carper," said Karichos, "I never did get you your hearing aid, did I?"

Larson ran across Mike Hoyt and the other American consul staffers; one day Peter Rombaut flew in. Larson learned that all the men with whom he and Carper shared the room at the Hôtel des Chutes arrived in Leo without injury, among them the planter Dubois.

"My whole life has been changed," he was still insisting. He seemed glad to have gone through the horror of Stan in order to gain an acquaintance with God and His book.

Word came positively that Bob Latham, the friend of the folk at Kilometer 8, had been murdered. As an immediate aftermath to the killing of Hector McMillan, Simbas sought out Latham and hacked him to death with a machete in his yard.

Refugees arriving from Stan said the place was now a city of the dead. The buildings bore few scars, but death permeated the air. Twenty-five Simbas were shot in an administration office near Lumumba Square the morning the mercenaries arrived in the city. Their bodies were sprawled for days afterward on the blasted ruins of the monument to Patrice Lumumba.

Another whose naked corpse was thrown on the heap there was the demented Kingese. This first chief of Stanleyville under the Simba regime, who had ordered the extinction of religion, was shot one day by a South African mercenary as he ran from a forest near Stan, shouting, *"Mai mai,* Mulele!" He was one of the few of the top rebel command to be caught. Gbenye, Soumialot, and General Olenga, news reports said, had escaped to neighboring countries and were dickering for new supplies to carry on the rebellion.

Dogs without masters ran wild in Stan; they routed among the unburied bodies. Shops, homes, and offices were completely sacked. Every safe in town was blown open and robbed. Who had done this? Not the rebels; they fled the center of town too quickly. And not many African citizens were moving about. This was a war of the mercenary soldier.

The government had hired these soldiers of fortune to put down the rebellion and to snatch helpless victims from dangerous situations, and for the greater part they did their jobs with skill and courage. And to the same degree as their daring they felt that whatever they laid hands on belonged to them to help compensate for all their trouble.

Among the mercenaries were oddballs, characters with real color, men who had joined up to get away from home, to make money, to obtain a license to kill, unlovely specimens of mankind who could laugh while they shot down innocent civilians. There was also a sprinkling of dedicated men who felt they were fighting for the right and every day risked their lives in doing it.

Whatever the motive, whatever the conduct after the battle

ended, without the mercenaries constitutional government in Congo by now would have died, and perhaps every foreigner with it.

The rebel propaganda had been so persuasive that it continued on without any effort to direct it. The people saw the foreign soldiers in the hire of the Congolese government. They did not know that most came from South Africa, Rhodesia, and Kenya. Instead, they saw the color of their skins and heard them speak English and were impressed by the word passed by the knowing ones:

"See—the Simbas said Americans roamed our country and killed our people." To many of the Congolese every mercenary came straight from New York City.

Larson shook his head in dismay over one eyewitness account of happenings in Stanleyville. The stadium there was again the scene of people's courts. Now it was the turn of the nationals to ask the public jury to decide whether a captured rebel should live or die.

"Was he a good Simba?" If the crowd clapped, the man would be set free. If the crowd booed, the fellow was summarily shot.

Some said the government cleanup had executed five hundred. Scores were toppled off the Tshopo Bridge and washed downstream by the falls.

At least the shootings were not dismemberments, and the bodies dumped in the river were eaten by crocodiles and not by cannibals.

During this period the world recalled afresh the atrocities the Nazis had committed in their death camps against the Jews. The statute of limitations for punishing war criminals neared; German officials reinspected Auschwitz and other camps in their deliberations on whether to extend the punishable period. Somehow there seemed to be a strange and ominous parallel between those horrible days of Nazi savagery and what the Simbas had perpetrated in the interior of Congo.

By no means could the inhumanities be laid simply to racial

hatred. What the rebels did to foreigners they did in greater number and sometimes in more perverse degree to fellow Congolese. Neither was bitterness toward other nationalities the overriding cause. Rather, the outworking of rebel purpose seemed to indicate that both racism and nationalism became tools in the hands of men who were determined by any means to set up and continue their own regime.

Deliberate killing made up a part of the strategy, and one wondered if the plan shown to Sonia Grant in October—to wipe out missions and Christianity—was not getting serious consideration on the part of Simba leaders. The timing of the incident at Isangi would seem to say it was.

A belated report arrived from this Catholic mission eighty miles downriver from Stan. It revealed that three members of the mission were killed five days before the paratroopers made their first landing.

On the very day after Gbenye pulled back Paul Carlson and the seven other Americans from certain death at the hands of the angry mobs in Stan and decided to save them for bargaining, rebel troops carried on their carnage at Isangi. They beat and tromped on a priest and two nuns. First of the three to die was Sister Mary-Antoinette, a fifty-two-year-old American from New York.

Ten others were designated for execution that day; several times the rebels began to carry out their intentions. Each time at the last moment, however, some small providential event kept them from it.

Once in a while the planeloads of refugees included rescued missionaries. One night the folk from Ekoko and Aketi mission stations arrived. Dorothy Scholten, the first of the missionaries to be widowed in this affair, was safe. Her five young children and the other workers from the two stations also came in unharmed.

Betty O'Neill had promised Bill Scholten at the time of his arrest that she would stick by Dorothy to care for the children. One day after Scholten died a Simba offered to exempt her from arrest because she was not American. This Irish nurse refused, however, and chose prison in order to stay near the young widow who needed her.

WEC missionaries John and Dolores Gunningham arrived on one plane. They told how John had been rescued by a mercenary column just scant minutes before he was to walk a log bridge, and by that walk to be dropped by the fire of a machine gun into the river. There he like others would have become food for the crocodiles.

Aubrey Brown, also of WEC, arrived with his family by a near escape. The rebel captain of their town planned to transport him at four o'clock to Paulis, where he was to be killed. That noon Brown locked his family in their house and while he waited they prayed for a miracle.

It came at one thirty—in the form of thirty mercenaries.

One UFM couple, the Kerrigans—who had been in Congo almost as long as Kinso and his wife—had found a temporary home in the tin-mining town of Bunia. Other missionaries evacuated the area, but Mrs. Kerrigan was determined to stay on.

Almost against their will they were finally evacuated to Leopoldville.

"We had fine fellowship with the Christians at Bunia," she said the night of their arrival. An enraptured audience sat on the upper veranda at the mission hostel and listened while she talked. "Good Simbas and bad Simbas often visited us. When the good ones came, I let them in because making inspections was a part of their job."

"What did you do when bad ones showed up and demanded to get in?" someone asked her.

"Humph!" she snapped. "I put my foot down and said, 'You can't come in. Not talking that vile talk and waving that gun around, you can't.' "

And none of her hearers doubted that in the four months they lived among the rebels Mrs. Kerrigan ever met up with more than she could conveniently handle.

Most of the traffic between Leopoldville and the interior of Congo moved in the direction of Leo. Yet one flight to the far north, into the Ubangi region, drew more than ordinary interest. On board in a plain wooden casket rode the body of the slain Paul Carlson.

The remains of the medical missionary had been flown out of Stan on that first day of rescue. In ceremonies at the Leopoldville airport two marines draped an American flag over the casket. The body could have gone to America for full honors and a hero's burial. But Lois Carlson decided otherwise.

Her husband belonged to Africa, and in Africa his body would stay.

The DC-4 of Air Congo landed on the dirt strip of Gemena, a government post that was to be the transfer point in Paul Carlson's last journey. Missionaries and African Christians placed the hallowed box into a truck for the forty-mile trip to Karawa, where the doctor once had practiced the healing arts and learned to speak in Lingala.

The road to Karawa ran through thick forest and palm groves and beside coffee plantations and towering brown anthills. In their grass-roofed mud huts strung along the way people heard the truck coming, ran to the roadside to meet it. Already reports of the death of *Monganga Paulo* had penetrated the jungle, and the simple tribesmen of the region felt keen sorrow.

"He saved my life," a man called out at one place. A woman showed her respect by removing her kerchief and clasping her hands behind her head. The truck hardly lingered any place; it was necessary that the burial party arrive before sundown to select a site for the grave. A young African pastor who joined the party en route shouted to all they met in the road:

"Here is the body of the doctor who died. Come to Karawa for the burial tomorrow."

At Karawa stood a large mission station sponsored jointly by the Evangelical Covenant and Free Churches of America. In only minutes after the truck arrived there hundreds of Congolese gathered. The Karawa station, as well as stations elsewhere in the

Ubangi, were now without resident missionaries. Because the area was considered too vulnerable to rebel attack the missionaries had moved across the border to the Central African Republic.

Those who brought the body to Karawa greeted their Congolese friends in silent, solemn embrace. It was the first meeting for most of them since early in September. One who had accompanied the body all the way from Leo and had brought the doctor's New Testament for Mrs. Carlson, said to the sad throng which stood on the steps of the cement-block church, "I am grieved to come back under these circumstances."

A small African humpback spoke up, and the deep serenity of his voice came clearly through the gloom of semidarkness:

"We don't understand now, but God's will has been done."

Pastor Matthieu Bangi had come from Wasolo, from where the doctor was taken in September.

"He liked us," he said. This short, simple appraisal of the relationship between them said much and said it with eloquence.

The following morning a small plane ferried in Lois Carlson and her two children, Wayne, nine, and Lynette, seven, and a few missionaries from the evacuation quarters. They flew to Gemena, then traveled the same bumpy road to Karawa. During the funeral Lois Carlson spoke to the hushed throng that overflowed the church.

"God has called my husband, Paul," she said. "I leave his physical body here as a memorial and as a reminder to you whom he served. I know he would have chosen to stay with you."

There remained only the procession down a palm-lined lane to a tiny burial ground that contained the graves of missionaries whom disease had felled in previous years. There his bearers lowered Paul Carlson's body into the earth. To the African, it made a difference where a man was buried; he wanted to rest among people to whom he belonged.

Paul Carlson was in the right place. He had arrived home in the Ubangi. Forever until the crowning day he would be one of theirs.

18

Triumph
in Tragedy

Christmas approached. Almost three dozen Protestant missionaries
—most of them of Unevangelized Fields—stayed hostages of the
rebels. Priests, nuns, merchants, planters, and other aliens in many
locations remained under rebel dominance.

The situation had never been more desperate.

Gradually the number of refugees at Union Mission House
dwindled. Families or remnants of families flew to their homes in
the United States or England or Germany or Canada or wherever
home was to wait out the uncertainties of the present and the
probable worsening of conditions in the near future. Al Larson and
Jean and the Dick Sigg family stayed on. They vowed not to leave
Congo until the last of their folk were liberated—or dead.

Those who had met to pray and plan on the Mission House
veranda now joined other bands of faithful intercessors in scattered areas of the world—in England, for example.

The London office of UFM is quartered in a house in placid
Ealing Common. There the staff and close friends of the mission
gather each Christmas season for a time of happy get-together.
This Christmastime, however, the usual spirit of good fellowship
slipped quietly into the deeper communion of petitioning prayer.

And in the United States—at the UFM office near Philadelphia —clothing for the destitute refugees poured in like an avalanche. With their gifts the people offered their prayers, for those who had come out of Congo and for those whose fates were still unknown.

President Lyndon Johnson communicated his sympathy to the sorrowing. In different communities attention focused on different missing missionaries. In Virginia, the people felt great concern for Mary Baker; in Western Canada, for Chester and Dolena Burk; at Mildmay Mission Hospital in London's East End, where they had trained, for Ian and Audrey Sharpe and Jean Sweet; in Northern Ireland, for Ruby Gray; in Perth, Australia, for Laurel McCallum.

Père Charles Schuster arrived in Luxembourg. After treatment for his chest wounds he got together with his boyhood parish priest, the fat and jolly Père Kinsch. The elder man was a city pastor now; in his plain but cheery apartment the two met to speak of old times and of violent days in Congo. Often they prayed for their confreres who were still held captive and for the bush people who nowadays had to get by without the regular visits of the good gray priest.

In the Central African Republic where Paul Carlson had left his wife and children, Lois recuperated from wounds that were as deep and painful as if they had been inflicted by tribal lances.

All over Northern Ireland a former missionary to Brazil, Joe Wright, alerted groups to pray. In country and city churches ministers climbed the steep steps to their very high pulpits and reminded their people of the names and needs of the remaining hostages.

Bob and Alma McAllister were now home in Belfast. Their experiences at Kilometer 8 put them on the front pages of the newspapers. Churches invited them to speak on the lessons that could be drawn from Congo. The many members of their two families tried to help the McAllisters forget the recent distresses by smothering them in natural Irish hospitality.

One evening Bob and Alma gathered with the relatives for a singsong. For two hours they sang old favorite hymns and drank tea and ate generous portions of cake. At nine o'clock Bob turned on a radio.

"It's time for the news from BBC," he said. "Maybe there will be something new from Congo."

There was—news that was both bad and good.

Three Protestant women and eleven Catholic sisters had been freed by a mercenary force in Bafwasende. The McAllisters listened intently to learn their identities . . . Louie Rimmer, an Englishwoman of sixty-five and a missionary to Congo since 1928 . . . Olive McCarten, a younger woman from England . . . Dolena Burk, from Western Canada.

"Are there others?" whispered Alma McAllister, hoping so hard there would be more.

The announcer said, as if he had heard her searching question, "The nuns and the three Protestants are the only ones accounted for."

Where were the others?

Had Bob Latham been able to make a second trip to Boyulu, the mission station on the old slave trail east of Stan, fewer missionaries would now be in the hands of the rebels. But he had transported only five persons to Kilometer 8 before the Simbas confiscated his truck. Personal contact with Boyulu was thus cut off.

The eight missionaries and Heather Arton, the schoolgirl visiting from England, carried on their teaching and training of the young, and caring for the physical ills of the people. But they carried on under a siege of terror.

The rebels at first gave no evidence of a defined policy toward them. The first encounter in August provided a preview of the confusion and inconsistency that was to come. Truckloads of Simbas rumbled in to the mission station; they looked fierce in their leaf coverings and daubs of white paint and wielding long, sharp spears.

"Grab these people! Tie them up!" the rebels said as they jumped from the trucks.

"Why do you want to tie us?" asked the bewildered Chester Burk.

A Simba spoke up that they always tied government officials.

"But we're not—"

"Isn't this the government station of Bafwasende?" asked the rebel leader.

It was not. The Simbas apologized, climbed back in their trucks, and drove off for the post five miles further along the road.

Many times in the days following the missionaries experienced torment at the hands of the ordinary soldiers, or the *Jeunesse* who clung to them. But when they happened around, the officers usually ran the soldiers and troublesome youths away, and for a while the torment let up. Sometimes the rebels created hardships for the missionaries because they were missionaries, and at other times they showed them favor for the same reason.

Mostly, however, the treatment was not good. In mid-November, though none was American, the Boyulu missionaries were arrested and interned in Bafwasende. Here occurred an answer to Ione McMillan's prayer. It was Laurel McCallum who by her readings from her *Daily Light* devotional and her transcendant spirit managed to buoy them up.

While held in Bafwasende John Arton and Chester Burk heard the Simba guards talk about the help the rebels were receiving from Peking and Moscow. All the prisoners heard speeches that Simba officers delivered to crowds that gathered outside their place of imprisonment.

"Plant big gardens," the officers advised. "Next year people whose skins are different, and whose eyes are different, will come. They will buy your produce, and then they will buy your gardens. They will give you a good price."

Some of the officers spoke of having been out of the country for training. These were the most polite of all the rebels. Never did they lose self-control in the presence of the foreigners. Yet the prisoners felt these cool, designing men to be deceptive and actually the most dangerous of their captors. It seemed they knew they could not stir up the villagers against the missionaries in terms of religion, so they chose to fight them in the guise of politics.

"These foreigners say they love you," the officers said to their men. "They lie to you. They are not in Congo because they love you and want to help you, but to exploit you."

One officer seemed so different from the others. A guileless young man named Jean Pierre, who was no more than thirty, he had switched from the national army to the Simbas to stay alive when the rebels captured the tin-mining town of Bunia. He frankly said to his prisoners that the Simbas were very wrong to pillage and kill the way they did.

After guarding them for three days he was pleased to tell the missionaries that the rebel chiefs had decided to let them go back to Boyulu.

"Do you mind if we sing?" asked Olive McCarten, expressing the joy of herself and her colleagues.

"Sing," said Jean Pierre. "I know some of your songs."

Before their release they sang English and Swahili hymns, and this drew several soldiers as listeners. Each time the singing was about to be stopped, a Simba would ask that they continue.

Finally one soldier asked, "Aren't you going to have the teaching today?"

He had attended mission services at some time in his life. The missionaries took the opportunity to tell their guards the Gospel. One young Simba said he had been a schoolboy at a mission station; he asked Dolena Burk to pray for him.

Palm leaves stuck from his waist and the *dawa* fetish hung from his neck. The cuttings on his forehead indicated his full allegiance to the rebel witchcraft.

"If you mix Christianity with your sorcery, how can I pray for you?" asked Mrs. Burk. "What would I say to God about you?"

"If I am involved in something I shouldn't be, pray that God will get me out of it," he said. His eyes welled with fear as he realized that other Simbas standing about had heard him.

He stiffened. "That's all I'm going to say about it," he said. "But pray for me."

Yet no other in that group of Simba soldiers appeared to blame him for his doubts. The expressions on some of their faces even seemed to indicate he was speaking their thoughts.

The missionaries left the prison at Bafwasende for their houses at the Boyulu station; these buildings now became their prison. The rebels assigned thirteen Simba guards to watch them night and day, not to enter their homes, but to stand at the windows and stare in continually. Such surveillance became difficult for the nerves.

Hardly had they got used to this arrangement when two rebel officers drove on to the station in a small automobile. The day was Tuesday, November 24, and they had fled Stanleyville ahead of the attack by paratroopers. They rushed up to the Simba guards.

"The foreign people in Stan are all in prison," they said in great agitation. "Why aren't these people in prison?" They demanded that all nine of the mission personnel be transported to Bafwasende at once.

"In your car?" asked John Arton, trying to hold in his amusement. But the newcomers were too upset to listen. They insisted that everyone on the station should get into the car at once.

Reasoning finally prevailed. More practical-minded rebels sent to Bafwasende for a second car, and the missionaries had time to pack their bags once more.

This time imprisonment took place in a large house that had belonged to a Belgian *commerçant*. Upon arrival the soldiers relieved their prisoners of luggage, watches, eyeglasses, shoes. All surrendered their glasses, that is, except Jean Sweet. This young first-term missionary was extremely handicapped without her thick lenses. As the guards began collecting glasses, she took hers off and slipped them to Olive McCarten, who dropped them in a pocket of her dress.

"Go into that other room," the guards then ordered. Olive took Jean's hand to lead her.

"Why are you leading her?" a Simba demanded of Olive.

"She can't see without her glasses," she replied.

"Where are they?"

She produced them from the pocket. He ordered Jean to put them on. He was a small fellow and easy to be picked out of a large group of soldiers, but the missionaries marked him for more than his stature. He was one who now had something to say every time a new guard came around and remarked about Jean Sweet's glasses.

"Oh," the little fellow would say, "she's blind without them. You should see her try to walk! You'd actually be sorry for her."

The room to which the Boyulu folk were led was already crowded. Seven priests and eleven Italian Catholic sisters sat in a space about ten feet square. The caps of the nuns had been removed, revealing lovely hair and youthful beauty.

For two days and nights the rebels kept up a drumfire of insults and minor persecutions. Boys not yet in their teens entered the overcrowded room to menace with their knives. They forced both men and women to kneel, then pressed lighted cigarettes into their mouths. At times they permitted no one to speak; the softest whisper brought stern reprisal from the guards. Each time a new guard reported for duty he rapped several of the prisoners on the head with a stick.

At one point a Simba challenged a nun, "Do you believe in God?"

"Yes," she replied resolutely, "I believe in God."

He struck her, perhaps to see if God would ward off the blow.

Another time a guard tossed off jauntily:

"There is no God."

"There is, of course there is," a number of the prisoners replied. He then smiled and said, "I merely joked. I know God lives."

If some of the rebels had failed ever to come in contact with God or His people, they had opportunity now to see under the most trying of circumstances the resolute faith of these who did know Him. Sixteen-year-old Heather Arton stanchly refused the comforts she might have enjoyed in order to stay with her parents and ease their burden in whatever way she could. The Simbas saw in Sister Lucia a fearless soul. She met their cursings with a firm rebuke.

"Curse all you want," she would answer. "God will have the final say."

And to cheer her fellow prisoners within earshot she would

smile and whisper, "Never mind. God *is*."

On the third day of their imprisonment—November 27—the women were summoned from the room. First, the Simbas made them pick grass in front of the house. Then they marched them barefoot to a nearby river. For the elderly Louie Rimmer a beating could hardly have been more cruel than the sharp stones which cut her feet.

The Simbas allowed the women to bathe, even waited some distance away to afford them privacy. Then they ordered the prisoners to return to the house.

"Sing something," a guard commanded Dolena Burk and Olive McCarten, who led the procession up from the river. Since jeering spectators lined the route, the women were not sure whether he jested or meant what he said. They began to sing "Onward, Christian Soldiers," and others behind them joined in.

The song lifted their thoughts from their burning feet; it made the march to the house more bearable. Shortly after they settled in the house again fighter-bombers of Tshombe's national air force, piloted by Cuban mercenaries, suddenly buzzed the encampment. Panic broke at the appearance of the planes. The Simba guards ran in every direction.

"If one of us is killed today, ten of you will die," said an extremely nervous rebel soldier. He ran to join his comrades under some bit of cover.

The prisoners heard the explosions, and the Britons among them knew they were not bombs, having been through the blitz of World War II. One who watched through a window saw two rockets drop in the river where the women had washed, one on a nearby plantation, and one in the forest. It was safe to say that inaccurate aiming had done no damage.

Actual results of the rocket firing meant little, however, to the Simbas. The prisoners in the house believed that rebel anger was too intense to stop short of violence.

How right they were. In a few moments several rebel soldiers rushed into the house and pushed the captives out onto the veranda.

"We've got to kill you," one Simba shouted, almost beside himself.

"Yes, now you will die!" screamed another.

"Disrobe! Disrobe!"

Gun barrels poked at the helpless prisoners, and because of them they began to remove their clothing. The Simbas started Chester Burk and John Arton and the seven priests in a rapid walk toward the river.

"Chester!" cried Dolena. They were almost trotting, nine abreast, prodded by men with submachine guns toward the river. Dolena shuddered at what was implied in the disrobing, even more than the angry predictions of the distraught soldiers. She had heard that often the Simbas took a person's clothing before they killed him. And there before her, her husband in only his undershorts was being marched away. Her own disrobing no longer seemed to matter; nothing mattered now except that Chester was being taken from her and she would never see him again.

"Chester!" she called.

But he was not permitted to stop, nor even to turn to answer her call.

On the veranda the Simbas separated three nuns from the others, three who had nursed in the village hospital. But the three were determined they would not be separated.

"If one will die, we all will die—together." The young, plucky Lucia spoke. She tossed her hair out of her face and in her defiance she was never more beautiful.

The Simbas, however, held the persuasion of brute force. They beat the nuns, pulled and shoved them, and brandished spears until they achieved the separation they wished. Wheeling to the Protestant women, they pointed, seemingly at random, at Dolena Burk, Louie Rimmer, and Olive McCarten.

"You and you and you," they shouted. "Follow the men to the river."

A total of twenty now were walking into the jaws of death. Without explanation, one who seemed to be the leader boomed out the order for the Protestant women to turn back. The guards who accompanied them relayed the command and at spear point chased them all the way to the house on the run. The nuns, too, were recalled.

"We'll kill you tomorrow," the Simba chief promised.

Just as Dolena Burk stepped up to the veranda the three women and Heather who had been held back were now being pushed in the way from which she had just returned. They must have been inside—she hadn't seen them as she ran up the path. And now she passed them on the steps so quickly that she had no time to speak even a word with them. But what was there to say? Laurel McCallum's eyes said it all:

Good-by. All hope of our living has vanished.

Dolena reached the doorway to the house. The muffled noise she heard in the distance made her stumble through it, choking, half-blind, but fully alert to its meaning. A volley of shots from the river told her everything.

The shots were no random shooting of guns. How many had fired, she did not know. But there had been several, and they rang out just as the shots always rang out at the command of an executioner.

She glanced quickly back to the path. Laurel McCallum, Jean Sweet, and Betty Arton and her daughter Heather were passing from sight. They now followed the men to the river, and no one was calling them back.

That evening the guards gave back the clothing to the eleven nuns and the three Protestant women who remained. The nuns demanded the guards to inform them of when they were to be killed.

"Oh, we're done with killing," an officer replied.

"Then you admit you shot my husband and the others," Dolena Burk said.

But to this charge he would not reply directly. However, in a day or so other women in the area wore the clothing of those who had been marched to the river. And further confirmation was provided by the wife of the colonel who commanded Bafwasende.

She stopped by the house where the number of prisoners was now cut in half. She had been born on the Boyulu station and so wished to inquire about a missionary she had known there.

"How is Mrs. Engelson, the nurse," she asked.

"You mean Mrs. Arton," corrected Mrs. Burk. "The Simbas killed her and her teenage daughter."

"Oh, yes," the colonel's wife replied. "My husband did tell me that. He said the girl need not have died. But she was so stubborn. If she had consented to the requests of the soldiers—"

Two days later the fourteen women prisoners walked under armed guard through the town toward a plantation which the rebel chiefs had told them would be their new place of detention. Officers started them on their way, but turned them over to the soldiers. The march was marked by one vexation after another. But each woman knew that what was occurring here in the town was nothing in comparison to what they could expect at the isolated house deep in the forest.

To get to the plantation they had to pass the Catholic mission at the edge of town. It was here that the nuns had lived and served; they were well acquainted with the neighborhood. Just beyond the mission the Simba officers had taken up residence. Sister Lucia let it be known from where she walked at the rear of the line that she was going to halt this procession before they went beyond that point of no return.

In front of the mission she dropped to her knees.

"Help us!" she shrieked. "We're being beaten!" She shouted at the top of her voice. She wanted to make sure the officers in their houses up ahead heard her.

Others knelt also and joined in her wailing.

"Stop them from beating us!" they pleaded.

Sister Lucia thought she was screaming a lie. The young soldiers and members of the *Jeunesse* had reviled them, but she had not seen any lay hands on one of the women. But under the circum-

stances she felt that her lie was no more than a venial sin. It wasn't
even a lie, however.

Up front a Simba soldier was right then in the act of slapping a
nun. And from where they lounged in their nearby quarters, the
officers heard the screams of the nuns. They ran to the road to see
what was happening.

"Kill us here," Sister Lucia said, and she wept enormous
tears.

"We will not," said one of the officers abruptly. He guessed that
the youth had been troubling the women; he chased them away. To
the women he said, "All of you go over to that house and stay
there." He pointed to a fairly large mud house just beyond the
mission. "I'll send Captain Jean Pierre to set your guard."

It was amazing how quickly Sister Lucia was able to compose
herself. Soneone asked her what had caused her to call out that
they were being beaten when she herself did not know they
were.

"Why," she said, shrugging off the intended praise. "The Lord
told me to do it."

Captain Jean Pierre, whom the women from Boyulu had met
during their first imprisonment and remembered for his kind treatment of them, soon proved that he relished his new assignment. He
vowed not only to guard the women, but to save their sanity as
well as their lives.

"I don't like to see you sit around so quiet," he said to Dolena
Burk one day in their current prison, the mud hut near the officers'
quarters. "What you people need is organization—military organization."

He proposed to provide it.

"Mama"—this is what he called Mrs. Burk—"you will be
Grand Elite of the Week." That meant she would supervise the
cleaning of the house and preparation of the meals. He designated
Sister Lucia as *Médicin Provincial*.

"I will expect a report on the physical condition of each person
in your company every day," he said.

Sister Lucia snapped to attention, returned him a smart Simba salute, an extended arm from the chest.

A few days later he entered their house to bark in jest:

"What report does the *Médicin Provincial* have to make this morning?"

"A sister is sick," replied Sister Lucia.

"What remedy do you recommend?"

"A trip to Rome."

He coughed and turned away, beaten in his little game.

"No," he said, facing her again and trying to look stern. "The medicine is too strong. You will all go to the dungeon instead."

In more serious moments he said he would lay down no rules except one: Stay out of the way of the Simbas.

One evening he said to the women, "Let's sing outdoors." He allowed them to set chairs near the house but in a position where they could enjoy the clear full moon.

The nuns sang some of their songs. Then in a pleasant voice he sang with "Mama" and Olive McCarten and Louie Rimmer the hymns that he said he once had learned at a mission in north Congo in more peaceful years. It was the nuns' turn again, and they sang a song to the tune of "Nearer, My God, to Thee."

"Mama," he said. "That's our hymn, too."

After they finished, he requested "Silent Night." They all sang it—some in Italian, some in English, some in Swahili.

Jean Pierre slept on a low native bed at the door of the prisoners' house. On the floor near him an oil lamp burned all night. Sometimes Dolena Burk awoke in the night, her soul burdened too heavily to sleep soundly. She would look over their company and marvel how peaceful life could really be in the midst of so great a calamity. Once she awoke with a start. She felt something crawling on her face. Something bit her on the leg. She reached across the sleeping Jean Pierre and turned up the wick on the lamp.

Driver ants!

The house had been invaded by voracious driver ants. They fed only on living creatures. Dolena looked to a corner where a chicken they intended to eat the following day had been half devoured.

"Jean Pierre!" she called. She shook him awake. Others in the house were now slapping at the ants, and soon all were wide awake. Guards who remained outside during the night roused up at the commotion.

"What is happening in here?" they demanded as they rushed to the door. Checking inside, they discovered the answer. Everyone was up and scratching and trying to get away from the ants.

"Go outside," Jean Pierre said. Especially did the white-robed sisters rush to the road in front of the house and begin stomping and shaking themselves furiously. The section of the room where they had lain held the greatest concentration of the ants.

The moon shone brilliantly. Its rays picked up the white habits of the dancing nuns, transforming them into luminescent but comic ballerinas. What a sight to behold! The nuns laughed. Though the biting of the ants stung, they enjoyed the funny spectacle they made in the middle of the road in the moonlight. Dolena and her companions laughed. So did the Simba guards. For half an hour the barriers that separated captive from captor disappeared. This first taste of freedom in many weeks was delicious, even if the portion was small and fleeting.

One of the Simbas doubled over in hilarious laughter as he watched the sisters shake the ants from their clothing. Then suddenly he stopped laughing. He, too, began to shake and squirm. He provided the others with the occasion for unrestrained merriment. He had stepped into the middle of a patch of the swarming ants.

Jean Pierre relayed the news in a "military communique" that someday his prisoners would stand a chance of rescue by Major Mike Hoare's mercenary column. But from what others said the women lost their optimism of ever getting away alive.

"If *les mercenaires* come near Bafwasende," an unfriendly officer warned one day, "we will kill you."

The three Protestant women thought the worst would come when one night a disgruntled officer—a Colonel Kisangi, who habitually popped up almost everywhere to cause trouble— abducted them and carried them away in his car to a house on the other side of Bafwasende. But faithful Jean Pierre! He alerted his superior officers. With the young captain they sped after the women and brought them back unharmed.

And then on December 18 the mercenaries came. They arrived in the morning, speeding into town so fast that they caught the rebels off guard. They came by way of a back road through the jungle. On that road their quick-moving column overtook a car, which by standard procedure they filled with lead. In inspecting it later they found a letter addressed to the Simba commandant of Bafwasende. It read:

"Mercenaries coming. Kill every foreigner at Bafwasende."

The massacre did not materialize, of course; had the timing varied slightly it may well have. Even the arrival of the mercenaries guaranteed no safety for the women.

Loud and unidentified gunfire on their road sent the occupants of the prison house searching for cover. Someone slammed shut the door. Dolena Burk, at that moment carrying a plate of food to Louie Rimmer, peeked through a crack in the door. What she saw caused her to drop the food and freeze with a sudden paralysis.

"Mercenaries!" she cried.

"Les mercenaires?" asked the nuns, disbelieving.

"Yes, but they've already gone by," she said. She wanted to weep. She had seen the last of a column of vehicles speed by their house.

Some of the sisters began to moan. To be bypassed—what could be worse? The flyover of planes had caused the Simbas to kill mercilessly some three weeks earlier. Now that the hated mercenaries had traversed their area, would the rebels not carry out their threat to kill again?

The Simbas, too, had heard the firing of mercenary guns. They fled into the forest. Only Jean Pierre remained at hand. He came running to the house.

"Quick!" he said breathlessly. "I will hide you in a banana grove before the Simbas can return. And then I will see if I can run after the mercenaries to call them back to take you."

Obediently because they fully trusted him, the fourteen women followed the young captain along a path to the banana trees. Just as they were about to enter, out from the grove strode the irascible Colonel Kisangi. A Sten gun hung from his shoulder. He stopped. Jean Pierre and the women stopped dead in their tracks. He said nothing, only stared at the young officer and his strange company.

"Ohhhh," gasped a nun. Surely, he would kill them all. He had only to lift his gun and at point-blank range to mow them all down. Jean Pierre was no help to them now. He was not armed. He seldom carried a gun. He likely would die with them because the talk was getting around how this young captain was showing too many kindnesses to his prisoners.

Dolena Burk looked at the colonel and noted his eyes were glassy, his face was showing no emotion at all. Why did he not say something, why not curse them, why not kill them and end this silent, stupefying torment? He moved no muscle, did not even blink. He just stood fixedly and stared at them.

"Ohhhh," sighed another sister, and her slight gasp seemed to break his spell. Still he said nothing, made no noise. He merely turned from them and walked back into the grove.

He was gone! But so was their hiding place. And two other Simbas had emerged from hiding. One bore a knife, the other a bow and arrow. The man with the knife had none of the silence of Kisangi. He nearly raved as he said he ought to kill the women at once.

Jean Pierre spoke up to him. "Why do you want to kill them?" he asked. "If you want to fight, why don't you go where there are men who are armed and who can put up a fight with you?"

The words took the fellow aback. He grumbled, but put up his knife and slunk away. The young captain ordered the Simba with bow and arrow to leave. He then said to the women he would march them into town to make contact with the mercenaries who, from the sound of firing, were still there.

On the way to the road they met another soldier. "What are you doing here?" Jean Pierre demanded. "Get back to your post."

Turning to the woman, he said, "I'll go with you . . . I will protect you on the road. When we get to the mercenaries, will you speak a word for me?"

"We will. Of course we will," the women replied together.

It was an odd procession that filed down the road toward town. A captain of the Simba army led his platoon of hardy warriors— the battles they had fought, and won, were of the spirit, but what battles they had been!—all in his little troop marched with arms raised high above their heads in surrender.

The mercenaries saw the women approach. They broke toward them. Thinking there was no one left in this place to rescue, they were about to move on, but here was the prize they sought, walking toward them behind a rebel officer.

"Save him," the women pleaded in behalf of their friend.

"We'll save him," a mercenary officer replied. "But whether he gets by the national army—that's another thing."

One who found paper and pencil wrote a letter praising Jean Pierre's kindness and consideration and the frequent risks to his own life to save theirs. All the women signed it.

That afternoon a helicopter arrived to fly the women to Stanleyville and thence to Leopoldville. In Stan, Dolena Burk listened to a radio report and it further burdened an already saddened heart. The broadcast reported that a young rebel captain—name unknown—had been captured by the mercenaries in Bafwasende and turned over to the national army. Since he was a Simba he of course was executed.

Mike Hoare's mercenaries had sped to another concentration of missionaries. But when the troops reached the river-crossing town of Banalia they found no one; not even a local villager had remained in the area who could relate the recent happenings.

But down at the ferry slip on the south bank of the Aruwimi River the mercenaries picked up clues that spelled a tragic story. Strewn at the water's edge were the blood-stained habits of three nuns, the clothing of a priest, and the blood-soaked clothing that foreign children wear. There was fresh blood on the slipway itself.

And providing evidence of the identity of the victims, who by virtue of the pattern had been thrown to the crocodiles, the driver's license found on the bank bore the name of Missionary Dennis Parry.

No rain had yet smeared it. What appeared to be multiple slayings had probably occurred not more than two hours before the mercenaries arrived.

At the telltale signs of mass murder a few of the hard-bitten hired soldiers wept openly and without shame.

Did this mean that Mary Baker was dead? And perhaps Margaret Hayes, her partner at Bopepe in recent years? And Pastor Bo Martin, might he not have died with them?

If the assumptions were correct, were Dr. Ian Sharpe and Audrey his wife and their three children dead? They had been a family who prayed for many years for the Africans before they ever set foot on Congo soil.

There were others: Dennis and Nora Parry and two of their children. Did it mean that the other two in school in England were now orphans? And Ruby Gray, whose identification card and Bible, the last possessions a missionary would surrender, were discovered near the river.

It certainly seemed to mean the deaths of all these.

In the closing weeks of 1964 the toll in the family of Unevangelized Fields Mission stood at twenty. Nine from other societies were dead, and some were still missing. At least seventy among the Catholic missions had lost their lives. Paul Carlson was right in his final letter home: This was the century of the Christian martyr.

The loss struck many locations in Congo, many mission societies, many nationalities. Might not this scattering be in God's providence to spread the coals of evangel fire in Congo and also in a world that finally found its concern?

An early reaction, and one to be expected, was voiced by those who spoke of the defeat for missions. But who looking at the Cross would not have seen defeat—only to be joyously jolted by the victory of Resurrection?

Well, the corns of wheat had fallen into the ground and died. And because they had, a day of resurrection, of a better resurrection, would dawn for many.

The news that Louie Rimmer had escaped Bafwasende reached her brother's home in Blackpool, England, at a time when he was out shrimping. A reporter asked his wife what she thought about her sister-in-law's close brush with death.

"Why, young man," she replied, "I'm not surprised that she survived, because she has such an indomitable spirit. The missionaries were ordered out of Congo during Independence days, but Louie returned as soon as she was allowed to.

"I for one haven't the slightest doubt that she'll do the same again."

With all hope dashed that any more of his people would be saved, Al Larson said it was time to go home. First he and Jean would fly to London to look up Kinso. Then Al and Kinso would travel throughout England and Ireland, as they had traveled together over much of Congo. Their goal would be to visit the families of every British victim of this latest example of man's inhumanity to man. Then he and Jean would fly to the United States to do the same there and in Canada.

Following this, Al would join the other missionaries who had come through the recent difficult days and go up and down the land to raise up fervent prayer for the Congo Church and to recruit young people to take the places of those who had died. They would seek out physicians and printers and writers and teachers and nurses and evangelists and anyone dedicated to the will of God and the spirit of pioneering who could help bring a new generation of Congo to Christ.

And anticipating that there would be much planning and praying and preparing to do with his brother in the Lord, Asani Benedict—and perhaps to be even more of a brother to him be-

cause of the presumed loss of faithful Bo Martin—Al Larson
would not be away from Congo for long.

In fact, in anticipation of that happy day of return, before he
left Leopoldville he bought himself a round-trip ticket.

EPILOGUE

Al Larson and Kinso returned to Congo late in April, 1965, a few weeks
earlier than Larson had planned. They hurried to Leopoldville and thence
to Stanleyville in response to the news out of rebel territory that one of the
missionaries who had been presumed dead was alive.

Margaret Hayes, the English nurse who worked with Mary Baker at the
Christian village of Bopepe, was separated from Mary and the other prisoners at Banalia. She was hidden by friendly Congolese for several days, then
when her freedom threatened the safety of the villagers she surrendered to
the Simbas. They assigned her to care for rebel wounded. She spent some
time at the Catholic school at Buta, where Dr. Carlson had stayed for
nearly a month.

From behind rebel lines Margaret Hayes was able to dispatch a letter that
confirmed the deaths of her fellow missionaries at Banalia.

"I alone am left," she said. A prolonged dry season at Banalia had pre-
served the missionary documents found at the river. Thus, while it appeared
that the victims had been killed shortly before the mercenaries arrived in
December, the massacre actually took place on November 25.

Larson and Kinso flew to the Congo, hopeful that they could work for
Miss Hayes's release.

The Congolese national army and Major Hoare's mercenaries had retaken
most of northeast Congo from the Simbas by spring, and in this had the
help of villagers who turned angrily on the rebel régime. Yet the Simbas
retained the area north of Stanleyville. It was not possible for Larson to
drive even five miles out of the city to his home at Kilometer 8. He received
reports that "the hangar" had been burned and the main house ransacked
and turned into a Simba headquarters.

News did filter through from rebel territory that the church, though dispersed and suffering, stood true, that revival fire was burning. In the heart of
Stan, LECO was again open, a busy distribution point for Christian literature. Radio was back in use also, penetrating the rebel pockets with the
Gospel. Asani, returned to Stan, preached again by the broadcasts.

Al Larson returned to America in June to prepare his decimated field
force for a renewed thrust. Yet once more he had come back with a new
burden; not only was Bo Martin dead, but also Malenza the houseboy.

Thousands around the world found a ground for rededication to the work
of God in Congo in the words of Margaret Hayes's letter: "We can't leave
our field high and dry! We *must* have workers, and if God wills it, when
and if I am released, I would like to return. Think of the poor scattered
flock of Christ: My heart breaks whenever I think of it."

She was to have her chance. In June soldiers rescued Margaret Hayes and
her fellow prisoners.

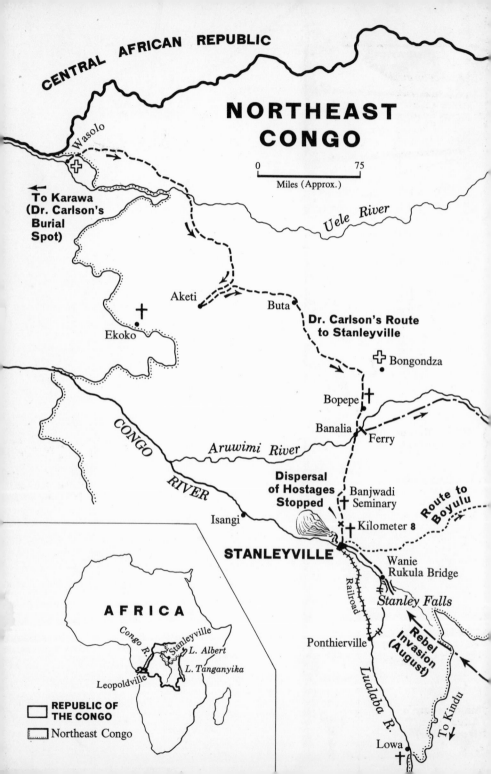

CENTRAL AFRICAN REPUBLIC

NORTHEAST CONGO

0   75
Miles (Approx.)

Wasolo

✚

← To Karawa
(Dr. Carlson's
Burial
Spot)

Uele River

Aketi

Buta

**Dr. Carlson's Route
to Stanleyville**

✚ Ekoko

✚ Bongondza

Bopepe ✚

Banalia   Ferry

Aruwimi River

**Route
to
Boyulu**

**Dispersal
of Hostages
Stopped**

Banjwadi
✚ Seminary

CONGO

RIVER

Isangi

× ✚ Kilometer **8**

STANLEYVILLE

Wanie
Rukula Bridge

Railroad

Stanley Falls

**Rebel
Invasion
(August)**

Ponthierville

Lualaba R.

To Kindu ↓

AFRICA

Congo R.

Stanleyville
L. Albert
L. Tanganyika

Leopoldville

Lowa ✚

☐ **REPUBLIC OF
THE CONGO**

☐ Northeast Congo